Data Literacy

Achieving Higher Productivity for Citizens, Knowledge Workers, and Organizations

Peter Aiken

Todd Harbour

Technics Publications

115 Linda Vista
Sedona, AZ 86336 USA
https://www.TechnicsPub.com

Edited by Emily Daw
Cover design by Lorena Molinari

First Printing 2021

ISBN, print ed. 9781634629584
ISBN, Kindle ed. 9781634629591
ISBN, ePub ed. 9781634629607
ISBN, PDF ed. 9781634629614

Library of Congress Control Number: 2021943383

Advance Praise for Data Literacy

"Literacy" is far more than the ability to read and write. Its definition implies much about our capacity to obtain and master knowledge generally and offers an opportunity and grounds for the basis of mastery. Data Literacy provides an amazing framework that will allow a mobile data spreader to move from a crawler to a walking knowledge worker to a running data professional should they so choose. Another masterpiece from the visionary that taught us that data is 'soil' not 'oil'!

Michael Leahy
Maryland Secretary of Technology

~~~~~

"Data." The word itself places a different image in your mind today than it did 20 years ago, which makes sense. Data is different. Aiken and Harbour present a thorough view of how data has become an anthropological movement and what organizations and individuals need to do. Data has entered all aspects of society. Aiken and Harbour present a thorough treatment of what you need to look out for and what to do about data in all of its forms.

John Ladley
Thought leader and author of *Data Governance: How to Design, Deploy, and Sustain an Effective Data Governance Program 2nd Edition*
~~~~~

Making good decisions about anything takes good data. This book is a great reference for those who are seeking to understand the critical role of data in the evolving landscape of technology, business, governments, and your own day-to-day life.

Suzette Kent
CEO Kent Advisory Services, former Federal Chief Information Officer/OMB

~~~~~

Finally! A book that explains Data Literacy in simple terms providing real-world context to a concept defined and debated by data professionals, executives (CDOs), business analysts, academics, and consultants. It provides relatable examples for everyone to identify bad data behaviors and learn good data hygiene. It presents clear and actionable activities to raise data acumen through tiered teaching curriculum and phased organizational actions. It is a must-read for executives and managers responsible for enterprise data management programs and strongly encouraged for all adults, especially parents.

Maria Vorheh
KPMG, Director, Fed CIO Advisory, former CDO FBI

~~~~~

A thought-provoking look into the vast impacts of data illiteracy coupled with a practical approach to maximizing data's value through improved data literacy.

Catheryn Clay Doss
CDO Federal Reserve Bank of Richmond, former CDO CapitalOne

Acknowledgments

We dedicate this book to the 'father' of information engineering, Clive Finkelstein (1939-2021). We are grateful to have benefitted from countless hours of his generous mentorship. This text is a small contribution toward his overall vision.

It's not possible to put together a published work of any kind without lots of assistance. We benefitted from our share and want to thank all who contributed, with a few special recognitions. These resources served as major sources and we gratefully build on their previous successes:

- Our longtime friend, editor, and collaborator Juanita Billings
- Cathy Doss, CDO Richmond FRB
- Micheline (Mitch) St Clair of Data Governance at Plan International Canada
- We include several lists from our colleague Chris Bradley, whose own work in this area continues to be inspiring. Thank you, Chris, for permission to use these.

- We have benefitted from the review, input, and contributions of our colleague John Ladley. Thank you, John!

We also acknowledge the following sources for their research groundwork. Our efforts build specifically onto solid accomplishments by:

- The Data Literacy Project—a joint effort of Qlik and Accenture: https://thedataliteracyproject.org
- The Data Journalism Handbook 2: https://bit.ly/36HdIAH
- 2015 Strategies and Best Practices for Data Literacy Education Knowledge Synthesis Report available at: https://bit.ly/36KkEwO
- 2013 core data competencies by Prado and Garcia-Quismondo available at: https://bit.ly/3BfMn6P

From Todd:
I would like to thank my wife, Roxanne. Her contribution to this book goes well beyond its pages and into the very fabric of my life. She is my rock, my core, and my soul. She is the reason I strive for (but never reach) perfection.

From Peter:
This is dedicated to my father, who provided me with the foundational engineering and architectural concepts that have been requisite to all my subsequent lessons. I miss you, Dad! (Benjamin Haynes Aiken 1932-2020)

Contents

Foreword by Richard Stengel

We are living in the greatest information revolution in human history. Even greater than the advent of the printing press.

It's estimated that 1.7 MB of data are created every second for every person on earth—that's the equivalent of 7 billion Gutenberg bible's worth of information created every second. Every day, more than 300 billion emails are sent. Google processes 6 billion requests every 24 hours. YouTube watchers consume 4,333,560 videos a minute. In total, some 2.5 exabytes of data is generated every day. 1 exabyte is equivalent to 3000 times the content of the Library of Congress. No wonder some data scientists have conjectured that 90% of all the data in the history of the world was generated in the last two years.

And these numbers are growing exponentially. Today, 5 billion people worldwide have the most powerful information engine in history in their pocket. And every swipe, search, text, keystroke, click, like, and purchase creates more data. Everything you do on your phone or computer—and we haven't even factored in the Internet of Things!—creates more data and more information. Every person with a smartphone can access more information than anyone in history until now.

And yet.

And yet, a recent poll showed less trust in science and facts than in the days before computers and the internet. 43 million Americans have low literacy skills, and 8.4 million Americans are classified as functionally illiterate. In the past ten years, average reading proficiency scores across the country have declined. In the face of a worldwide pandemic, there are millions of people who seem not to understand—or trust—the basic tenets of science. For the last decade, there's a growing tsunami of disinformation that people seem incapable of deciphering. Even though the amount of data is growing, Peter Aiken and Todd Harbour write in their important and illuminating book, data literacy seems to have stagnated. When there is more data, more facts, more information—more knowledge—instantly available than at any time in history, millions of people depend on intuition, superstition, and conspiracy theories.

Ok, but first, a basic question. What is data?

Data are the units of information used in the digital economy. In science, data is a body of facts, but in the digital world it is bits and bytes of information which may be true or not. As Aiken and Harbour note, data is unique (it keeps its value), non-depletable (you can't use it up), non-degradable (it's accessible forever), regenerative (it can be used over and over), and its cost diminishes with use. What oil was to the industrial age, data is to the information age.

But people are afraid of data. One study showed that more Americans would rather pay their bills than work with data. In the 21st century, data can and should enable people to make better and more informed decisions about every aspect of their lives. It should improve productivity and competitiveness. It should make us all better citizens. Lack of data literacy makes us susceptible to manipulation, misinformation, and disinformation. It is a threat to our society and to democracy itself. Part of citizenry in the 21st century should be data and media literacy.

Data—your data—is what makes billions of dollars for the platform companies. Your data, *every bit* of it, has value and it's making them rich. Online platforms and providers collect just about everything they can about you and analyze it for a variety of purposes: to optimize engagement (keeping you online); to personalizing advertising (selling you things); to license to third parties (to sell you more things); to predict your behavior and that of others. There's nothing too small for them to know. Every second you're online or on your phone, you're giving your data to someone who is monetizing it. Shoshana Zuboff has written that we are living in the age of surveillance capitalism.

But the problem is, masses of people are not aware of this. Millions of us have traded security and privacy for convenience. That's a dangerous bargain. It opens us to manipulation, deception, and outright piracy. Hacks and ransomware attacks depend in part on data illiteracy.

So what can you do? For one, be vigilant. Distrust and verify. Be careful about giving access to your data. Be skeptical of any requests for information. Don't automatically give apps access to your location, your pictures, your contacts. Do so only when it makes sense. Why give a restaurant app access to your camera? You shouldn't really give anyone full access to your contacts. Don't open texts from people you don't know. Everything you say or do online pretty much exists forever, so think twice about what you post or tweet.

Becoming data literate is not just about protecting your privacy and security. It's about protecting our democracy and your participation in it. "Governments are instituted," the Declaration says, "deriving their just powers from the consent of the governed." Don't consent to giving away your information and your agency. Don't consent to being fooled by the disinformationists. Use data to make better choices, choices that are both in your interest and the interest of the nation. Data is democratic. It's available to all of us. Use it wisely—and don't let others misuse it.

Richard Stengel is on-air analyst at MSNBC, (Former) Under Secretary of State for Public Diplomacy and Public Affairs & Editor TIME, (Author) Information Wars and Mandela's Way (more at) https://richardstengel.com.

Introduction

Any incoming mobile call, text, shared selfie, e-mail, 'like,' or file exchange (as small as a bit) are all data requests, and your response (or lack of) will also be recorded as data as well.

Data Lesson #1

We believe all citizens working in today's Internet enabled world want to become data literate but have few resources to do so. Mastery of this book's content can be a step toward your personal and your organization's data literacy.

We envision three types of readers with intertwined goals:

- individuals reading to learn how to better manage their own data,
- individuals hoping to learn what their organizations should do to improve organizational data literacy, and
- data professionals interested in what they can do to help move our profession, the citizenry, and society forward.

We must do more to address the widening gap between the data literate and the data illiterate among us. We need a citizenry who understands how to use data to better grasp concepts in any arena, whether in science, economics, justice, society, research, or anywhere else.

Lack of data literacy is a direct threat to our citizens. Not understanding data and data concepts is both a root cause and an unrecognized, necessary skill set preventing many citizens and organizations from achieving other successes. Those who remain data illiterate stay as "perpetual, involuntary data donors," or PIDDs. PIDDs are unaware that they are the products of an increasingly powerful set of interests focused on transforming goods, services, ideas, nature, private, personal data, and people into commodities or objects of trade (commodification)—for profit and largely without regulation or oversight.

This is by design, as we learn from Shoshanna Zuboff's influential book, *Surveillance Capitalism: The Fight for a Human Future at the New Frontier of Power*. Her phrase "surveillance capitalism" refers to a class of organizations dependent on PIDDs for data to fund their organizational growth. The outrage over these conditions should continue to increase as citizens become increasingly aware that the purpose of the industry focuses on selling increasing amounts of, and more effective advertising. Finally, lest we forget, advertising's goals are to influence behavior–ideally to control behavior. These same PIDD control techniques have been in use for at least a decade, increasing instances of bad behavior, creating audiences for targeted misinformation efforts, and ultimately influencing voting and other important decisions.[1]

The surveillance capitalism business model requires PIDDS to remain victims, giving up their data so that they can be targets for advertising and much worse types of data influencing. Combined, these data collections and collectors are "a distributed and largely uncontested new expression of power which constitutes hidden mechanisms of extraction, commodification, and control that threatens core values such as freedom, democracy, and privacy."[2]

The goal is control over population segments. This is achieved by guiding customers' data inputs to produce desired outputs. Citizens are coerced into giving up their liberties as companies limit their choices, feed them disinformation and junk news, or simply misinform them about products.

We describe a great and still growing need to combat data illiteracy—not only for data professionals (who largely are not as data literate as they could be), but also for all citizens. This book will provide an objective means of improving both your individual data literacy and that of your organization. If enough individuals and organizations expand and improve data literacy, all citizens will benefit.

Part 1 outlines the case for increased data literacy. Part 1 begins by presenting foundational data literacy lessons that are currently covered obliquely in textbooks or training. We hope teenagers and adults can use them to avoid becoming PIDDs, unknowing stooges of surveillance capitalism. It then makes the case that modern life operates with less friction when citizens are more data literate. It lays out the challenges that arise from simultaneously increasing data across all dimensions while not increasing data literacy during this period of unprecedented growth. We argue that current approaches to data education are ineffective, with increasingly devastating consequences for citizens. We next present a small business case for increasing organizational and individual data literacy, focusing on specific characteristics of knowledge workers.

Part 2 presents readers with the tools to protect themselves and their private information in the 21st century digital economy. This structured approach to data literacy is in the form of a Digital Civics Framework (DCF). The DCF illustrates the size and scope of the data literacy challenge and orders a requisite list of citizen data knowledge areas (CDKAs). Data characteristics, competencies, commonalities, and CDKAs align with five framework actors. At the end of Part 2, you will understand data literacy requirements delineated as 30 specific CDKAs and how they must work in concert to achieve meaningful results. We include suggestions on how individuals and organizations can achieve mastery over these CDKAs, thereby increasing their productivity and enabling them to teach the principles to others.

Part 3 describes how to use the DCF to organize and develop remediation responses to improve individual and organizational data literacy. We offer an overarching approach and practical remedies for overcoming each data literacy obstacle for MDS, ADS, knowledge workers, and data professionals. These lessons present ways to improve performance for many organizational workers. We also highlight vital data-literacy barriers to show how they are impediments to social initiatives. The next two chapters outline twelve steps required by organizations and resulting organizational data management programs. The final chapter envisions a world of data literacy to help motivate movement towards it.

Society's relentless movement to digitize requires elaborating citizenship's rights and responsibilities concerning the digital framework surrounding them. If things keep going as they are (stagnated data literacy progress at the very worst time), unscrupulous organizations and governments will continue to suck up the unknowingly "donated" data contributed by billions of unsuspecting citizens. These same citizens are also unaware that contributing their data also makes them vulnerable to the control and influence exerted by their data.

As we watched politicians and the media talk about data during the COVID-19 pandemic, we saw that neither addressed the underlying principle *that all problems are data problems*! Failure to address this fundamental citizen knowledge gap will continue to hurt society. We are still optimistic and envision other types of societal improvements that result in higher data literacy rates—societal structures that are more resilient, better able to handle the next world-wide emergency, and more capable of raising aware, informed future generations. We are also aware of the accuracy of George Box's famous aphorism:

> *All models are wrong— some are useful!*[3]

We hope this framing and further refinement of data literacy are useful!

Peter Aiken and Todd Harbour (Fall 2021)

PART I

Why Learn More About Data?

Dabbling in Data Is Dangerous.

The key to improving organizational data literacy is to improve data education and citizen data literacy levels. Our experience shows that most underestimate data complexities and the work it takes to gain value from it effectively. Many consider data scarily complex–most don't know that they don't know. Over our careers, we've seen more organizations fail than succeed because they didn't exert discipline across their organization or apply enough resources. We believe the same principle must now hold true for society. Unless governments take data seriously and fund data literacy efforts, society could fail as well. Nor is it just the government's problem: we believe all citizens must individually invest in increasing their own data literacy—if for no other reason than understanding that being a PIDD is undesirable. (As we will detail in Chapter 5, the good news is that most individuals are willing to become more data literate.) Citizens who remain data illiterate will lose control of their data and their privacy. Only by becoming data literate can they learn how to control—and protect—their data, their privacy, and their very freedom.

Part 1 answers the question, "Why do we need to learn about data?" This section supplies background on data basics, data growth, and data education that helps readers to appreciate data and the consequences of not taking it seriously. You are encouraged to treat data both as an asset and a programmatic organizational investment. We also encourage readers to make explicit and deliberate decisions concerning data: data should be part of your everyday thinking. Realize that society is increasingly dependent on data even though people underestimate how it drives our financial systems, power grid, and news and information services. As Rick Stengel stated so well in the foreword to this book, data are the units of information used in every aspect of the digital economy.

- Chapter 1 lays out a framework for understanding data as an asset that must be used and protected—much as we do anything else of value.
- Chapter 2 describes data as foundational to modern life and society.
- Chapter 3 describes the massive increase in data availability and usage and new societal capabilities as well as new citizen capabilities.

- Chapter 4 provides evidence that current approaches are just not cutting it: societal data debt is increasing by all accounts.

- Chapter 5 offers a starting point for a solution to increase the productivity of knowledge workers.

CHAPTER 1

Data Bootcamp

Outside the data community, general knowledge of data and data concepts is relatively scarce. This chapter provides the basic, non-technical knowledge of data that we believe all **adults** need to function in society. It argues that data must be seen as a personal asset first that citizens should not have to fight to protect.

Defining data assets

The first thing that any adult needs to understand about data is that it is an asset. Most of us could list common corporate assets, such as real property, financial investments, inventory, knowledge, and skills—even reputation and goodwill. However, few citizens would consider data as an asset either for themselves or for their companies. This section sets out to correct this foundational misunderstanding.

How do we define data?

When defining data, it is good to understand that data results when pairing a fact and a meaning usefully. One fact that many understand is the meaning of the number 42. In more than 30 years of discussing data with groups worldwide, there has always been at least one individual in the group who remembers the book, *The Hitchhikers Guide to the Galaxy*, and that the number 42 represents "the meaning of life, the universe, and everything." Inevitably, someone in the audience who didn't read the book becomes bewildered and confused at this point. What does 42 have to do with anything? Isn't 42 Jackie Robinson's jersey number? (Yes.) That is the same fact paired with a different meaning.

At its most superficial level, data is any combination of a fact and a definition. After pairing "42" with "the meaning of life," a person has context and understanding. Together, the combination of fact and meaning constitute a bit of data. However, most citizens don't have the luxury of studying the data in their lives.

Specifically, we recognize that your organization's data is complex and detailed. It's also deceivingly simple. After all, data represents everything in binary terms: true or false. That's pretty simple. So, why is data confusing, and why do citizens have a tough time talking about it? This confusion is a common problem. The lack of data knowledge and experience amplifies miscommunication among citizens. Typically, the groups involved are data citizens and non-data citizens. That is, some people understand data concepts, and others don't. We recognize that bridging the gap between citizen groups is one of this book's most significant challenges.

For most, data can be confusing because it is complex, detailed, and taught inconsistently. Knowing how to read and interpret data takes discipline, practice, and education.

Even those who often work with data know only part of the picture. For example, data scientists often discover useful data maintenance utilities instead of learning various classes of tools and when to apply each as part of their educational programs. For many, data is like the story of the blind men and the elephant.

Figure 1.1—Encountering an elephant in an uncoordinated manner[4]

As the story goes, the man who felt the elephant's trunk thought he touched a snake. The man who felt the elephant's torso thought he touched a wall, and the man who touched the elephant's leg thought he touched a tree. Without the benefit of their combined observations, each man thought he felt a different thing. Like elephant parts, numerous sub-disciplines comprise data. In the data world, different citizens work according to different specialties. Some citizens focus on collecting data, and others focus on analyzing data—some do neither.

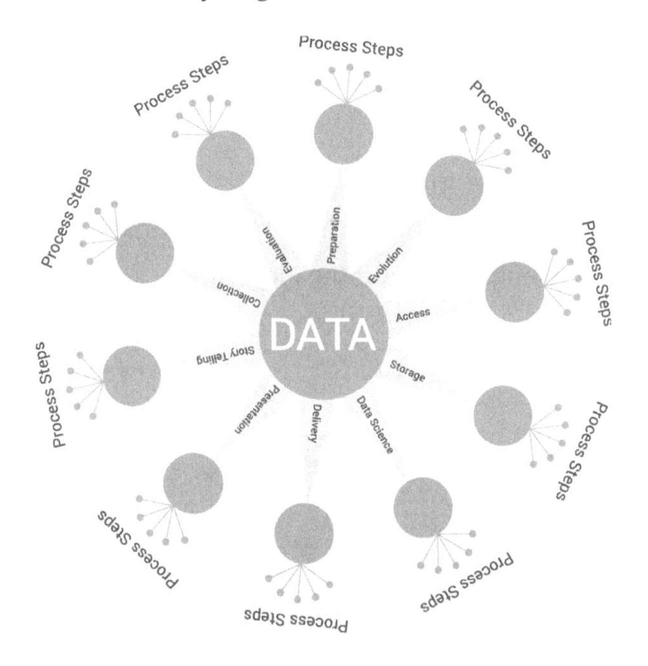

Figure 1.2—There are many more data views

These jobs don't overlap or even collaborate. They principally work in separate universes, interacting with one another only on occasion. Some examples:

- Some collect data and think data is a set of business processes and financial transactions.
- Some protect data and think data is a set of logistical controls applied to data assets.
- Some store data and think data is a calculation of data growth.

Data is an asset

Before diving into further concepts, let's do a few quick exercises to get you thinking about data and information in your own life. Get out a blank sheet of paper and don't read further until you have completed these three activities:[1]

1. List types of personal information that are in your house. (Here are two to get you started: insurance policies and photographs.)
2. List examples of data that others have about you or your family. Make sure to record the data that relates to you or your family.

---

[1] This terrific introduction to data is reproduced with full credit for and permission from our colleague Chris Bradley, chris.bradley@dmadvisors.co.uk.

3. List bad things that could happen to your data if it's controlled or accessed by someone else.

When you are ready, compare your list to the list below.

1. Types of personal information:

insurance policies
house deeds
bank statements
credit card statements
photographs
personal videos
walking maps
books
school work
kitchen calendars
address book
diplomas and certificates

2. Data others have about you and your family:

pension funds
loyalty points
credit card transactions
bank transactions
school records
timesheets
mortgage payments
tax payments
hotel visits
shows and club visits
university records
medical records
charity contributions
club memberships
land registries
electoral rolls
company payroll
credit ratings

3. Bad things that could happen:

identify theft
children's school details revealed
reputation damage
suggestions of improper behavior
sensitive medical information
mortgage statement goes next door
mortgage shows arrears incorrectly
credit rating fault stops loan request
loyalty points reset to zero by mistake
pension fund calculated incorrectly

What you've just cataloged and read are some of your *data assets*. Assets are classes of resources controlled by the organization from which future benefits are expected to flow. Data assets are those datasets from which the organization hopes to benefit. Because we do not consider and protect our data assets, millions suffer the effects of data breaches, politicians do not support data reform legislation, and society trudges along with expensive technologies that do not serve needs. People need to be aware of their data: where it is located (both physically and electronically), who has access to it, its veracity, and what it means to them in today's digital world.

Data is strategic

The advent of personal computing is gradually increasing citizen awareness of data as an asset. An early manifestation involved the ability of citizens' digital bookmarks for their Internet browsers. Back before Google, when a citizen found a useful website, they tended to bookmark the site to allow rapid access in the future. Before Internet-wide search capabilities, bookmarks were a list of Internet sites that people knew, understood, and trusted. People, organizations, and technologies all stored bookmarks using different formats. As a result, moving and exchanging bookmarks was challenging. Early computer users paid much attention to the management of their bookmarks. However, as people migrate more bookmarks to the cloud, the tedious and time-consuming process of migrating other data from computer to computer decreases. Migrating to the cloud also represents an initial whitelisting solution offering bookmarks vetted by someone reputable. While better-designed device data migration and search has relegated the bookmark problem to history, this approach to managing data complexity was automated and incorporated into the device upgrade process.

The opposite of opt-in is opt-out or blacklisting. Today, many browsers come with blacklisted sites, and when users try to visit them, the system will alert users with warnings and disclaimers. Understanding how and when to apply both black- and whitelisting is key to some approaches to increasing data literacy and managing data complexities. For example, ContactsOnlyMode, a concept we will introduce in Chapter 7 as helpful to mobile data spreaders, is a whitelisted-contacts-only approach to introducing novice users to the Internet.

Like any personal or organizational asset, data must be used strategically. As previously noted, in its most basic form, data is simply facts and numbers. But to be useful, people must organize data into models: intricate, detailed, and complex data designs.

But in many cases, these data models, designed by ill-equipped or unqualified designers, have hard-to-find, irreversible and permanent flaws, and inefficiencies. These remain hidden throughout development but inevitably surface much later. If experts do not find the problems early enough, these foundational problems make their way into production systems. By then, it's often too late or too costly to fix. Some fearless organizations try to make the repairs. However, they typically can't recover their investments. Still, some try to use flawed systems in a production environment. Almost always, they suffer the worst. They suffer unnecessarily from lots of small defects. The costs of these defects add up rapidly. We call this data debt.

The laws of physics do not apply to data

Unlike other business assets, data does not conform to the laws of physics. Organizations understanding this can produce quality data and reliable decisions. Most organizations have conflicting (and often competing) datasets, definitions, and uses—in other words, too much data debt.

One governs data using a relatively small number of "data physics laws." These limit potential data combinations to specifics such as

one-to-one,
one-to-many, and
many-to-many

depending on the various combinations of technology comprising the solution. These supply certainty to problem solutions that are quite different from solutions in other domains such as software, networking, security, and more. As such, this profession attracts problem solvers who like to work in worlds with reduced uncertainty. Understanding this data characteristic is crucial to understanding data's importance to systems (and hence society's) design. Here are a few examples of data characteristics:[5]

Unique	It will retain its form and value for some time
Non-depletable	Can be accessible forever (or at least indefinitely)
It can't be used up	Worthy of further organizational investment
Non-degrading	Valued in conjunction with other organizational asset valuations
Durable	Difficult to visualize without practice
Strategic	Has almost unlimited uses and low inventory, transportation, and transmission costs
Invisible	Can be misused and misinterpreted
Non-rivalrous	Can be copied for free
Regenerative	Impossible to clean up if it's spilled
Difficult to control	Data centers are going green
Eco-friendly	

Data is not the new oil!

If you Google "data is the new oil," you will find more than five million references. Like crude oil, data can be drilled (mined) and refined to provide value. Others have extended the metaphor, noting that, just as oil changed entire economies and how its citizens lived and worked, data is driving similar kinds of changes today.

While these transformative properties are fascinating, this is absolutely the wrong way to think about data assets. For instance, oil conforms to a product-use cycle. After one uses it, one must get more oil to obtain additional value and, when that oil is gone, one must replenish the supply. This process continues until one no longer needs or has oil. There is no concept of reuse whatsoever about oil. It's finite and predictable and, when it's gone, it's gone.

For data, on the other hand, this process works almost in reverse! After paying for a collection, the relative cost of using the data diminishes with each subsequent use.[6] Data increases in value the more people use it. Therefore, organizations are encouraged and financially rewarded to reuse data. Likewise, increased use obviously won't destroy or harm data. Organizations keep data in the original electronic format, where it will stay unless someone deliberately changes it. In this way, data is durable (capable of generating flows of goods and services over time), and **organizations should treat it as an**

investment rather than an expense. Further, the price of oil fluctuates in response to market forces. Data assets are responsive to market forces but can also be made more valuable by simply doing a good job managing them and carefully increasing scope, granularity, timeframes, combinations, etc.

Data is the most powerful yet underutilized and poorly managed organizational investment. When one compares data to other organizational assets, one quickly sees that data is unique. Most often, the characteristics that make data unique also warrant a strategic approach to its utilization.

A better way to conceptualize data is to change the word "oil" to "soil." Prepare well a solid planting bed, and you will find that you can use that foundation to plant good things in it and produce repeated good results. The timing also functions as a better analogy—one doesn't grow tomato plants on Monday and expects to harvest ripe tomatoes on Friday. Data, like soil, requires preparation, persistence, and patience. The physical size limitations of the areas suitable for planting also speak to relevant data considerations—especially when planning data reuse.

Social media: Your data is someone else's asset

In the grand scheme of things, social media is one of the critically important new entries but exists at an extremely low level of maturity. We can summarize social media in the context of the history of communications:[7]

Year	Invention	Impact
500-1500	Pigeon Posting	Sending messages using carrier pigeons
1792	Telegraph	Electricity beats pigeons for both accuracy and speed
1836	Morse Code	Improves telegraphy system
1836	Pneumatic Mail	Improves point to point workflow
1875	Telephone	Gradually improves person to person communications
1891	Radio	Improves broadcast communication
1969	CompuServe	Improves computer to computer communication
1971	First email	Ray Tomlinson is generally credited as having sent the first email across a network (Wikipedia)
1978	First BBS	Bulletin board systems permitted groups of users to meet and chat
1989 1994	WWW First Blog	World Wide Web begins At links.net by a Swarthmore student
1997		3 degrees of separation general awareness – demonstrating the "Kevin Bacon-ness" of everything

While many citizens do not recognize data as an asset, one industry has: social media. In this case, however, the data that social media companies profit from is not their own—until we choose to give it to them.

> *In modern capitalist society, technology was, is and will always be an expression of the economic objectives that direct it into action.*[8]

There's an adage that suggests that if you're not paying for a product, then you *are* the product.[9] In other words, the company is profiting from your use of the product or service by using your data. This is how you become a PIDD. Citizens unfamiliar with this relationship allow big tech to continue to exploit them. And the US judiciary system has allowed this system to stand. US Magistrate Judge Paul Grewal struck down a lawsuit because users opted into a free service on the tacit understanding that the providers would mine and monetize user data. Judge Grewal noted in the decision:

> *By now, most citizens know who Google is and what Google does. Google serves billions of online users in this country and around the world ... With little or no revenue from its users, Google still manages to turn a healthy profit by selling advertisements within its products that rely in substantial part on users' personal identification information ... in this model, the users are the real product.* [10]

We know the names. We hear them daily. They are Facebook, Apple, Amazon, Netflix, and Google, known by the acronym "FAANG." FAANG is a scary name, and it is a scary concept. Not long ago, these companies supplied goods and services much differently from what they do today. For example, look at how Facebook has described itself over the years:

Year	Description
2004	Facebook is an online directory that connects citizens through social networks at colleges.
2005	Facebook is an online directory that connects citizens through social networks at schools.
2006	Facebook is a social utility that connects you with the citizens around you. Facebook is made up of lots of separate networks, things like schools, companies, and regions.
2007	Facebook is a social utility that connects you with the citizens around you. Upload photos or publish notes, get the latest news from your friends, post videos on your profile, tag your friends, use privacy settings to control who sees your info, join a network to see citizens who live, study, or work around you.
2008	Facebook is a social utility that connects you with the citizens around you. Use Facebook to keep up with friends and family, share photos and videos, control privacy online, reconnect with old classmates.
2008	Facebook helps you connect and share with the citizens in your life.
2009	Facebook gives citizens the power to share and make the world more open and connected.
2013	Facebook's mission is to give citizens the power to share and make the world more open and connected.
2017	Facebook's mission is to give citizens the power to build community and bring the world closer together.
2017	Facebook's mission is to give citizens the power to share and make the world more open and connected.
2019	Facebook's mission is to stay connected with friends and family, to discover what's going on in the world, and to share and express what matters to them.
2020	Facebook's mission is to give citizens the power to share and make the world more open and connected.

Source: unknown

What started as a college-age project quickly evolved into being one of the world's most powerful tech companies. At its outset, Facebook ran like many new Internet based offerings. Wide-eyed and eager to explore the power of the

Internet, Facebook touted social connectivity and sharing. But there were early hints in 2004 of what Facebook would become. Over the next few years, Facebook expanded its user base and became one of the world's fastest growing and wealthiest companies. Mark Zuckerberg, founder and CEO of Facebook, noted that 4,000 "dumb f*cks" were willing to surrender personal information to join his new and exciting network.[11]

What is social media?

To fully understand social media motivations, one must start with an understanding of the basics. What is social media? Merriam Webster defines social media as *electronic communication forms (such as websites for social networking and microblogging)*. Users create online communities to share information, ideas, personal messages, and other content (such as videos).

Of course, the key to understanding social media is to realize that social media companies have ulterior motives. They are for-profit businesses. Consider that in 2017, Apple, Facebook, Google, Verisign, and VISA all earned more than $1 million per employee![12] These earnings represent vast leverage that is unavailable to those unable to achieve these efficiencies. Thus, the opportunities for organizations to shape and mold the behavior of others are great.

How do social media companies get us to give them so much of our data? The answer is a number of tricks ranging from valuable services to clickbait and many other forms. If you've spent any time on social media at all, you're familiar with these tropes of "clickbait," the article photos and headlines that drop tantalizing hints about what lies beyond. Jeffrey Haidt has excellent research on this and some of the physical, psychological, and social consequences of what social media is doing to people. Clicking these articles is designed to give the user a shot of the neurochemical called dopamine. Dopamine isn't about pleasure; it's about the anticipation of pleasure. It's about the pursuit of happiness rather than happiness itself.[13]

The same principle applies to why we hand over so much of ourselves to social media. For example, we post a selfie to anticipate the number of "likes" and "follows" it will get us. Or we continue the infinite scroll through our feed, far past the point of boredom, with the expectation that we are surely one flick of the thumb away from pleasure.

Social media companies get their revenue from advertisers. Facebook and Google reap a substantial percentage of their income from it. Consequently, those companies are motivated to create as many ways as possible to "hook" people and keep them on their platforms.

Consider this: social media companies encourage online conversations to harvest data from the participants.

Encouraged is a misnomer— social media companies engineer their sites to manufacture and promote engagement to elicit the largest amount of information a participant will surrender. The platforms are purposefully addictive and designed to motivate users to produce data.

Other people gaining from social media include influencers and the companies who hire them. In 2018, companies that used influencer marketing got a 520% return on investment.[14] Since Instagram reached 1 billion active users, many young citizens rely on influencer recommendations for their purchases. These influencers often have fewer than 100,000 followers, but they are still responsible for most posts. Influencers and social media comprise just the latest attempt to skirt regulation and scrutiny. (It used to be okay to advertise cigarettes on television to children!) We will see an increasing focus on these influencers who use social media more effectively.

User data

The key to online advertising lies in the collection of user data. "User data" is everything an organization knows about its users. The industry often breaks user data into three main categories: explicit or declared data, implicit and inferred data, and third-party data (that is, data obtained from a data broker).

Declared data is anything a user voluntarily gives a recipient. User data is the kind of information citizens present when they sign up for services. Think of it as user profile information. Online providers ask for this information like your name, age, location, gender, and likes and dislikes. Companies condition users to surrender this type of data without thinking about the ramifications.

Implicit data is data that provider organizations collect without needing the user's direct input. Browsing history is an excellent example of this kind of data. Online providers want to know how long you stay on a webpage, what ads you click, how you move your mouse, and what songs you have in your playlists. In principle, organizations collect about everything you do online and analyze it for different purposes. This is the basis for the Google Analytics product.[15] Some websites use it to maximize revenue—others to perfect the citizen engagement experience.

Inferred information is data that makes assumptions about you based on a combination of declared and implicit data. Complex algorithms categorize users and determine if a system should present an individual with a clothing ad or a travel ad. Once organizations process user information, they prepare it for resale. Third-party brokers sell data to other organizations that, in turn, enhance their data and use it to target new customers.

Social media can consume countless amounts of time as users engage in new and seemingly different content. It's critical to understand that, outside of a few not-for-profits, social media companies exist to find new ways of extracting data from the users. To put these remarks into perspective, consider these objective definitions of success: Money changes hands based on 1) data existing on a screen where a user might notice it and, 2) even more, if a user clicks on a word or image and moves to a destination URL. This flimsy value proposition is defined as *engagement* and provides a very squishy foundation for future investment.

Protecting your data

To make responsible decisions about their online information, users must understand the possible consequences of posting online. To qualify to work for some law enforcement agencies, citizens have to hand over the passwords to their social media accounts. Giving authorities your passwords allows them to read what you wrote and posted historically and reveals all of your conversations. The agencies justified asking for passwords, showing a need to understand the individual applying for work at an intimate level.

Some citizens protect their data, but others have no idea that social media companies actively harvest their data.

Most citizens unknowingly supply data to feed the Data Matrix (more in Chapter 2). Before venturing into the Internet, citizens must understand the various aspects of some of the following factors:

- cost of managing
- time commitment
- lost customers
- long-term commitment
- outside support
- getting attribution right
- executive reviews
- digital trail
- cost of analyzing success
- the cost of screwing up
- social media management platforms
- tying into web analytics
- remediation for social media gaffs
- digital harassment
- opportunity cost

Most realize that today's citizens are more likely to experience social networks than learn data literacy. Therefore, we advocate those responsible adults keep communication channels open via periodic citizen data discussions (more on this in Chapter 6).

Internet of Things

The Internet of Things (IoT) is an even more horrifying intersection of data demand and data illiteracy. This term describes any device connected to the Internet. These machines are unique and different from the common idea of a computer. IoT devices are small computers that measure tiny and unique things. For example, IoT devices measure how fast something moves or how much power an electric device consumes, in addition to many other useful (and profit-producing) pieces of information. Another difference between ordinary computers and IoT devices is that users do not directly operate them. Instead, other electronic machines—like smartphones, tablets, and notebook computers—control them. We noted some of these standard IoT devices below:[16]

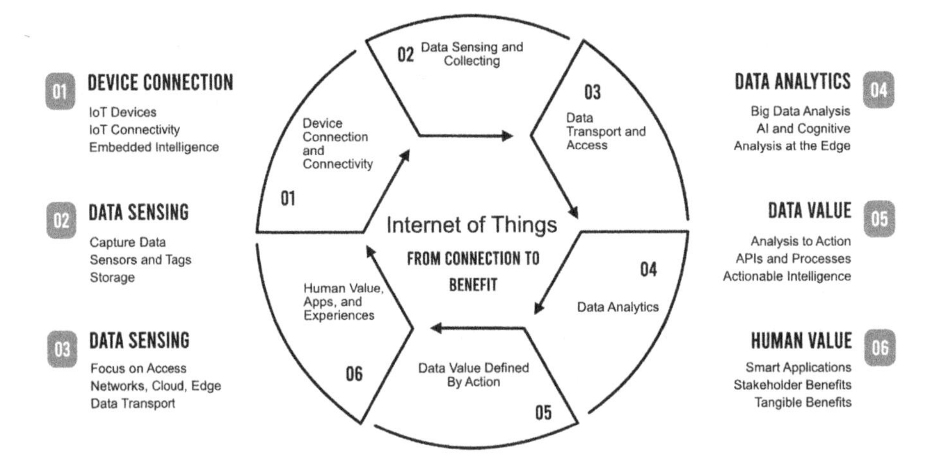

Figure 1.4—Depiction of the Internet of Things

digital control systems
toasters
cochlear Implants
connected appliances
refrigerators
soil monitoring
building energy systems
wearable technology
smart factory equipment
surveillance cameras/baby monitors
shipping container and logistics tracking
smart phones and speakers
wireless inventory trackers
vehicle-to-everything connections (V2X)
emergency notification systems
ultra-high-speed wireless Internet
biometric cybersecurity scanners
smart home and security systems
autonomous farming equipment

A more troubling aspect of IoT 'computers' is that they are not recognized as such by most, and that the software developers have proven so notoriously poor (security-wise) that entire product lines have been places on the US Government watch list. These devices are often in occupied areas which permit a very high degree of invasion of personal space. This opens literally billions of unsecured devices with access to human behavior data.

When organizations deploy billions of IoT devices worldwide, the sensors create a mesh that allows people to monitor and control almost anything imaginable. Farmers can manage giant combines in the fields. Parents can monitor their children while they sleep, and homeowners can control the temperature in their houses while they are away on vacation. As time goes on, inventors will use these and more advanced versions of these prototypical sensors to deliver more creative and socially helpful capabilities. However, no matter how useful these devices are to society, there is a downside.

Probably one of the best examples of such a problematic IoT device is Amazon's Ring Camera. The Ring service offers customers some remarkable capabilities. For example, the system's camera can show the owner if someone is at the front door. The system can lock and unlock doors. The system can record video for later viewing and sharing—and much more. Most importantly, these devices share their data, so Ring collects a lot of data about you, your property, and your surroundings. What is disturbing is that it's not clear where that data goes and who has access to it. Where this a trivial or one-time amount of data, most would shrug it off. But it's not an insignificant amount of data, and the systems collect it 24/7. The amount of information that Ring and other IoT devices collect about people has already reached a level where many are concerned about their privacy.

End user license agreements (EULAs) like the Ring agreement allow a corporation and its employees unfettered access to private property at will. By agreeing with the EULA, people permit Amazon to surveil anyone who signs it. IoT devices are collectively raising questions about how tech giants like Amazon collect data from each device. For example, EULAs give Amazon and law enforcement permission to view video collected on Ring cameras—any time they want. Not surprisingly, Amazon already developed specialized software that "stitches" video information together.

When combined with video from other Ring cameras in the same neighborhood, the software allows law enforcement (and anyone else) a realistic view of neighborhood activity. For example, Ring video footage could show a thief going from house to house. By most measures, this is a remarkable capability and crucial in helping law enforcement keep our neighborhoods safe. But there are other considerations that many don't understand or notice, such as the failure of general-purpose facial recognition or why more chatbot conversations are not yet satisfactory. What helps people understand the up and down sides of these capabilities? Data literacy.

Chapter conclusions-Data lessons for adults & knowledge workers are foundational

Most citizens are not aware of the value of their data or the harm resulting from it falling into the wrong hands. Worse, today's 'data professionals' do not know that they approach their data knowledge from substantially different perspectives and are unaware of other aspects of data and the process of obtaining value from it. Moreover, when organizations poorly design data for system use, data debt increases. Mix in a lethal combination of products (social media and IoT) designed to extract data and PIDDs scarcely have a chance against surveillance capitalism. Worst of all, this is being done for the sake of advertising (when treated charitably–at its worst it is about population control). This data bootcamp chapter concludes with the next two data lessons.

Data is more complicated than people understand. Most encounter data from one perspective and do not discover other areas. This leads to incorrect perceptions, misunderstandings, misfires, and, most importantly, misallocation of resources. As our colleague, Lewis, often said, "You can't productively dabble in data!"

Data Lesson #2

Data is a valuable asset! Be conscious of what you have and what you do with it.

Data Lesson #3

CHAPTER 2

A Data Illiterate Society

This chapter describes the necessity of everyday citizens becoming data literate. First, we will use the COVID-19 pandemic as a collective focus for the type of problems that arise when decision makers lack an understanding of data. Then, we will define data literacy through a series of comparisons to similar skills, illustrating the need for a standardized scale for data literacy. We will describe the problem of data debt and the danger of the data matrix to the common citizen.

The Pandemic illustrates the problems of a data illiterate society

We began this book in early 2020 when COVID-19 put much of our world under strict quarantine. There was much confusion, fear, opinions, defiance, hysteria...and errors. Much of the fear and confusion arose from an inability to understand what we call *pandemic math*. It goes like this: *If the demand for beds at a 48-bed hospital doubles every day, at what point does anyone notice that the beds are growing scarce?*

- Day 1, 3 beds were occupied.
- Day 2, 6 beds were occupied.
- Day 3, ¾ of the beds were available.
- Day 4, ½ of the beds were available.
- Today, no beds are available.
- What should the hospital do tomorrow?

Consider the following analogy. Societies exert control over pandemics by *flattening the curve* associated with the rate of infection. However, if people don't understand flattening or doubling daily volumes, following the rationale for pandemic decisions will be challenging. **The pandemic has shown us that data illiterate citizens cannot understand the consequences of their actions in society.**

Various health officials tried to use data combinations to manage expectations throughout the pandemic,[17] but these officials had severe problems standardizing data collection and analyses across the country.[18] The ability to recognize change is essential if a state expects to improve its ability to measure real-world phenomena and make proper policy decisions. Everyone involved must understand data—and information derived from the data—to manage crises and grow in times of prosperity.

We began this book with the shocking idea that 2020 would be known as the year the AI/ML algorithms[19] ran out of data suitable for AI training purposes![20] Specifically, meaningful advances in artificial intelligence (AI) depend on learning algorithms built using real-world data. In her influential book, *The Big Nine*,[21] futurist Amy Webb argues that only a handful of companies do data well enough to provide training to AI programs. She makes the case that the U.S. must be a leader in the field as a matter of national security. Webb's concern underscores the real crisis, that AI algorithms are starving for data of sufficient quality to carry out the desired training. Consequently, data-needs are preventing necessary algorithm training and impeding new AI capabilities.

Using test data helps solve some of the problems, but history has shown that testing data is inadequate, incomplete, and unreliable. We saw this over the first part of the year 2020. Then, researchers presented exaggerated predictions and had to adjust their models to align with real-world measurements. Never had nations used models to set national and international policies at this scale. What many have learned is that math was not the problem. **Data was the problem**.

Looking back, it's clear that researchers could have built much better models using high-quality training data assets. However, those data assets didn't exist. Why? The conflict between science and individual liberty was playing out in a battle over data. This situation prevented people from effectively evaluating different approaches in a consistent and even-handed manner. This illustrates that politics and social concerns taint every measure (more data) we identify.

It is no surprise that many offered varying predictions. Until the COVID-19 coronavirus appeared, these models were just that—models. Trouble ensued when a data illiterate media, political leadership, and private citizens failed to understand the issues and data related to the various models. We contend that increasing the general population's data literacy, especially those in leadership roles, will prevent the type of data-based misunderstandings such as those that occurred in the pandemic.

The reality is that most citizens do not understand much about data. They hear people talk about data on the news, but they don't know where information comes from or how systems work with it. How do people use data? Why should I care? More importantly, citizens don't understand how data affects them on an individual level. Without that understanding, citizens can't begin to ask questions about data, let alone find the answers to their questions.

One important consequence of this is a communications bottleneck. Many are unable to consider the vast sums of storage, processing, interpretation, and more. It can be challenging to have a substantive conversation about data with someone who must make important decisions but is data illiterate.

If an individual lacks a fundamental understanding of the topic and the data, the communication can require enormous effort. Data literate participants must translate their ideas into a simple and understandable form for the decision-maker who must also engage. The data literate person must take the extra step and offer more information to help others understand data. In the end, the added effort may or may not result in effective communication. Lack of effective communication often dooms policy efforts. This task of converting or translating information falls entirely on the (always too) few data experts available. For example, suppose a data expert sees that their organization has poor "data hygiene." If the person's superiors are not data literate, trying to convince them of the need to change data processes may prove too difficult. The poor practices continue and, unfortunately, continue to impact global health.[22]

Data literacy is a range (as opposed to a binary measure)

Society knows that a literate population functions better than an illiterate one.

Society invests significant resources in improving literacy. Education systems develop programs to be sure that our children can read and write. However, we have not yet invested similar resources in data literacy. To become more data literate, citizens need to understand the value of data and the remarkable things that we can do with it.

What is literacy?

The Data Literacy Project shows that employees with strong data literacy bring:

- 3-5% greater market capitalization
- $320-$534 million in higher enterprise value
- positive impact on margin, return-on-assets, return-on-equity, and return-on-sales.[23]

But what does data literacy entail, and how is it measured?

The *Cambridge English Dictionary* defines the term "literate" to denote a person who can read and write. For example:

The man was barely literate and took a long time to write his name.

However, there are other useful definitions. For instance, "literate" also describes someone as having a good education and competent writing abilities:

He wrote a literate, colorful column and reviewed plays.

It can also describe a person as having a basic skill or knowledge of a subject:

They wanted to make sure their child was computer literate.

We believe these are excellent and helpful definitions—all from https://dictionary.cambridge.org/us/.

When evaluating traditional literacy, we may speak of someone having a "twelfth-grade reading level" or a "second-grade reading level." This creates a range rather than a binary condition. The same must be true when describing data literacy. We believe there must be a standard scale that denotes data literacy progress. We can't accurately measure an individual's data knowledge, skills, and ability across society without these measures. We define in Chapter 6 a framework that permits objective specification of data knowledge optimized for differing citizen data literacy needs. These CDKAs are simple and objective.

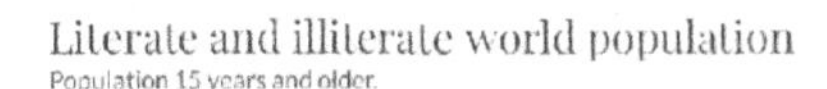

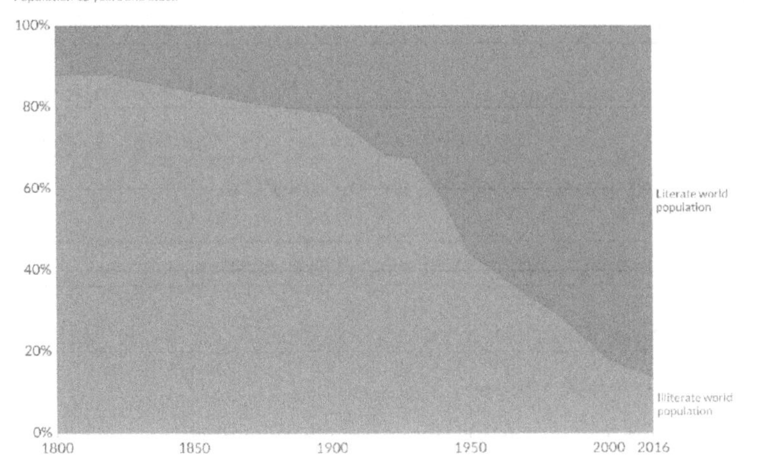

Figure 2.1— Literate and illiterate world populations (age 15 and up)[24]

> *From a historical perspective, literacy levels for the world population have risen drastically in the last couple of centuries. While only 12% of the people in the world could read and write in 1820, today the share has reversed: only 14% of the world population, in 2016, remained illiterate. Over the last 65 years, the global literacy rate increased by 4% every 5 years— from 42% in 1960 to 86% in 2015.*

Is it like computer literacy?

A related term is "computer literacy." People apply this term to describe someone who uses electronic devices like computers, tablets, and smartphones. This term's application expanded quickly to include other activities, including word processing, surfing the Internet, and attending online conferences. For example, consider how we apply the term computer literacy to describe someone.

A computer literate person can turn on a computer, tablet, or smartphone, use it to process words, surf the Internet, and place a Zoom™ call.

The problem with using this definition is that computer literacy initially reflected necessary operational skills, but no more. For example, a computer literate person probably has no idea that leaving equipment connected to the Internet makes it susceptible to hijacking.

Foreign actors regularly commandeer citizens' computers and repurpose them for nefarious activities while citizens become unwitting agents for foreign criminals. That same "computer literate" person may be unaware that the machine is taking part in nefarious acts such as distributed denial-of-service attacks on the country's military. But as we've seen, the public often fails to realize that their behavior puts them at risk for a growing range of injuries. It is such a serious challenge that the FBI was authorized to directly remove malware from public and private MS Exchange servers in the aftermath of the SolarWinds hack.[25]

How about financial literacy?

The concept of financial literacy has achieved a more cohesive understanding due to the coordinated efforts of professional societies and substantive funding. A typical definition of financial literacy is understanding and effectively using various financial skills, including personal financial management, budgeting, and investing. The term is well-understood within the profession and generally seen as a useful societal goal. Country music singer and songwriter Charlie Louvin said it well when describing his and his brother's stage performance costumes as a tax deduction:

> *"Of course they're deductible, but before you can deduct them from your taxes, you have to deduct 'em from your income."*[26]

If you don't appreciate the wisdom of this statement, you may benefit from increasing your own financial literacy. Clearly, Charlie Louvin was financially literate!

Like financial literacy, data literacy involves both practical and theoretical considerations.

Is it like learning to drive?

Consider driving. Most people agree that if someone only knows how to use a car's ignition, they can't safely operate a vehicle on a public road. Turning on a car's ignition is necessary to drive a car, but it's not enough to safely drive the vehicle on public roads. Before taking a vehicle on public roadways, a person must prove an understanding of road rules. However, that's still insufficient. Student drivers also must pass a practical exam.

This test proves that a student can control the automobile under real-world conditions. Together, these tests give the government and public confidence that drivers know how to drive their vehicles safely. Successfully passing a driving test is an objective level of driving performance. This same level of performance will serve the driver well for a lifetime. This isn't to say that one cannot improve their driving abilities—improving from driving literacy to driving acumen might improve traffic patterns.

As in the above cases, data literacy requires knowledge of basic functions (what data is) and the ability to put that knowledge to use to protect oneself and others.

Do we need "levels" of data literacy? Yes—five of them!

> *By 2023, data literacy will become an explicit and necessary driver of business value, demonstrated by its formal inclusion in over 80% of data and analytics strategies and change management programs.*[27]

Everyone produces data. Today, citizens share aspects of their lives with many others. Yet few citizens are data literate. Data illiterate citizens do not understand the consequences of their actions in society. Thus, society developed into a two-tiered system: 1) citizens interested in and becoming more data literate and 2) citizens who are not. While these represent endpoints on a range, we believe that this social dynamic will play a pivotal future role. It is difficult to imagine that the surveillance capitalists will find a profitable future with less than half of the population falling into category 2—it isn't practical with fewer citizens taking part. Surveillance capitalism has a personal stake in keeping data literacy rates low, a goal that is a direct attack on our fellow citizens. Increasing citizen data literacy will allow citizens to fight to keep and monetize their own data rather than allowing others to profit from it.

It is easy to declare someone as data literate, but it is another thing to prove it. This stems from trying to precisely define the single term, *data literacy*. Ordinary interpretation suggests that data literacy is someone capable of "reading, working with, analyzing, and arguing using data."[28] Unfortunately, it is not useful as a measure as it lacks objective standards. As a result, citizens make self-assessments about their data literacy, and society has no way to confirm or refute those claims. This contrasts with other disciplines such as reading, in which we have ways to measure a person's competency through objective measures.

We believe proving someone's data literacy isn't a binary assertion: either literate or illiterate. Instead, we should measure data literacy against a range reflecting objectively measurable aspects. The range moves from *data literacy* to *data proficiency* to *data acumen*, just as children move from spelling "cat" and "dog" at a kindergarten level to writing multi-page research essays at the twelfth-grade level.

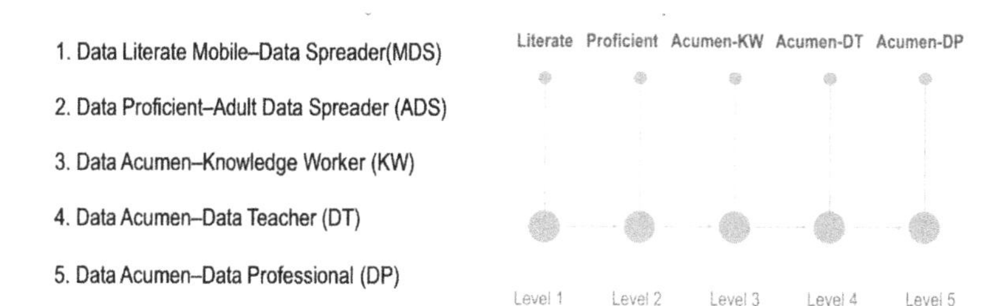

Figure 2.2—A refinement of term data literacy

Each ranking level represents an objectively higher level of data competency. The measure allows us to make objective assertions about someone's data competencies at each point along the scale. This kind of tool has many different uses. For example, it would allow employers to discriminate among applicants, tailor position descriptions, and compare applicants.

In Chapter 6, we will describe these levels more precisely in the context of a Digital Civics Framework. For now, it is sufficient to understand that these five levels more accurately and objectively reflect the challenge associated with improving citizen data literacy and achieving a more manageable understanding of facts (data values).

Exponential effect of bad data decisions

It should come as no surprise that most decision-makers are not data literate. If decision-makers are data illiterate, they will make bad data decisions. Any decision which does not include a holistic study of data creates a cascade of problems across society. Contributing to such bad decisions are outdated and irrelevant materials, scant technical expertise, and disinterested decision-makers. The impact of bad choices is the poor-quality data and mistreatment of organizational data assets. If organizations rely on these data assets to make serious data decisions, uninformed decision-making increases significantly. The question for most organizations addresses how to break out of the cycle. Increased citizen data literacy will help.

Protect your data

Organizations are trying to get your data. Your organization's data has value. Secure it, obtain a copy, back it up, and test the backup system. Yet, many will keep asking you to give it away for nothing. Most importantly, you can't secure what you can't manage, and you certainly can't manage things that you do not know about.

As a Knowledge Worker (KW), you should have an essential awareness of the concept of data = value. Consequently, you are the proverbial first line of defense against someone trying to steal your organization's data.

It's always the KW who connects the fact that cyber breach attempts occur on Thursday afternoons, and that there is always a red Volkswagen parked outside the front of the building on Thursday afternoons.

Unless you are an exhibitionist, it turns out that you can apply the same approach to your organizational data and your own data! No one should ask for someone else's data without a good reason. Here are some excellent reasons for sharing your data:

- Doctor obtaining a medical history
- Warning delivery personal about aggressively licking dogs
- Bank requesting income data as part of a credit card application

Here are some terrible reasons:

- The mattress company receives a feed containing the dates and times of each mattress activity at a customer address, the number of people using the mattress, and the amount of moisture recorded before and after the exercises.

- The robot vacuum company receives a data feed describing 1) the layout of each room vacuumed by the robot and 2) changes to these rooms, 3) the amount and type of things swept up by the vacuum.

- The smart thermometer company receives a regular feed of the audio in the thermostat range, mostly if the company 'forgot' to tell customers there was a microphone in their thermostat!

Citizens and KWs should try to understand the nature of data requests and draw upon neutral expertise to assist with these types of decisions. Still, they should also learn that a reasonable default answer is NO—particularly to continuous streams! With devices, a good practice is, for example, for an application to request to track your location and offer three choices: 1) always, 2) when using the app, 3) never. Not showing the second choice "when using" should be an immediate red flag: Why does the company behind the app want to always know your location, even while you aren't using it? It gives rise to rumors such as "Facebook is listening to all your conversations!" Of course, granting access still presents the subsequent challenge of understanding what data the app acquires and how it's shared.

Citizen "Data Smarts" are required to interact with organizational data machines and (indirectly) with the data matrix

Citizens require specific data capabilities to interact with two increasingly common concepts: an organizational data machine (ODM) and a data matrix.

What are "organizational data machines?"

An ODM is any operation in which an organization collects and processes data (often combined with other acquired data) to produce expected outputs in a factory-like production format.

Figure 2.3—An organizational data machine—this is the perception that most citizens have of organizational data processing.

Governments, companies, or other organizations run data machines. For example, a tax authority collects taxes and citizen information, processes funds against specific accounts, and produces more collection notices, confirmations, and refunds. The tax authority may use multiple computers in various locations, but from the citizen's perspective, it acts as a single ODM. Another example would be a local retail outlet's customer loyalty program, which takes in information about its customers through sales and in turn, feeds information back to the customers in the form of targeted advertising.

Citizens can interact with an ODM in the following ways:

1. exude data to be ingested by an ODM,

2. receive data outputs prepared by an ODM, and

3. participate in the creation or operation of an ODM.

Most citizens exude data as perpetual, involuntary data donors (PIDDs) and receive data, often unconsciously, from various ODMs. Some citizens also participate in the processing of data (the primary operation of the ODM) and fewer still in the creation and evolution of ODMs. These ODMs are created by someone trying to make money in that manner.

ODMs have an enormous impact on our society, but currently, there is no standardized method of credentialing those who work with ODMs as there is for crime lab technicians or CPAs. As a result, organizations fuel their ODMs with low-quality data. That data is then poorly managed and processed, leading to outputs that fail to support organizational strategy. This comes at an ever-increasing cost to citizens. Such situations are seen all around us: 1) inconsistent COVID-19 data processing has resulted in many reports documenting erroneous virus-related counts, 2) citizens fail to realize that technology solutions only account for only around 10% of data challenges, and 3) teachers address data topics incorrectly.

Knowledge workers are involved in planning, building, or maintaining system data as the feed or process data that has encountered the ODM. Currently, they are not qualified data management professionals—nor should we expect them to be currently. We hope this situation improves soon.

Increasingly burdensome organizational data debt

Imagine if when your mail arrived each day, you simply placed it all into a single basket each day and allowed it to accumulate over several months. Worse still, imagine that all the mail going through the US Postal Service piled up this way in a single, unorganized location. This is what is happening to organizational data.

This is referred to as "data debt," representing the time and effort it will take to return an organization's data to a governed state from its current ungoverned state. There is precious little trustworthy expertise around the concept of how to address data debt.[29] These challenges have lingered since computers began producing results, resulting in terabytes of data that have been collected but not processed in such a way as to be useful to anybody.

Many people are qualified to address localized changes in data infrastructure, just as most of us can sort our own incoming mail. However, far fewer individuals have the requisite background to either repair neglected or reengineer existing ODMs and sources—just as most of us wouldn't know what to do with the mail of an entire country. The results of unqualified individuals processing data badly or processing inferior quality data can both be devastating. Thirty years of incorrect *foci* have resulted in the existing data debt requiring massive maintenance, scrap, and rework to help organizations rework existing poorly or even irresponsibly engineered ODMs.

Low citizen data literacy in the face of expanding data demands and the number of devices deployed to capture it leaves few who are even aware of this critical lack of data skills. Furthermore, it leaves the supply of data in a mostly unknown state. Insufficient data and citizen data illiteracy manifest as multifaceted organizational challenges with a (mostly anonymous) common root cause. Efforts to fix these challenges have resulted in a disproportionate effort focused on improving business process systems. Yet, this excessive focus on business processes has resulted in the accumulation of data debt.

The combination of postponed maintenance and general lack of data literacy combine to make data challenges more daunting. Every effort to reduce data debt also reduces the quantity of redundant, obsolete, and trivial data (ROT), leading to conditions where it is easier for knowledge workers to perform.

What is the "data matrix?"

Data machine-data can be, and often is, analyzed for purposes beyond its original collection purpose. These unspecified, unknown, complex interactions comprise the **data matrix**. Much more of this type of data sharing is happening than most are aware.

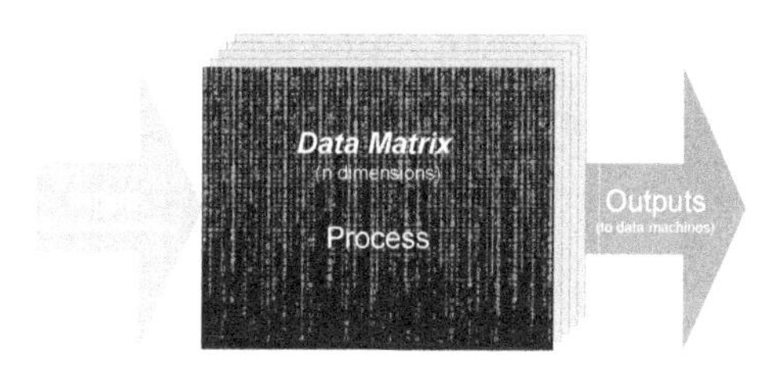

Figure 2.4—The data matrix (n-dimensional)

The phrase derives from surveillance capitalism. It is the physical embodiment of the "other parties" clause in each end user license agreement (EULA) that many of us simply ignore. A data matrix reflects business arrangements that work together to control the collection, use, and dissemination of data to generate profit and exert social influence. We use this term to highlight the largely unknown exchanges that occur out of sight and beyond the scope of the original data interaction of which most are unaware.

Businesses of all kinds use data to anticipate and address timely customer needs and notifying those customers of matters of interest—in addition to satisfying governmental and other requirements for reporting, and so on. Unfortunately, such capabilities are also available to bad actors, including data poachers. Often, these data matrix-based interactions do not exist for good for the citizen. When this is coupled with an inherently indecipherable EULA and fundamental opt-out bias, **the result is a system disproportionally impacting those who have the most to lose and are also the most unaware of the risks**. Much more of this type of data sharing is happening than most are aware. For example, according to the EFF, your next job interviewer may know that you called a suicide prevention hotline from the Golden Gate Bridge a year ago—all through the power of the data matrix.[30]

How the data matrix works

The data matrix exists for surveillance capitalism companies to harvest vast amounts of money. Consider the incentives to invest in data. The organization itself can be invisible. It can occupy an area of minimal public understanding and extraordinarily little regulation—how many citizens understand the power of the data held by Experian, Equifax, and Trans Union? Citizens need to understand that they are not always interacting with individual organizations when they work on the Internet. They are more likely interacting with a data matrix—and should act accordingly. Another typical tactic is for these actors to present end users with terms and conditions that are indecipherable. These agreements are enormous documents prepared in a way that is immensely difficult to understand. Often, a website will embed legal terms that cause the end user to surrender data rights. For example, a well-known company uses this strategy as part of its terms and conditions of usage. Buried in the terms and conditions document are statements that cause the user to grant the company license to use the user's information:

> *By submitting User Provided Content through any of the Services, you grant COMPANY a sublicensable, worldwide, royalty-free license to host, store, copy, publish, distribute, provide access to, create derivative works of, and otherwise use such User Provided Content to the extent and in the form or context we deem appropriate on or through any media or medium and with any technology or devices now known or hereafter developed or discovered. This includes the right for COMPANY to copy, display, and index your User Provided Content. COMPANY will own the indexes it creates. We will also have the right to continue to use your User Provided Content, even if you stop using the Services, but only as necessary for us to provide and improve the Services.*

The average end user would never notice this clause hidden amongst dozens of other similarly obscure and wordy paragraphs. Unfortunately, this renders citizens prey for unscrupulous data practices.[31]

Lack of data literacy permits pilfering from data owners everywhere. (Of note: the term *pilfering* typically implies a particular kind of stealing. What is pilfered is usually stolen stealthily—furtively, so that no one will notice—in small amounts and often again and again.) Society is dividing into two groups—with the data illiterate destined to become PIDDs fueling and otherwise contributing to what we call the Data Matrix, which has lately been responsible for publishing both disinformation and misinformation[32] by combining pilfered and legitimate data. PIDDs feed data acquisition programs that engage in publishing both forms of falsehood. The data is almost free!

Invisible, profitable, and with no regulation or oversight, the data exchanged via the Data Matrix powers the billions of nuisance data traffic—texts, mobile calls, and emails—that distract, invade, and collect. These comprise an increasingly disturbing portion of the Internet. More disturbing, the Data Matrix delivers not just junk contacts but **is also the primary amplifier/spreader of disinformation, misinformation, propaganda, and junk news.** The ultimate result of ignoring the Data Matrix is that citizen PIDDs will continue to supply the data fuel required to power it.

To give just a minor example: most well-crafted clickbait—designed to make readers want to click on a hyperlink, especially when the link leads to content of dubious value or interest—is carefully engineered to deliver periodic endorphins to those who click—mimicking the high delivered by drugs!

Data literacy progress has stagnated at the very time when we need it most facing an increasingly large data tsunami. If things keep going as they are, unscrupulous organizations and governments will continue to suck up the donated data contributed by billions of unsuspecting citizens. *These same* PIDDs *are also unaware that the very act of contributing their data also makes them much more vulnerable to the control and influence exerted by the data from the Data Matrix.*

We must do more to address the widening gap between the data literate and the data-illiterate among us. What is at risk is control of society! A lack of data thinking leads organizations to focus on more accessible and profitable academic disciplines like software development and/or data mining. Here are just a few:

- Many organizations still treat data assets as project assets. When organizations do not have a fair accounting of their data assets, they can't use them to their fullest potential.

- Lack of data awareness leads organizations to ignore the need for data programs and, instead, attempt to manage shared organizational data assets at the project level.
- Lack of data programs leads to increases in IT spending. Consequently, organizations expend resources on integrating and cleaning data or managing far more data than is necessary to work strategically.
- Lack of ability to prepare for future change by implementing a flexible and adaptable organizational data architecture also unnecessarily expends resources.
- A vague focus on efficiently and effectively supporting organizational strategy utilizing data assets leads to diminished organizational performance.
- Voluminous amounts of unmanaged data introduce complexity within an organization.
- Increasing amounts of time, efforts, and risk associated with IT projects threaten budgetary bottom lines.

- Inability to engineer flexibility and adaptability into architectures before production requires additional time and funding to correct adverse effects of such inability.

- Lack of ability to produce reusable data-focused work products requires duplication of effort, diminishes quality and reliability of information—and costs money.

- Increasing time spent understanding data and corresponding decreases time and costs expended for analysis.

- Lack of understanding of data assets inhibits any ability to consider (much less implement) data focused portions of organizational strategy.

- Reduction in the certainty benefits of engineered solutions is an adverse result of not understanding organizational data assets.

- Finally—and perhaps the most egregious, the resulting increased organizational data ROT makes everything worse.

In other words, with neither industry professionals nor academic programs placing a premium on data skills, we end up with few data practitioners in any given organization.

Chapter conclusions-We don't do this well yet

Additional data lessons to reinforce this chapter's content:

To be useful, the concept of data literacy must be considered a range (more literate or less literate) rather than a binary (literate or not literate).

Data Lesson #4

Citizens operating in today's world are dependent on smooth interaction with ODMs and data specifically.

Data Lesson #5

Organizations face data debt and low data literacy within the workforce. However, many believe that the net generation and digital natives are inherently more knowledgeable technically than past students. Although younger generations may be able to "do" more with their tech, they may not be any better equipped to deal responsibly with their data.

Data Lesson #6

Data moves between ODMs to form the data matrix–generally for the not for the good of the citizen

Data Lesson #7

CHAPTER 3

An Excess of Data

The headline from recent Pew Center Research is generally good news. In 2000, about 50% of US adults did not use the internet. In 2019, that number had plummeted to 10% (https://pewrsr.ch/3EPPkfY). With more citizens using the Internet, more citizens must understand data and what the relative risks are.

Without a practical understanding of data, Internet users are likely to be financially injured by predators at some time in their life. Similarly, these PIDDs could face a future where injuries are common and follow them throughout their lives. We believe the answer is making citizens data literate.

To begin this chapter, we share a story about a large public organization that recently improved its supply chain and human capital. We'll briefly review the lessons learned and evidence of the continually increasing data interaction across society. We'll show that these data interactions account for about 20% to 40% of an organization's typical IT budget. After, we'll demonstrate how technology can only solve part of the data problem. Last, we'll review some additional lessons learned.

A representative experience— Awakening to different types of data problems in a crisis

We want to share a recent story about an organization and how it encountered data issues by surprise and, more importantly, in bungled response to a publicity disaster. If a large public organization has as much trouble as we are going to describe, imagine the toll that data challenges take on individual citizens. Let's review how management learned of its data problems. The organization had a flagship product. During a televised event, the product suffered a catastrophic failure. Corporate officials asked many questions concerning the product's quality control systems.

When the company investigated the issue, they realized data was the root of the problem. The company discovered that much of the data required by the analysis came from other organizations. The company also learned that it needed to identify the pedigree for each data asset. The company eventually reverse-engineered the data, cleaned it, and updated the data with tags and further semantic details. Unfortunately, what should have been a relatively easy public relations response exposed internal confusion and imprecision. Not a good image to project.

These data problems and the resulting communications mess directly affected investor confidence, and, as a result, the company lost a billion dollars on Wall Street. Like the Target data breach, the impact of this catastrophe reached the board room. Attention from the board of directors positively impacted the data literacy initiative, ensuring program success.

This organization's experiences were unexceptional in our estimation. Unfortunately, far too many organizations go through roughly the same awakening processing and experience unsatisfying results.

Four basic data truths

A gospel for citizens to share as they begin to learn more about data is to understand what we call the *four basic data truths*:

1. Data volume is increasing faster than organizations can process it.
2. Poor data practices divert resources and reduce productivity.

3. Reliance on technology and current educational practices has not materially improved experiences and bottom-line improvements.
4. Data requires organization.

Data Truth #1: More data is a reality

> *The Library of Congress had 39 million books in its collection when it was created in 1800. Today the Internet generates 100 times that much data every second!* [33]
>
> **Information Wars by Richard Stengel**

Our favorite set of illustrations of this concept comes from Domo, a cloud-based integration vendor. Its work presents different Internet statistics illustrating the dramatic increases in data over the past few years. Every year, Domo releases an insightful infographic showing data growth as compared to the previous calendar year. Domo's research shows how much and what kinds of data people accessed during the preceding year using an intuitive form. To help people understand the problem, Domo standardized all measures to *data events per minute.* For the entirety of 2020, every minute of every day:

- Zoom hosted 208,000 participants
- Netflix streamed 400,000 hours of video
- YouTube users uploaded 500 hours of video

- Consumers spent $1M online
- LinkedIn users applied for 69,000+ jobs
- Spotify added 28 songs
- Amazon shipped 6,659 packages
- Users spent $3,805 through mobile apps[34]

The amount of Internet data continues to grow at staggering rates. Most data created since 2002 has been digital, and most of it has been created recently.[35] The rate of increase is perhaps more revealing. The following characteristics combine to increase data growth:

- The number of Internet users is increasing.
- The number of devices per person is increasing.
- The number of devices connected to the Internet is increasing.
- The data matrix is relentlessly pushing to find and integrate more data about citizens.

It is irresponsible for any nation to increase the data burdens on its populace without providing the knowledge, skills, and tools required to manage it.

There is an infodemic (information epidemic) spreading a digital disease: misleading or factually inaccurate information. Gone are the traditional news and information sources. Today, the Internet is the source of people's knowledge. And with this change, there is an explosion of potential news and information sources. Many are small, focused news outlets, but others are not—some exist specifically to promote a business or political agenda. Websites like Media Matters, Center for American Progress, Breitbart, and Common Dreams are just a few websites that offer readers highly partisan news and information. With more websites appearing every day, the likelihood that someone encounters factually inaccurate or incomplete information grows, and with it comes the fuel for national discontent and discord.[36]

Data Truth #2: Very few organizations account for data interchange costs

Datasets transferred between ODMs via the data matrix are data interchanges. Many seem free, but only because few of us know how to account for their hidden costs. Not paying attention to data interchange costs has enormous consequences. Moving data from one system to another isn't cheap. It's a complicated and time-consuming task that consumes considerable resources. These costs affect citizens and organizations in several ways. The most obvious is money. The more times an organization processes a data asset, the more money it spends on human and machine resources. It makes sense that the fewer times an organization must process a data asset, the more efficient the organization is. If an organization processes data repeatedly, the organization must dedicate more resources for each data interchange.

To better understand this relationship, let's go back to the beginning—before there were computer systems. In those times, creative citizens made individual applications that were genuinely inventive and technologically advanced for the time. For example, consider the typical set of systems for most organizations—they consist of disparate applications with tightly integrated datasets (as depicted). While these applications produced locally optimal solutions, the lack of programmatic coordination resulted in a hodgepodge of standards and rigid data exchange, limited to pre-specified instances. As a result, poor data practices combined with suboptimal data models and a new idea was born. People came to call these dated systems "legacy systems."[37]

With perfect hindsight, the original architects of these, the existing legacy systems, missed an opportunity to inject standards much higher and more efficiently. Suppose the original data models for these legacy systems were better. They would have likely persisted, given organizational reluctance to change them. However, it is difficult to criticize the first efforts of these inventors.

The general next wave of attempts to get more from organizational data focused on extracting, transforming, and loading transactional data from the legacy environment, consisting of business intelligence, data warehousing, and lake technologies. This duplicated data is revised, tortured, and munged until the organization obtains satisfactory results. Unfortunately, the insights gleaned from this process are rarely transmitted back into the legacy data management environment.

As our colleague, Tom Redman, is fond of saying: hidden data factory costs are scattered across an organization (2016). Most do not recognize, organize, or account for these activities; they must nevertheless repair the data defects to function. We describe these functions in a single word: waste. The challenge is to make the costs of this hidden repair visible! These unorganized, unrecognized, and unaccounted for operations represent many of the efforts for which companies pay their knowledge workers. This is time wasted in uncounted ways instead of addressing these issues programmatically.[38] We have documented these hidden sources of expense previously and will describe a representative case below.[39]

Employees of companies often engage in "shadow IT," a process that puts company and customer data at risk. Shadow IT uses information technology systems, devices, software, applications, and services without the explicit approval of the company's IT department. Shadow IT has grown exponentially in recent years with the adoption of cloud-based applications and services. One of the biggest reasons employees engage in shadow IT is to increase efficiency. A recent RSA study reported that 35% of employees feel like they need to work around their company's security policies to get their jobs done.[40] For example, an employee may discover a better file-sharing application than the one officially permitted. Once one employee begins using it, other members of their department may do the same. While it's clear that shadow IT isn't going away, organizations can minimize the risk associated with it by educating end users and taking preventative measures to watch and manage unsanctioned applications. As they work their way up the literacy levels, organizations try to recognize and account for the costs of these individual data repair factories. Only when they analyze and understand these costs can they build systems that address deficiencies programmatically.

Data Truth #3: Technology can't solve most of the problem

While technology can solve many problems, it cannot solve every problem. This should come as no surprise to anyone. But when the risks are high and people get nervous, they revert to what they know: they look for magic solutions using technology. Despite people's faith in technology, these solutions have not materially addressed the gap between citizen data processing capabilities and the amount of data necessary to process daily. The gap is growing, and technology is reaching its limits. Figure 3.1

reports that more training is still focused on how to use the tool instead of how to use the tool to solve a problem.[41]

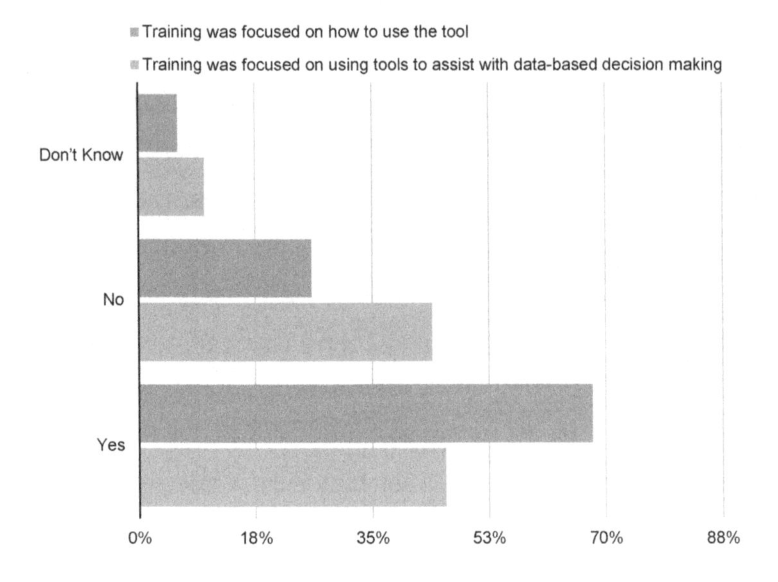

Figure 3.1—The gap is growing

The gap is growing, data literacy among citizens is stagnating, data debt is increasing, and technology is reaching its limits. We're now in the post-big data era, which ushered in a new wave of thinking and processing data. Organizations treated many of these problems as IT projects instead of innovation projects—and most wound up in the same "not meeting expectations" category as other ill-fated IT projects.

Our colleague, Randy Bean, conducted an excellent quality annual survey, who repeatedly asked the same or similar organizations to quantify the challenges met as they faced the principal challenge to becoming data driven. The result, consistent for years, indicates that citizens, process, and culture issues dominate—by almost 90+percent! However, the ultimate argument for investing more in proven data practices is the widespread lack of data to train advanced algorithms required for AI apps. Talk about being out over our skis! In a 2020 study by Harvard Business Review, findings reveal that technology investments occur at people's expense and process issues.[42] Diagnosing data challenges can be difficult because the IT system or process is conceptually closer to the user experiencing the challenge. It's only natural to blame the messenger for a wrong message.

Challenge to Becoming Data-Driven	2018	2019	2020	2021
People, Business Process, Culture	80.9%	92.5%	90.9%	92.2%
Technology	19.1%	7.5%	9.1%	7.8%

Figure 3.2—Technology must occupy a much less prominent role

Data Truth #4: Data requires organization

Better organized data increases in value. To see the truth in this, imagine getting value from this book without the aid of regular pagination, indices, tables of contents, headings, and more. Its contents might be inherently useful and valuable but understanding it would be more difficult. Then imagine trying to find a particular piece of information again after you'd read the book the first time—it would be next to impossible!

Our experience indicates that organizations lose 20-40% of their IT spending to poor data practices. Poor data practices are costing organizations much money, time, and effort. The number one cause is data's tendency to follow Pareto's law that avows 80% of organizational data to be redundant, obsolete, or trivial (ROT). The only argument we get is from colleagues in the business who suggest that the actual number is greater than 80%. Improving organizational data involves ending data ROT (most of a community's data) and improving the remaining 20% to make it fit for use. The question to ask is which information should we eliminate? These statistics suggest that the best way to improve organizational data assets is to decrease corporate ROT and increase the remaining data quality.

Organizations must standardize more of their data, or costs will continue to rise. One way to control costs is through data normalization. Normalizing data is the most basic way to determine its fundamental value. If information isn't semantically and syntactically standardized, organizations will spend unnecessary money to process it. Untreated, it contributes to the organizational data debt and causes the cost of everything to increase. Surprisingly, many miss this primary point, often claiming standardizing data takes too much time and money. We understand that organizations are under tremendous pressure to deliver, and we know standardization costs money. However, as the saying goes, you can pay me now or pay me later. It matters not—if organizations want to leverage their systems, organizations must build their solutions on solid foundations free of semantic controversy and confusion.

To avoid confusion and higher costs, we recommend two methods of data standardization: 1) standardize the limits of data, and 2) standardize the arrangement of data. These two make it possible to determine how accurate, scalable, and valuable any given plan/outcome would be.

Chapter conclusions-Data are drowning us

Citizens are drowning in bad data and bad data practices at the individual, workgroup, and society levels. The first step addressing the challenge is deciding where efforts can be most effective–in this case, a sizable percentage of the human population. Next, we present a scaler approach to the concept of data literacy–transforming it from a binary condition to a graduated concept. These citizen data smarts are the 'eyes' through which non-data literates view concepts such as ODMs and the Data Matrix. When viewed against the four data truths, it becomes clear that society will require a sustained effort just to 'tread water.' This is not occurring and too many citizens are data illiterate. Still, more data lessons help illustrate challenging scale dimensions.

Ninety percent of the US is online, increasing the importance of improving data literacy.

Data Lesson #8

Data and interactions with citizens are accelerating, posing a threat to those who are data illiterate.

Data Lesson #9

Delay in processing data impacts everyone, much as traffic affects congested commutes. We must get better at recognizing, accounting for, and addressing delays programmatically.

Data Lesson #10

This challenge can't easily be corrected and, more importantly, the data debt will require some real effort to clean up. (Professional ministrations are required to make up for past neglect.).

Data Lesson #11

Technology can only address specific parts of the data challenges. The other 90% consists of people and process challenges that currently are unmet.

Data Lesson #12

Disorganized data is useless data. Organizations must standardize and organize or face hidden costs later.

Data Lesson #13

CHAPTER 4

The Current Approach Ain't Cutting It!

Our educational system is failing to educate society about data. From what you've learned about the importance of data management in the earlier chapters, that should scare you!

In this chapter, we describe the root causes of society's failure to manage our data. Then we discuss the current ways that educational institutions and other organizations are attempting to teach data principles and why those methods are insufficient. Societies must develop more effective approaches. Creating such a system is difficult, but it isn't impossible. A few countries, including Saudi Arabia, Kazakhstan, and Mexico, have successfully introduced national student data literacy curricula. We outline a program that we think would address the debts in the United States and elsewhere.

Lack of progress towards citizen data literacy

What progress is society making towards data literacy? McKinsey Global Institute addressed this question in the now famous study: *Big Data: The Next Frontier for Innovation, Competition, and Productivity*. In this study, McKinsey suggested the United States needed more than 1.5 million additional data-savvy managers. McKinsey's study crystalized and energized the data science movement and helped produce more than 300 operations research, statistics, computer science, and other technically focused programs. IBM echoed McKinsey with its prediction that, by 2020, the US would need more than 2,720,000 data and data analytic **experts.**[43]

We are teaching data skills as an outgrowth of statistics—and supply isn't keeping up with demand. Consider the gap between today's data volume and our ability to process it. We've seen an exponential data growth in storage: 28% per year. At the same time, we've seen a more modest increase in data analysts: 5.7% per year.

Output from all these new data science programs doesn't make a dent in the demand for data talent. To give you an idea of the scale of such a challenge, consider the need for information security professionals. The lack of data experts is a widely acknowledged problem as well. And like data analysts, society is working to create a larger pool of security experts in response to the growing body of data across the nation. This approach doesn't seem to be working either, however. Despite the industry's best efforts to increase between 2017-18, the number of clicks on posted cybersecurity jobs decreased! The lack of interest in cybersecurity jobs left a shortfall of thousands of jobs and could not have happened at a worse time. Between 2013 and 2015, we saw increases of 70% in cybersecurity attacks and 242% in data breaches. Suppose supply isn't close to meeting demand in the whole cyber industry?

How can we expect the current approach to address an ever-widening gap? The data world is far less organized than the cyber area—exceeding its size by at least a factor of 10. We need to catch up, but now we can talk about flattening (not the curve but) the rate of increase in the gap between the data analysis requirements and capabilities.

Federal literacy tracking

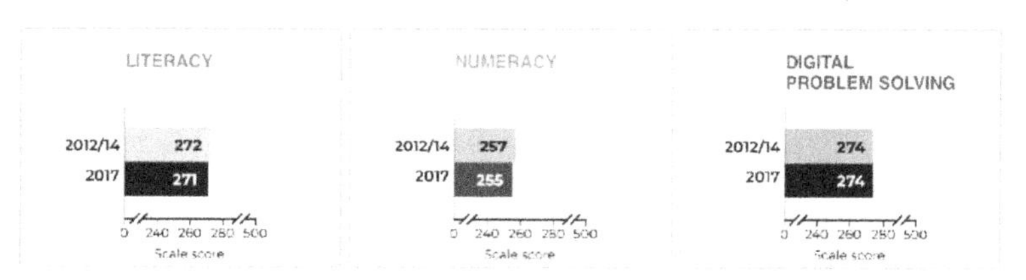

Figure 4.1—Tracking literacy by the US Federal Government

Happily, the federal government has been keeping track of some data that we can use to assess US literacy. *The*

National Assessment of Adult Literacy[44] measures literacy, numeracy, and digital problem-solving among American adults aged 16 or older. The organization considers these three competencies as critical for 21st-century society and the global economy.

- Literacy: the ability to understand, use and respond appropriately to written texts.
- Numeracy: the capacity to use mathematical and computational skills.
- Digital problem solving: the ability to access and interpret information in digital environments to perform practical tasks.

While none of this measure data literacy, as surrogates, they are informative. The essential takeaway from this data is that there was no literacy growth from 2012-14 to 2017. Quoting from the report: "Between 2012/14 and 2017, there were no statistically significant changes in the percentages of adults performed at each proficiency level in any of the three ... domains." Showing no meaningful literacy change is virtually the same as moving backward!

Industry and data literacy

Organizations are struggling with the concept of organizational data literacy. Despite increasing data and technology investments, the percentage of firms self-identifying as data-driven declined from 37% in 2017 to 24% in 2020.

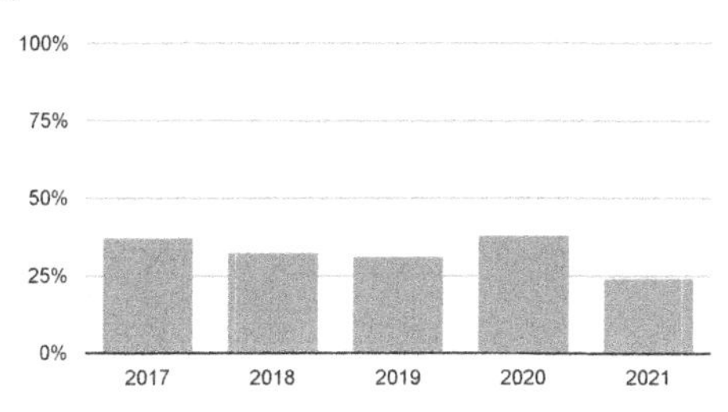

Figure 4.2—Lack of progress towards organizational data literacy

Other interesting findings include that most organizations have failed to:

- forge a data culture (86%)
- create a data-driven organization (86%)
- treat data as a business asset (39%)
- compete on data and analytics (41%)
- address issues that cause data to undermine key initiatives (66%)
- increase the scope of their data effort beyond departments (70%)
- have their data leadership report outside of IT (58%).

The most interesting finding was a self-assessment of the challenges facing data initiatives as 10% based on technology and 90% based on workers and processes. In conclusion, Bean and Davenport write: "Firms must become much more serious and creative about addressing the human side of data if they truly expect to derive meaningful business benefits."[45]

Still, outsiders (non-data citizens) do not want to hear about or discuss the complexities of the various challenges and solutions. Most also lack the architecture and engineering backgrounds required to review the highly automated solutions required. This lack of foundational education makes students unqualified to participate in solution development materially. Since schools teach data so unevenly, data professionals interact with others with varying depth and correctness of data knowledge. One can conclude that everyone learned data management by themselves without uniform guidance. This is an inefficient learning method fraught with problems.

Root cause analysis and insights

To understand the magnitude of this challenge and the vastness of the data debt, we present a root cause analysis of the challenges we face on the facing page.

This data-focused approach will require a very fundamental shift in organizational approaches to problem-solving. In the past, organizations have:

- Organized around strategies—make great products, provide excellent strategies, etc.
- Invested resources in systems and technologies to help them to achieve their strategic objectives.
- Implemented systems as combinations of hardware, software, processes, citizens, and data.
- Considered data as an afterthought during the conversion process.
- Allowed poor data to negatively impact other system components.

Q1: Why are so many organizational technology experiences so poor?
A1: Misunderstanding of data's role in IT
Q2: Why do so few understand data's role in IT?
A2: Little, if any, focus on enterprise-wide data use in the educational system.
Q3: Why is the educational system not addressing this gap?
A3: Lack of recognition by the system
Q4: Why has the system not yet been made aware of this deficiency?
A4: Lack of understanding at the executive-level
Q5: Why do they not understand?
A5: Little, if any, focus on enterprise-wide data use in the educational system.
Q6: What unit of measure should we use to assess progress?
A6: Understanding the challenge better, we now know that progress can be meaningfully measured across years as opposed to weeks.

Complaints, in the form of business challenges, are lodged against either the system or the process. Unfortunately, the data's role in these challenges is most often under-recognized or ignored altogether. Instead, remedies are applied at the system or process level, further increasing the system's complexity and brittleness (for example, placing multiple duplicative control systems for priority edge processing instead of centralizing controls for efficiency).

Good data versus good data skills

Seeing these problems arise, businesses have awoken to the necessity of acquiring good data. However, as we saw in Chapter 3, most organizations have more data than they know what to do with! The problem is that far too many data initiatives focus on getting useful data. However, producing quality data proves to be a difficult challenge and is only partially addressed by this book.

Unfortunately, good data constitutes only part of the requirements. Organizations must also have the following, which we have found that almost none of them do:

- Well-organized data of known quality.
- Workers who know how to use it to best support strategy.

In organization after organization, we find the legacy data environment treated as a black box. Workers extract, transform, and load data into warehouses without any idea what happens to the data next. But they don't stop there. After loading data into various data stores, those same workers populate dashboards, alerts, and other reporting technologies. Many of these systems function well and are finely tuned, well-engineered data environments. However, 100% of organizations we have dealt with failed to communicate the lessons learned from the analytics practice's challenges back to the black box. This represents a failure to provide a valuable feedback loop. Organizations have not yet learned the value of a data literate workforce.

Evaluation of the current curriculum

Only data is experiencing such rapid growth that it requires us to rethink what's been happening. Our colleague, Micheline Casey, has a great saying that we're fond of repeating, "There will never be any less data than right now!" Despite this dramatic rise in data volume and role, society (broadly comprised of social, political, and economic dimensions) has failed to respond. Data is conspicuously missing from not just high school and college curricula but as a business competency. Data's absence from the formal educational material leads to smart but under-informed individuals making decisions that have not generally led to good data outcomes. Poor data outcomes increasingly hurt society in many small ways. Ultimately, the system can't take anymore—data exceeds our ability to manage it to the detriment of society.

So how can we fix these problems? First, we must understand what a qualified data scientist does, and that isn't always easy.

One problem with the term "data scientist" has been summed up by Eric Siegel, author of *Predictive Analytics*:

> *Data science is a redundant term, since all science involves data; it's like saying, "book librarian."* [46]

Further, the term "data scientist" is vague. An excellent refinement to the data science movement has been the addition of a third-level qualifier. This type of qualifier indicates a specific area of subject matter expertise that the owner possesses, such as *healthcare data scientist* or *actuarial data scientist*. A "healthcare" qualifier represents a useful reframing of the goal from the process to the outcome and makes it easier to recommend specific educational- and industry-specific components.

The qualifications for data scientists are poorly defined and open to interpretation, and many people are under the mistaken belief that their main function is to build databases. Colleges and universities are quick to offer courses showing students how the latest technologies work, but those same schools rarely teach students how to manage their data. Unfortunately, there are only a few noteworthy exceptions. Most organizations don't yet consider data skills to be a necessary qualification for employment. This view is standard across corporations, with leaders believing that data skills are necessary only when building new databases. Consider that these topics are literally excluded:

- Database migration
- Implementing a software application
- Installing an enterprise resource package (ERP).

To execute these tasks, employees would not need to create a new database but would need to have a fundamental knowledge of how data systems work. However, these skills are frequently excluded from educational curricula. Three major problems occur when data scientists are improperly educated:

1. **They are not interested in learning about the industries in which they are employed**. Data scientists often don't know (or worse, care to know) about the company employing them. They care more about the process than the results. As with many technologically focused careers, this first generation of data scientists has proven more

interested in algorithms than in helping organizations improve their operations.

2. **They are not productive enough**. Data scientists spend 80% of their time migrating, converting, and improving data. Schools can improve this ratio by recognizing the need to teach more data management principles as part of core data science curricula and partner data scientists with capable and qualified data mungers at a ratio of 10 data scientists for each data management professional.

3. **They have little or no experience munging data**. All data scientists will describe their work in Parito terms—something like: I spend 80% of my time preparing the data and 20% doing the required analyses. Increasing familiarity with munging techniques and toolsets helps improve overall throughput.

2020 data munging (preparation) market study

A report from Dresner Advisory Services[47] provides the following information regarding organizations' current use of data munging approaches and technology.

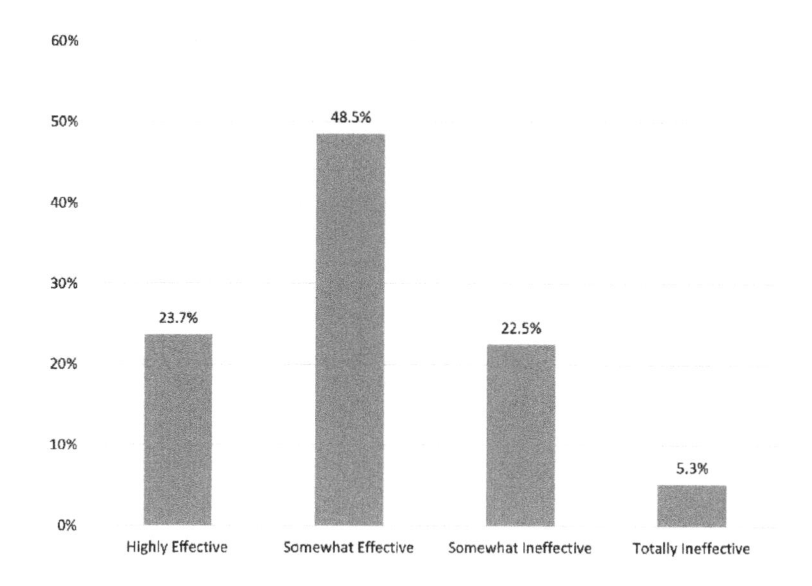

Figure 4.3—Data-preparation approach

Some high points include:

- In 2020, nearly half of organizations (49%) say their current data-preparation approach is "somewhat effective."
- Combined with those that report "highly effective" data preparation, the total figure nears three-quarters (73%) of respondents.
- The remaining respondents, about 28%, report only a "somewhat ineffective" or "totally ineffective" approach to data preparation.

Overall, the responses imply a growing maturity of data preparation, likely in the context of increasing self-service and user autonomy.

A majority (62%) of respondents say they "constantly" or "frequently" make use of data preparation. We can't distinguish whether end user efforts are individual or repeated practices. Still, overall usage of data preparation is high, with a total of 84% reporting at least "occasional" data preparation activity. Only about 16% of respondents "rarely" or "never" perform data preparation.

The mean frequency of data preparation in 2020 increases noticeably with organization size, from a low of 3.3 at small organizations (1-100 employees) to 4.0 at substantial organizations (> 10,000 employees). Combined "constant" and "frequent" usage is highest at enormous organizations (75%). After that, it decreases to a low of 54% at small organizations. "Constant" users also increase in number with organization size.

This approach isn't new. The authors of the report "The New Decision Makers: Equipping Frontline Workers for Success" use the term *frontline workers* (in its pre-pandemic usage) to focus on employees who are the first contact between organizations and customer service. These include sales clerks, nurses, flight attendants, maintenance workers, electricians, store managers, service technicians, field salespeople, and more.[48]

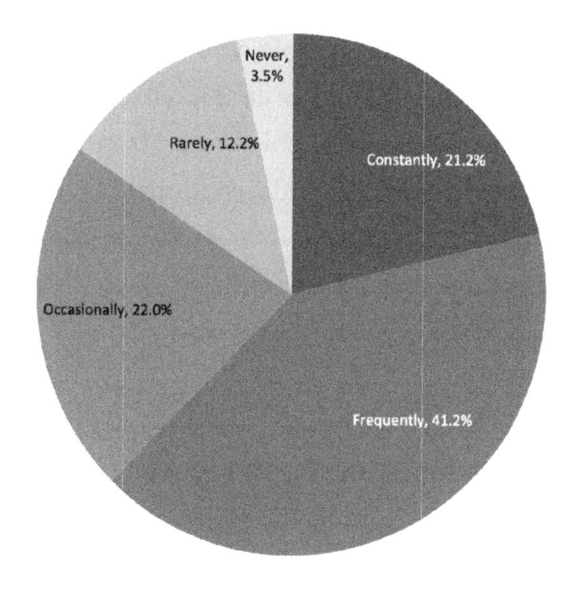

Figure 4.4—Make use of data preparation

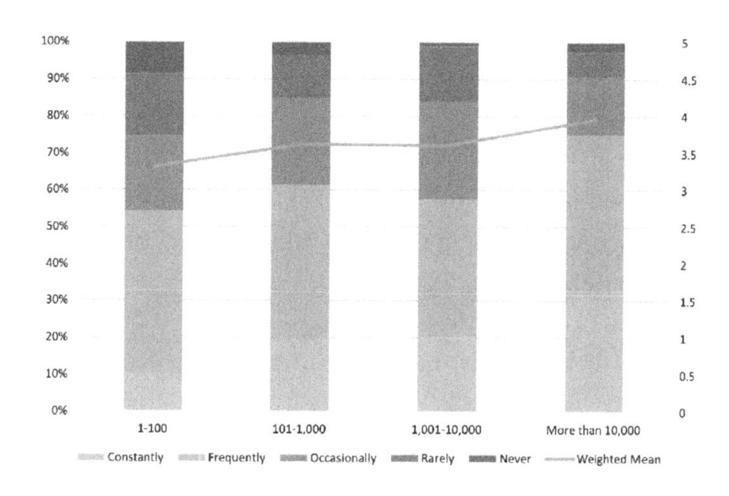

Figure 4.5—Mean frequency of data preparation

Referring to their approach as *The Two-Sided Coin: Empowerment and Enablement*, there are two critical aspects of creating an empowered and data-driven enterprise. The first involves a culture shift. Leaders are more than twice as likely as followers (51% versus 23%) to say a data driven culture is a critical part of their organization's corporate strategy. For data-driven decision-making to become ingrained in the culture, a move from hierarchical to a more distributed way of working is required. Many refer to this as the democratization of data.

Weak data management foundation

> *17% of US knowledge workers report a significant amount of time was spent in mainstream education learning how to use data in the workplace, versus 52% in India.*[49]

Why are so many professionals unequipped to deal with data effectively? Data education occurs in several ways, but none deliver effective or efficient results. Instead, the current data curriculum does not address foundational data concepts. Data skills, like algorithms, often take a back seat to technology skills.

The lack of any comprehensive data literacy efforts isn't surprising. Most approaches are fundamentally flawed—incorporating data development into existing software development methods. This flaw is so fundamental that the only way to obtain positive results is not to share any data between projects.

Today, data management relies on a few scientific, research, architectural, and engineering principles not taught in most science, technology, engineering, and mathematics (STEM) programs. Most educational institutions don't address this educational debt, thereby contributing to society's data debt. As a result, few students understand the contents of this book, for example, by the time they graduate from high school. Instead, students enter the workforce with strong technical skills but no foundational understanding of data thinking and best practices. Often, those who have strong data knowledge and expertise come from disciplines such as accounting, process improvement, and others outside the field of data. There, they learn about data strategy and temper their theoretical learning with relevant realities. Because people don't have formal data education, workers confuse data problems with IT problems. Consequently, people regularly reach for IT first to solve data problems.

Data literacy isn't considered a necessary workforce skill

Because decision-makers don't know how badly they need data specialists, educational institutions do not focus on producing them. What we've seen appear is a commercial approach to education that focuses on what the industry thinks it needs at the expense of the more comprehensive educational needs. For example, we routinely see universities offer courses in programming at the cost of foundational data concepts. Lacking any foundational knowledge regarding data and its management, students enter the workforce ill-equipped to deal with the data explosion.

For educational institutions, this approach makes fiscal sense and is easier to deliver. Focusing on market-driven academic demands also allows universities to optimize education along select lines of business. Universities can focus on higher-yield offerings without delving into the areas that require critical thinking and sound judgment.

Existing scientific foundation

So, if students want to learn about data, where can they go? One underutilized resource is the Library Science community. Data professionals have two "blueprints" created by professional associations: The *Data Management Maturity Model* (*DMM*)[50] and the *Data Management Body of Knowledge* (*DMBoK*).[51] Organizations rarely bother to understand data until they use it. Such an afterthought creates all preventable problems: the practice costs more, delivers less, takes longer, and presents a higher risk. One example occurs when IT projects expect data to have been identified, specified, and documented, but it isn't. In programmatic terms, physical data structures must exist before any software projects can incorporate them correctly. Suppose any organization expects to reuse that data. In that case, they must first exercise data design principles that promote reuse over individual use. The DMBoK provides information to help with data use and reuse.

Uneven teaching and research approach

Academia has no shortage of good intentions. However, we must acknowledge that the quality of instruction around database design and technologies is uneven and unbalanced. Data design has never been an easy course to teach. If you have done this type of teaching professionally, you probably understand this already. If you know data design, you have not likely given much thought about explaining it to others. If you haven't done database design work, it's unlikely you are qualified to perform this work.

Here are three examples of data management challenges faced when teaching in higher education settings.

Outdated textbooks: Naturally, textbooks provide students problems to solve. Some problems have exact answers and are easy to grade and correct. For example, students are often asked to calculate the time it takes for a storage disk to access data. The problem gives students technical parameters for the exercise: 512 byte/sector, 12 ms seek time, and a disk rotation speed of 5400 RPM. The issue also indicates the disk can transfer data at a rate of 4MB/second. By most measures, this is a functional problem for students pursuing a technical degree. There is only one problem: modern devices rarely use spinning storage disks; they use solid-state storage.

Unqualified staff: A college student brought a database assignment home to a parent for assistance. The parent was a data professional with decades of experience. Surprisingly, the parent couldn't decipher the homework instructions and called one of us for assistance. I couldn't understand the instructions either. The student returned to class with a set of clarifying questions for the professor. The responses indicated that the professor was not qualified to teach this class. This finding prompted a call to the instructor's boss, the department chair. Instead of fixing the problem, the department chair responded, "I am not really worried because that professor will be retiring in a few years." After the escalation of the two responses to the dean, the school replaced the professor mid-semester, and the department chair wound up in hot water.

Faulty curriculum frameworks. Consider how schools teach the concept of operations in curricula. Methods—the purposeful things that get stuff done for us in today's SOcially, LOcation-aware, MObile (SOLOMO) society—are described and taught as comprising five components: hardware, software, citizens, processes, and data. The growth of data is far outpacing the growth of the other areas, but it has not received proportionately more attention.

Disproportionate focus on technology

Additionally, most educational programs focus on technology rather than data because many view technology and data as the same subject—*which they are not*. Most curricula are biased towards technology and consider data a subset of technology. This serves to conflate the two topics and confuses students and everyone else. Focusing on technology at the expense of data has resulted in the chaos that we experience today. A focus on data overlaps and reinforces data requirements that society must address before selecting any technology.

Schools treat data management as a collection of technical industry standards and courses sprinkled across various academic programs. As a result, finding organized data management knowledge is difficult. And as we previously saw, academia continues to produce graduates who are data illiterate. Worse still is what academia does to students who receive an IT education. For more than three decades, academia specified that students pursuing computer science, information systems, and computer engineering receive exactly one course about data. That's it. Instead of focusing on data, these courses taught students precisely one skill, building a new Oracle database! Ironically, building new databases is the most unlikely task a graduate will face on the job. Almost no one makes new databases from scratch today. Most people work on legacy datasets where reverse-engineering skills are more useful than data engineering skills. Consequently, when new graduates realize they need to understand data, they must find that knowledge elsewhere.

What are the solutions?

Decision-makers face discussions like the one on the following page. Of course, we disagree, but organizations must be realistic about the size and shape of the challenge. Societal data literacy should continue to be measured annually. Some organizations may benefit from quarterly measurements. Society must recognize that the current leadership will rotate to other positions by the time results from a societal data literacy effort are recognized.

Let's consider an example. School lesson plans present information that students must know. Specific lesson plans structure information to develop a thorough understanding of the field and address different needs at an organizational level. Though comprehensive in a traditional sense, most lesson plans do not recognize the role data and technology play in society. However, before students discuss any lesson plan, we must first focus on sustainability.

If	Attempting to manage data properly has been more trouble than it has been worth ...
Then	Stop trying!
If	¾ of knowledge workers feel insufficiently prepared to get data to support their organizational mission (and) Initial measurements paint a dark picture regarding data self-sufficiency/data-centric dreams
Then	Addressing this gap would seem highly and generally productive!
If	More citizens are using the Internet than ever before (and) The existing workforce has not been provided requisite data knowledge/skills (and) Universities/high schools are still not providing the requisite knowledge/skills (and) Current supply isn't close to meeting demand (and) Data continues to increase.
Then	how can we recover with our incorporating professional ministration to make up for past neglect?
If	Previous literacy effort have been unable to agree on common definitions/measures
Then	A different approach is required!

Over our collective careers, we have seen only a handful of organizations capable of sustaining the goals of any lesson plan. The only reason to continue investing in a data program is that data helps achieve a return on investment made in every lesson plan. Hence, organizations should partake in annual effort recalibration at the minimum.

We address this topic in more detail in Chapter 14. We're confident that no one is overtly against increased citizen data literacy. It doesn't hurt to have a strong business case to present to civic leaders, showing that increased investment in organizational data literacy improves both top and bottom lines. These improved economic benefits are the subject of next chapter.

Chapter conclusions-Data lessons on volume, educational effectiveness, and required effort

Measured as best we can, citizen literacy stagnates in a time of vastly increased data and data hype. The gap between the amount of data available for analysis and the ability of society to analyze it is increasingly unresolvable. Citizens report tangible interference with job performance because of data discomfort. Worse, this illiteracy has caused data fixes to go undiagnosed. Failure by the education systems to address this has left at least three generations of graduates without awareness of the nature of the challenge. Specific data lessons from Chapter 4 are:

Data is increasing at an incomprehensible rate. Yet, when needed most for data literacy to be holding steady (and more importantly, not growing), it is unavailable for use by the essential citizenry, and it's just as bad or worse with organizational data literacy.

Data Lesson #14

Data education occurs via any number of means, but none deliver results efficiently or effectively, as evidenced by the unimproved longitudinal scores.

Data Lesson #15

This challenge can't easily be corrected, and, more importantly, the data debt will require some real effort to clean up. (Again, professional ministrations are required to make up for past neglect.)

Data Lesson #16

CHAPTER 5

Increasing Knowledge Worker Productivity

Our society is a vast source of untapped potential, as this quote from the Data Literacy Project indicates:

> ***DATA-DRIVEN CITIZENS UNDERPIN A PRODUCTIVE WORKFORCE*** *One of the most significant challenges for organizations in the digital age isn't capturing data but turning data into actionable insights to empower employees to make more informed decisions, improve productivity, and drive competitive advantage. To succeed in the data revolution, business leaders enable their employees to become more confident and comfortable using data insights to make decisions. Using data to make business decisions will help firms grow by as much as 5% in enterprise value.*[52]

As noted, data illiteracy plagues organizations and workers everywhere. As in data security, a small, repeated investment in the form of annual training can go a long way toward preventing undesirable outcomes. This chapter explains how increased data literacy will make knowledge workers both happier and more productive. It outlines current findings about how knowledge workers prepare and use data to better support organizational strategy.

What is a knowledge worker?

Peter Drucker coined the phrase "knowledge worker" (KW).[53] Today, it describes a range of educated and skilled workers, including software engineers, lawyers, and others who must "think for a living." Most of these professionals must consider data inputs and make decisions based on their processes. These are the citizens whom we most need to be data literate. Since they make good money, investments in data literacy will result in increased payouts for organizations and their employees

Interestingly, as organizations increase digital achievement, traditional stereotypes give way to evolving realities. For knowledge workers? In the past, people did not consider trucking a destination for KWs. But truckers who are data literate will achieve more success, and the profession currently shares the 'think for a living' characteristic with other knowledge professions. To tease the trucker as KW thread further, where does all the truckers' data come from? In-cab constant monitoring and multiple video surveillance and Internet of Things (see Chapter 1) functionality combine to create a very mobile knowledge worker who must submit to continuous monitoring as a condition of employment.

How much can we increase KW productivity?

Research shows that one in ten organizations does a "good" job with their data.[54] This means that 90% of organizations lack a foundational resource to the business in the modern world. Increasing data literacy among KWs is key to increasing productivity. *We believe that doing so can increase KW productivity by 10-40%.* Let's look at some specific factors limiting KW productivity.

The human component of productivity

Consider these statistics[55] about employee attitudes towards data:

- 74% of employees report feeling overwhelmed or unhappy when working with data.
- More than half would rather do household chores (53%) or pay bills (52%) than work with data.
- 36% of those overwhelmed employees (74%) report spending at least one hour a week procrastinating over data-related tasks.

- 36% say they would find an alternative method to complete the job without using data.
- 14% would avoid the task entirely!
- 36% of employees report spending at least one hour a week procrastinating over data-related tasks.
- 59% of employees exhibit symptoms of burnout when working with customer relationship management (CRM) systems, 54% when working with resource planning, and 63% when working with communication tools.
- 14% of employees report feeling overwhelmed when working with data at least once each day—rising to half of employees once a week.
- Procrastination and stress from information, data, and technology issues cause companies to lose an average of more than *five working days* (43 hours) per employee annually.

Clearly, this apprehension of data represents a real barrier to organizations trying to build a data-driven culture. We believe that data literate employees will not drag their feet—data literacy would help reduce this lost productivity.

The process component of productivity

But reduced data anxiety isn't enough on its own. Organizations must also create systems and processes that allow those KWs to be more effective when working with data. Consider these specific measurements and findings from the oft-cited McKinsey report—in the context of the average KW working 250 eight-hour days annually:

- KWs spend only about 10% of their time creating new knowledge and content. Roughly one-third of their time is spent reworking and recreating knowledge that already exists. That totals 82 days per year. We propose that more efficient and effective data retrieval systems reduce wasted time by 20%, resulting in fifteen extra days per year!

- The average professional spends 28% of their time each workday reading and answering email. The average full-time worker in America spends a staggering 2.6 hours answering the 120 messages they receive per day.[56] Reducing email processing by improving KW data literacy could reduce email burdens by thirty minutes each day or fifteen days each year.

- Approximately 70% of KWs waste up to 60 minutes each day navigating between or within applications. Sixty-eight percent toggle between applications ten times an hour! Much of this app-switching occurs when one system needs data from another. Our specific objective is to reduce the average KW app switching time by five days per year.

Totals

To recap, here is what we believe that a data literate workforce could recover annually:

- 5 days from data-induced procrastination and sick leave
- 20 days from knowledge re-creation
- 10 days from email processing
- 5 days from navigating between applications.

Total: 40 days, or nearly 20% of KWs' work time

We conservatively rounded down each number. Expectations for the savings will fluctuate in the 10-40% range depending on a range of contextual factors. Even supposing the lowest end of this scale, any organization would be pleased with 10% increase in productivity!

Requiring data acumen of knowledge workers

The remainder of this chapter focuses on specific details applicable to all knowledge workers. Readers who already know this foundational material may find it repetitive and want to jump to the next chapter. We introduce a collection of data knowledge, necessary but insufficient for establishing a baseline for data literacy required of all knowledge workers (KWs). The collection includes:

- An assortment of motivations for increasing not just individual data literacy but also organizational data knowledge (this can only take place with a corporate data program)
- The data sandwich introduced as a conceptual goal and metaphor for a well-functioning organizational data machine (ODM)
- A series of topics illustrating this foundational data knowledge required of KWs.

Regaining that lost time will require some work upfront. All systems periodically need to be reengineered with the specific goal of system simplification. KWs represent the best source for uncovering hidden data inefficiencies and should be rewarded for providing improvement suggestions. Four representative data concepts can help KWs improve their productivity as each concept supports the provision of higher quality data more rapidly. We will describe each briefly below.

Learn about IDs to access information

How should organizations approach the process of using IDs (also known as primary keys) to access information? Often KWs share information, tips, and tricks amongst themselves. For example, we have heard repeated time after time that if a customer calls in and doesn't know their account number, you can look it up by their phone number. This should be part of the data literacy training provided to all KWs about how keys (i.e., specific data values) are used to access information and what key attributes are available to use.

There are two ways of discovering precise combinations of facts and meanings: searching and indexing. Both have advantages and disadvantages. The capability must exist to locate a specific piece of data when needed. For example, a team may be discussing the specifics of a particular purchase at a regular shopping destination. Even if they are to obtain a list of past purchases at the retail location, they are still likely to require a unique identifier (key) to view the list of items purchased during the specific visit. Many data machines require an ID (an authorized account) before personalization can occur.

Everyone should understand how to use these keys on the various components of the organizational data machine.

Understand the importance of required information

KWs need to understand why some systems require inputs—they can't be null. Those annoyances best exemplify required fields on the web highlighted in red—those fields that you thought that you did not need to fill. They represent data fields that require responses. There are two types. The first is a general comment field. If you put one character in, the field won't be empty, and the inputs will be added to the database. All that can be tested for in this required field is that something was input. Other types of required fields use algorithms to determine if the input is valid. For instance, a field may request an email address and refuse submissions that don't follow the format "@something.something." However, this does not always ensure valid responses. The input value

thisisnotwhereiwanttobe@googleismackerelfish.com

would pass the basic data input test. But in reality, this is unlikely to be a valid customer or organizational email address!

The second type of required field operates by selecting one choice from among multiple presented on a menu. Guidelines suggest that the initial (default) selection from the menu be null. If the input field defaults to null and restricted to not-null entries, the user will examine the potential menu choices and choose one. However, in far too many instances, an initial choice has been made. By default, the user is likely to leave the initial choice in place without thinking.

This sort of bad design leads to databases with entry names such as "FNU" and "LNU" (F/LNU = first/last name unknown). The use of these practices is common knowledge but not documented. For example, we have encountered paperwork listing a user's first name as FNU or LNU as a last name. In either case, the name was unknown at the time of data entry and, to submit the data to the data machine, someone had to enter a value to the required field. More importantly, many KWs have the skills and authorization to change FNU or LNU to the correct value (the actual name) but do not know they can make this happen.

Require maps and models

As a KW interacting with the organizational data machine, one will likely encounter a *data dependency challenge*. A standard structure used in data describes the concept well: parent-child relationships. In some data machines, it's a rule that parent data must exist before child data can live.

Master data records must exist before any transactions are authorized.

Data knowledge is important for organizations, too

Does the programming language known as COBOL mean anything to you? The language surfaced as a topic briefly during the COVID pandemic. During the crisis, several states' unemployment systems suddenly faced computing demands that were more than ten times their regular workload. Designers wrote their computer programs using COBOL and created systems capable of handling localized claims volumes. This might range from small numbers in the less crowded states to large numbers in densely populated areas. In some instances, systems could not meet the data processing demands, and the states had to figure out how to obtain the requisite expertise required to repair or face replacing entire systems.

Equal access to the system internals was required as hackers proved quite adept at fooling these old systems into paying criminals hundreds of millions of dollars for fraudulent unemployment claims. In many ways, the resilience of these "legacy" systems was available to those planning the various responses—capabilities understood because the data documentation was useful. The same type of organizational data knowledge is often tied up in a long-departed associate's head. It is in their head because that individual knows its value while the organization has not recognized its value. In general, organizations do not value KW data knowledge as an organizational asset. This is because of the generally low data literacy rate currently among citizens.[57]

What does that mean? It means that employees who do not understand data will not be able to use data to support organizational strategy. They will not be able to make decisions based on useful data. They will similarly be unable to use data to improve existing practices. Most importantly, they will be unable to approach new challenges from a data perspective primarily.

Another example supports better store management. The UK cosmetic firm Lush provides its shop managers access to data showing sales, stock levels, and freshness. This data enables them to make decisions to drive individual store performance. For example, it could be displaying products near each other that sell well together or offering more short-term, rather than long-term, promotions. Lush empowers its staff to make the decisions they see fit to increase profitability and reduce waste by giving its employees access to key data. They have seen an incredible response, with 70% of staff accessing the platform every day to review sales and stock and manage performance. This resulted in £1 million of lost stock savings in the first two years of providing data access to the staff.[58]

There's also a huge opportunity to use data-driven technologies such as artificial intelligence (AI) and machine learning in back-office operations. A classic example is forecasting, a practice that clothing retailers have long found a challenge. By deploying AI, retailers have the potential to process relevant data and determine the best forecast rapidly. However, it must then be the team's responsibility to read, analyze, and question AI-determined decisions to confirm that the company is on the right trajectory.

Making a better data sandwich

Improving the effectiveness of the organizational data machine is a crucial component of all KW job descriptions. The data machine functions better when the three capabilities (data supply chain, standard data assets, and data literacy) are synchronized. While they are necessary but insufficient prerequisites, they are additive, each building on the previous.

Objective KW and DP Literacy Standards: Organizations become data literate when applying these concepts at the organizational level. Rather than using workgroup-based practices, organizations can understand that a better method exists and encourage workers to achieve data literacy independently and support data supply chain methods.

Data Supply Chain: This is comprised of data decisions associated with the organizational value chain. By understanding data sources, uses, and flows, the organization can re-engineer aspects of its data supply chain to reduce friction resulting from what our colleague, Tom Redman, labeled "hidden data factories."[59] Only with this level of data literacy can organizations provide standard data to optimizable processes. And, only when enforced by organizational policy does such organization wide adoption occur. This results in better, more reliable, more predictable results that are available from workgroup or project-based results. Workgroups have less incentive to improve methods or data products once they satisfy project objectives. An organization's data assets improve when it designs and implements well-understood data supply chain logistics. Once in place, organizations ensure they do not deviate from standards unless through formal change processes.

Standard Data Assets: Just as we require a standard language for meaningful communication, organizations need traditional data assets to extract value. This means organizations must become more data-centric and, for example, begin documenting data assets using data based on organizational business glossaries or other similar techniques.

Combine these three elements and organizations can increase the number and quality of the data products they create. They can also improve the effectiveness and efficiency with which they can use data.

For organizations to succeed in today's global, networked environment, data assets must be viewed as the raw materials used to support evidence-based decision-making. Consequently, organizations need to fund and resource such efforts at the program level—as they do for any other organizational initiatives. The cost and risk of haphazardly doing this work always exceed the price of standardizing corporate data assets.

The first instance of data standardization using an example from the Canadian Social Security system. The challenge was to restrict the range of characteristics that data can represent. For example, suppose a collection of facts and meanings was to include gender information. A standard could state that the data must consist of the following and only the following allowable values and their English translations:

1. male
2. female
3. male soon to be female
4. female soon to be male
5. uncertain
6. doesn't know
7. won't tell.

The method uses seven values to represent gender. Do you need to represent more than seven genders? Facebook offers users 71 gender options (Williams, 2014). How does your design change if you need to describe more than two genders? To what level of specificity do you need to know when someone will take a new gender? The design describes men who become women and vice versa. Are there requirements for other combinations? All of the above and more must factor into the design of a data structure supporting the maintenance of this data.

Because of the appropriate use of data standards, a KW (a clerk) looking at the correct data field could know that this data conformed to the above data standard. The KW would see the value '2' and know that this record belonged to a female. Without the standard, we couldn't write programs to efficiently process the data to find, for example, the number of females in a population. Data standardization is often best paired with a data quality engineering initiative. Table after the table is profiled and evolved to conform to specified standards. These tasks usually cost organizations lots of money. Instead of paying lots of money to consultants, organizations should develop internal data capabilities of all kinds.

The second type of data standardization occurs when arranging individual data items, usually called data records. Standardization could permit a default configuration of data items to be delivered to any authorized Canadian Social Security System clerk showing data recorded about an individual. These could be given names such as Type-1 record and Type-2 record. Within the workgroups, KWs can share these record types and their respective contents. Let us suppose that neither contained information regarding the individual's gender, as discussed above. The decision and reasons to initially include or exclude this information may be documented but are more likely long gone. Reasons—from processing efficiencies to privacy to greed—drive the arrangement of these data structures. Far too often, there is no conscious arrangement at all. In all cases, once an infrastructure of application programs is used to access the existing collection of the data repeatedly, it's far more challenging to change the existing data structure than it is to change one program, much less many.

Changes are rarely made once the necessary data standards and structure decisions have been made (or not). Maintenance and corrective efforts are more often embedded in the application programs instead of at the data level. The world of data comprises vast collections of such data and structures in varying degrees of standardization. The process of making information conform to the desired standard is often taken on haphazardly without adequate planning. Because of volume considerations, we need to implement an engineering mindset to maximize the use of architectural constructs in the data.

Today, however, the exponential growth of data, combined with a low use of data standards and insufficient data literacy levels, means organizations have significant work ahead. As a result, organizations need to begin work now and invest in efforts to move data operations from being ill-defined to being regularized, standardized, and predictable. And as we have already said, the first step toward making this transition successful is developing a data strategy, a plan to move from a condition of confusion, disorder, and inefficiency to one of predictability, control, and efficiency.

Organizational data challenges are different. Note the differences between individual and administrative access to data. One of the most important is legacy (also referred to as "heritage applications"). We define legacy as any application that is currently running in production. Legacy applications and attendant complexity directly and negatively affect the speed at which citizens can access data. For example, when individuals access information and make simple queries with their mobile phones, tablets, and personal computers, they immediately receive results. However, running simple queries can take days or even weeks when citizens try to access an organization's information. So, what is happening? For personal applications, there is rarely any legacy involved. For organizations, the only time that there are no legacy applications is when the organization is at its very startup–when no previous systems exist. For organizations, legacy more often impedes the process of obtaining value from data. Notice the term 'legacy' is not as frequently applied to data. (It is never applied unless the origin/version of the data is known.)

Furthermore, when organizations acquire or merge with other organizations or simply update technologies, they face legacy barriers that can easily cripple critical business functions. As these organizations become more complex, they become less able to diagnose their own problems accurately. Over time, complexity and confusion mask the real underlying issues and lead experts to believe the root problem is an information technology (IT) problem. No matter the amount of resources organizations apply to this problem, it doesn't go away. The more complex and undisciplined an organization becomes, the more likely the problem is to resemble an IT problem.

The problem is one of **failing to standardize data management practices**. Compounding matters, organizations pay little attention to data quality and instead, first become enamored with data analytics and technologies. These efforts fail at a high rate because organizations spend inordinate amounts of IT resources versus investing in their data assets. Organizations need to establish and enforce well-understood directions (that is, strategy) to guide the management and usage of data assets.

Data and technology used in decision-making

Technology has completely transformed many working methods: ways we communicate, build customer relationships, measure success, and make decisions. However, the speed of such change(s) and the expectation for users to quickly adopt these new ways of working can be overwhelming. Often, organizations put technology in the hands of their employees and expect them to know what to do with it as if by magic. However, without proper training, employees can't use the technology to analyze data effectively.

Despite nearly all employees recognizing data in the workplace as an asset, few use it to make decisions. Only 37% of employees trust their decisions more when they make decisions using data. Almost half, 48%, frequently defer to making decisions based on "gut feelings" versus data-driven insight.[2]

---

[2] Statistics in this section from: http://thedataliteracyproject.org.

We find gut-feeling decisions at every stage in employees' careers—even more at senior levels. For instance, around two-thirds of C-suite executives, senior managers, and directors would go with their gut instinct over data-driven insight, compared with just 41% of junior managers and those below the last layer of management. Experience and intuition certainly have a role to play in business! However, executives should not lack the confidence to make decisions based on cold, hard facts. Clearly, the influx of new technologies isn't helping them develop that ability.

Reviewing the track record of an overenthusiastic adoption of new technologies is helpful when evaluating the cost of adopting new technologies. Take the Enterprise resource planning (ERP) industry, for example. Developed in response to the industry's demand for process standardization and mostly delivering on promised integration, ERPs still fail on most return on investment (ROI) evaluations because of how long they take to implement.

ERPs implement disruptive technologies with a long-established track record of making things worse for many years before the benefits accrue. Before that happens, organizations must deal with cost overruns, schedule delays, and undelivered functionality. There are many cases where the downturn in productivity due to the ERP disruption lasted half a decade or more. According to

Gartner, this kind of investment is an incredibly impressive "sell" given that the average tenure of CIOs is still hovering between 2-4 years. Any CIO advocating such an investment would likely be investing in the successors' successors' success!

The right question for the executive team considering the investment would be: If we invest (say) $1M in an ERP, how would productivity increase compared to funding the $1M in additional marketing or in some other capacity? ERPs are not inherently evil. However, considering the enthusiasm with which the community embraced them, you would have thought they were a pre-crime version of future bitcoin pricing knowledge. As it turns out, ERPs can help organizations with process standardization and are much more successful when implemented by organizations that can adapt to the ERP as-delivered/out-of-the-box (with zero customization) instead of modifying the ERP for the organization.

ERP investments are representative of the well-understood Gartner hype-cycle approach. Enthusiastic adoption, unrealistic expectations, and disappointment phases all precede meaningful implementation. A focus on data will do much more to improve an organization's ability to use data strategically than any technology investment. Increasing an organization's data literacy will be much more productive if you employ individuals capable of specifying their technology needs and, more importantly, using data to support organizational strategy! Organizations that can leverage this type of productivity increase will attain an advantage in the marketplace.

Chapter conclusions–Data lessons foundational to knowledge work

Providing the right data delivery improvements has proven difficult. The place where data literacy education will pay off most is a focus on organizational knowledge workers. There are lots of them and they are unproductive in unique ways that can be addressed through better data literacy. The productivity savings are anticipated and can be measured. Savings in the anticipated 10-25% range have excellent ROI. This is due to the last three data lessons.

KWs can be enormously more productive when equipped with the right data knowledge and skills.

Data Lesson #17

Foundational concepts for KWs include ID tags, data protection, required fields, and maps and models.

Data Lesson #18

More technology isn't always better! Consider the long-term ROI and opportunity cost prior to adoption.

Data Lesson #19

Now that you understand the importance of data literacy and how much work there is left to be done, we can move to Part 2 to describe the data literacy framework and accompanying citizen data literacy needs.

Part II

Educating Billions of Citizens using the Digital Civics Framework

As you learned in Part 1, there is a growing divide between the data literate and PIDDs. As a result, an increasing number of citizens become targets of deception and manipulation by those who understand how to use data that does not belong to them, to their advantage.

There are almost 8 billion citizens on the planet. Two and half billion citizens use mobile devices. There are 1.5 billion adult mobile users and 1 billion knowledge workers.[60] We believe that every one of these people should be data literate, increasing their contribution to modern society by better understanding how data affects their daily lives. We recognize this is a bold statement and a tall order to achieve. Part 2 presents our framework for doing just that: simplifying and formalizing a shared understanding of citizen data literacy needs. We need to educate several hundred million citizens to make any noticeable data literacy impact on society . We think we need to educate several hundred million citizens to make any data literacy impact on society.

Data knowledge should not be restricted to those in technical professions. We can provide all citizens with the knowledge that they need in an increasingly digital and data-driven world. Of course, citizens have different circumstances and therefore need different levels of knowledge to fulfill their roles in society. [61] Our approach addresses the needs at each level:

- Any person wishing to use a mobile device should meet a minimum data literacy requirement with periodic training updates (Chapter 7).
- All adult citizens should reach the standard of data proficiency with periodic training updates (Chapter 8).
- Knowledge Workers (KWs) must reach the standard of data acumen with periodic training updates (Chapter 9).

For this to happen, we must produce a class of thoroughly qualified data teachers to address the growing data deficit (Chapter 10). In addition, this work should be supported by data professionals doing broader research on today's problems (Chapter 11). Each level of the Digital Civics Framework must include all the knowledge and skills required at lower levels.

Chapter 6

Educating Citizens using the Digital Civics Framework

This chapter introduces the Digital Civics Framework (DCF). Civics is "a social science dealing with the rights and duties of citizens."[62] Society's inexorable movement to digitize requires elaborating citizen rights and duties concerning the digital framework surrounding them. The DCF:

- bounds data literacy requirements squarely in specific societal contexts—underscoring the roles played by five key types of objectively definable actors.
- permits the specification of literacy requirements common to each group's attributes and competency requirements.
- relates data literacy requirements to their societal components.
- describes where citizens can focus resources improve their use of data.

Different citizens have different data needs. These increase over time. For some, this means developing a deeper understanding of data computations and transformations. For others, that may mean becoming aware of the risks of making online purchases or posting a homemade video or a comment. Next, we describe the DCF attributes along the X-axis and the actors along the Y-axis. This chapter concludes with a description of two cross-level commonalities and their relationship to the corresponding citizen data literacy needs.

Level	Actor	Action	Affects	Produces	Using	In Order To	Surfing	CDKA
5	Data Professional	Leverages	Society	Insights & Invention	Experiences	Improve	Professional	27-30
4	Data Teacher	Influences	Students	Knowledge Workers	Pulpit	Catch up	Science	23-26
3	Knowledge Worker	Advances	Society	Profit	Automation	Contribute	Skill	18-22
2	Adult Data Spreader	Shapes & Molds	Children	Prepared Children	Guidance & Lessons	Vote	Sport	10-17
1	Mobile Data Spreader	Accesses	Themselves	Content	Time & Energy	Explore & Learn	Vocabulary	1-9

Figure 6.1—Digital Civics Framework

The data literacy scale and DCF actors

The DCF divides the population into five groups with different habits and needs related to data and the Internet. These five groups are:

mobile data spreader	MDSs include everyone equipped with a mobile device capable of connecting to the Internet. Caregivers should make base-level data literacy, with mandatory periodic reinforcement, a prerequisite to mobile privileges.
adult data spreader	ADSs are the set of all adults equipped with a mobile device capable of connecting to the Internet. Learning more about data (becoming proficient) is a prerequisite to responsible adult citizenship.
knowledge workers	KWs include anyone who interacts with an organization's data on a professional level. KWs should reach a higher standard of "data acumen," which can be objectively measured. A hiring need might be expressed as required KW level data acumen.
data teachers	Data teachers should possess data experience and teaching acumen and should also be capable of incorporating and providing feedback requisite to rapidly escalating societal needs. DTs should possess data acumen and be capable of the two-way feedback required to deliver the most effective data education.
data professionals	Anyone working as a data professional and maintaining requisite certification. In addition, they should be held to high ethical standards, and actively contribute to the profession.

Each group of actors is rated on a 1-5 scale based on its expected or actual level of data knowledge. The scale describes the data processing-related capabilities for each actor. For example, as described in our text, Mobile Data Spreaders (MDSs) are primarily younger (under 18) and inexperienced. They have limited abilities to manipulate data, exercise sound judgment, or protect themselves from malicious actors who could acquire their information. Thus, MDSs are ranked at a 1 on the competency scale.

On the opposite end of the range are Data Professionals (DPs). Ideally, DPs have a deep understanding of data and are experts at manipulating data. They also have the most mature understanding of how they and others can use it to their advantage. Therefore, they are ranked at a 5 on the competency scale.

Digital civics attributes

Across the X-axis, we have described data civics attributes in a narrative manner. Descriptors such as actions, effects, and goals help us understand categories of data users, what they do with data, and what their motivations are. We have described them using a format to indicate that an actor takes action that produces certain results, affecting a part of the population, to accomplish something. Each group is described in greater detail using this pattern.

```
Actor ( ) ➜ Action ( ) ➜ Produces ( ) ➜
        Affecting ( ) ➜ Using ( ) ➜ To ( )
```

actor — individuals who use data; the framework characterizes these actors in broad terms to account for the entire Internet-connected population.

action — the primary data-related activities an actor performs within a society.

produces — the output of an actor's actions; a product/digital output that an actor contributes to society.

affecting — the ways in which an actor's actions related to data affect self and others; when the actors interact with one another across society, they influence one another—positively or negatively.

using — the primary methods by which an actor affects society.

to — describes an actor's predominant reasons for using data.

Taken together, the competency descriptors and civic attributes provide a way to diagnose and understand social data literacy problems and plan data literacy remedies and initiatives.

Cross-level commonalities

In addition to each group's individual characteristics and goals, our analysis describes two further attributes: behavioral focus and ethical perspective. The information gleaned about these attributes contributed significantly to the citizen data literacy needs described in each chapter.

Behavioral focus

The behavioral focus of each group can be described either as *individual* or *organizational*. The two lower levels (MDSs and ADSs) focus primarily on their own Internet behaviors, while the three upper levels are concerned with the behaviors of organizations and individuals outside the organization. The "example" part of the Framework describes the types of activities a typical user partakes in online. Consider the approach that different people take to *surfing the Internet*. For many MDSs and ADSs, surfing is merely a form of entertainment. KWs are likely to be interested in improving their skills in some manner. DTs may focus on monitoring aspects of their profession. Professional and organizational considerations can more easily influence those who make their living as data professionals.

Can anyone influence an individual's data behavior? From a legal perspective, the answer is no, unless the individual voluntarily signs one or more Code of Conduct agreements (such as one required by their employer). These agreements can be weighty: there are numerous instances of specific individuals losing jobs because they obviously participated in the 6 Jan 2021 US Capital Riot. Other than that, we can't, of course, directly mandate how a citizen chooses to behave regarding their own data. However, we believe that with greater data literacy, individuals will self-regulate to a far greater degree.

Ethical issues in an information society

Data isn't inherently good or bad. However, people can frame it, edit it, and modify it to their liking. People can also use it for both ethical and unethical purposes. For example, people can use data to influence voters by citing outdated statistics or statistics extracted from a small or biased population sample. People can also use data to confuse others. For example, what does the phrase "take an additional 25% off our already half-off prices" mean? Is it the same as 75% off? Because data can be manipulated in this way, both citizens and organizations must use it responsibly and ethically.

MDSs and ADSs share a moral obligation to avoid being fooled. The data illiterate MDS-ADS combination is the most attractive and most accessible target of those who would cheat and manipulate citizens—surveillance capitalists. Make no mistake, attempts to deceive and manipulate the 2.5 billion MDSs occupy a large focus on the bad guys' concerted efforts. The Data Matrix enjoys the data illiterate because they can more easily be fooled and manipulated. We can't expect the citizenry to focus beyond the self and family. More importantly, we can't force them to take other positions. We can't hold citizens to conduct codes of conduct that conflict with rights. Individual freedom is the embodiment of this concept. The focus of the MDS is the MDS.

Actors at Levels 3-5 share a moral obligation to avoid trying to trick private individuals. As such, they are more likely than individual citizens to outline what responsible, ethical behavior looks like explicitly. Organizations will increasingly adopt and require their employees to support specific organizational behaviors concerning data operations. Binding employment agreements and CoCs hold KWs to data use agreements and ethical frameworks and provide required enforcement "teeth."

Society will require additional ethical considerations for DT and DP levels. DTs will be a necessary part of the DP certification and screening process. As such, society will govern these people with internally developed CoCs. These certification and screen processes need to incorporate peer performance reviews and short feedback loops to be effective. It is important to establish this foundational basis early as we believe it is likely that DPs will subdivide into specific groupings with appropriate practice-level ethical certification requirements. Additional reasons for needing guidance include:

- Open and transparent management of personal information
- Anonymity and pseudonymity
- Collection of solicited personal information
- Dealing with unsolicited personal information
- Notification when collecting personal information
- Use or disclosure of personal information

- Direct marketing
- Cross-border disclosure of personal information
- Adoption, use, or disclosure of government related identifiers
- Quality of personal information
- Security of personal information
- Access to personal information
- Correction of personal data.

Several factors might induce an organization to formalize its data ethics procedures. The closer an organization engages with AI, the more likely it will adopt an organizational ethical focus—as Google did concerning AI in 2018 in response to workforce 'requests.'[63] They may also do so to protect (or give the appearance of protecting) their customers' data:

> *Privacy is a fundamental human right. At Apple, it's also one of our core values. Your devices are important to so many parts of your life. What you share from those experiences, and who you share it with, should be up to you. We design Apple products to protect your privacy and give you control over your information. It's not always easy. But that's the kind of innovation we believe in.*[64]

Organizations do not always follow through with the ethical policies they set forth. However, an organizational focus on ethics creates an additional level of understanding among the KWs who govern the meta-processes required to identify bad behavior. They can perceive how assembling innocuous individual efforts into uses can violate stated organizational practices.

Throughout history, employees have been tested as to whether they will support corrupt practices. These tests now extend to include the evaluation of corrupt data practices. In the future, employees will be increasingly employed to fool or manipulate citizens, thereby following the lead set by the corporate ethical focus. We believe these data professionals should be objectively (highly) skilled with their use of data acumen in defense of all citizens. For example, suppose an employee observes corporate behavior that violates a user privacy agreement such as the one above. The employee should be empowered to do something about it!

Basic foundational concepts for ethical analysis and consideration encompass the following aspects:

- **Responsibility**: accepting the potential costs, duties, and obligations for decisions.
- **Accountability**: mechanisms for identifying responsible parties.
- **Liability**: permits individuals (and firms) to recover damages done to them.
- **Due process**: laws are well known and understood, with an ability to appeal to higher authorities.

Foundational candidate ethical principles suggest preferred behaviors.

- **Golden Rule**: Do unto others as you would have them do unto you.
- **Immanuel Kant's Categorical Imperative**: If an action isn't right for everyone to take, it's not right for anyone.
- **Descartes Rule of Change**: If an action can't be taken repeatedly, it's not right to take it at all.
- **Utilitarian Principle**: Take the action that achieves the higher or greater value.
- **Risk Aversion Principle**: Take the action that produces the least harm or potential cost.
- **Ethical "No Free Lunch" Rule**: Assume that virtually all tangible and intangible objects are owned by someone unless there is a specific declaration otherwise.

It will behoove all organizations to consider issues such as the data ethics canvas developed by the Open Data Institute and summarized in Appendix K.

Data conversations

At the individual level, we envision that each MDS should receive data knowledge from a responsible ADS. However, we'd expect that amount who do receive that instruction would roughly correspond to the number who get their "the birds and the bees" knowledge from their parents. Given that topic's track record—we won't expect stellar results from that method.

In early hazing rituals, fraternities often sent pledges to find a non-existent physical object. A common focus was the need for "left-handed smoke shifters" for camping. The pledge would run to other campsites asking if anyone had one. If they survived the process, they would then be permitted to play this prank on subsequent pledges—keeping the story and tradition alive. Our approach here is similar (without the pranking) to craft a series of data stories that will eventually become common knowledge.

To get citizens to care about their data literacy, it needs to be personal and memorable. We hope the following two stories will be just that.

Memorable story #1: Just hand me your system backups and I will restore them for you ...

Back when we were younger, separate bosses gave us each a computer and instructed us to back it up. After using the machine for a couple of weeks, the hard drive on the devices mysteriously failed. The boss requested our latest backup copy. If we had neglected the backup portion of our responsibilities (at least one of us had), it drove the lesson home through an awkward conversation. Likely, we both experienced the same ritual because it was a proven way of getting employees to back up their computer work!

Memorable story #2: The convincer

The second mutually experienced story involves a device that police use to help individuals remember to fasten their seatbelts whenever in a vehicle. The operator asks prospective or current drivers to sit in the chair and, of course, fasten their seatbelts. The device simulates a minor collision by rolling down an incline and hitting the full stop-bar at 5 mph. Anyone who ever sat through a ride on The Seat Belt Convincer became rigorous about automotive seatbelt usage from that point onward. The 5-mph crash is unpleasant enough that many deem the result to be unpleasant and to be avoided. One can draw other analogies for the teaching of defensive driving. Once the drivers have had this experience, the lesson stays with them for life.

We are not advocating deception or forced difficulty, but these shared experiences indicate a promising means of working toward increased data literacy. We need to articulate the benefits of increased data literacy and provide citizens with specific ways of improving their data literacy. Awareness will help support their usage.

Citizen data knowledge areas (literacy needs and responses)

The citizen data literacy knowledge areas (CDKAs) we present are built to strengthen each group of actors' behavioral and ethical focus. Each CDKA acts as an organizing principle by describing the specific vulnerability as a target of countermeasures and education. The goal of the CDKAs is to reduce the complexity of implementing the DCF. They are discussed in the remaining chapter comprising this Part. We have paired these CDKA clusters with reference-able and repeatable vignettes.

We present these in terms that can become standard and easily referenced, just like "the birds and the bees" conversation. This simplification reduces the number of resources needed to improve the average citizen's data literacy. Perhaps it presents an easy-to-tell story for those not data literate who can then decide how vital data literacy is to their individual lives. Each CDKA comprised of paired needs and responses.

Chapter conclusions–A problem well stated

Problem definition has always been a challenge. Data requirements are the most objective and verifiable requirements. Getting this more in-depth understanding of the challenge facing us as citizens is an important first step.

CHAPTER 7

Mobile Data Spreader (MDS)

> *Society [has a] misconception that citizens born post-1983, referred to as "digital natives" or the "net generation," have inherent technological skills and abilities. This misconception has resulted in a major skills gap in industry and the daunting realization that this must be remedied. (Manyika, et al., 2011).*[65]

Two and half billion people currently carry around an extremely powerful computing device, one that has continuous access to much of the world's accumulated knowledge, and that in turn almost continuously adds to that store of knowledge. In fact, the devices are so powerful that malware can easily highjack extra computing cycles without the user being aware.

We are speaking, of course, of smartphones and tablets. We call these citizens Mobile Data Spreaders (MDSs). MDSs must have some degree of data literacy to be able to operate their mobile device devices. However, it's essential to ensure that all individuals who connect devices to the Internet have at least an MDS level of data literacy.

All 2.5 billion mobile device users would, of course, fall into the broad category of MDSs. But for purposes of this chapter, let's zoom in on those who fall into the category of

MDS, but not any others: in other words, children under the age of eighteen.[66]

While some laws regulate children and their participation in certain Internet services, mobile access convenience has driven the "appropriateness" of mobile privileges to lower and lower ages. We believe that this trend will continue.

Every young person with a device possesses instant gratification capabilities combined with far more computing and amplification power than has been available in the past. Too often, this great power is given without context, without the requisite conversations, knowledge, and capabilities. The users are too often data illiterate.

This chapter elaborates on the characteristics of MDSs and the data knowledge that they need to avoid being fooled or manipulated by others on the Internet. It provides guidance and suggestions for ADSs to assist their MDSs in becoming data literate.

Mobile data spreader description

Actor: MDSs have superpowers: creative energy and access to high-quality data that they desire. While young compared to our other four actor types, MDSs aren't intimidated by technology and are skilled at information access. They are fluent in the latest digital vocabulary and can manipulate technology to their liking. Channeled and focused, MDSs have an abundance of energy, time, and creativity. They devote those resources to exploring and learning about any topic. For example, witness the mass of teenage musical prodigies on YouTube! Further, they can consume a far greater variety of media than was possible in our day. Rather than being limited to AM or FM radio, today's youth can watch someone interpret the masters on a YouTube video called "ISOLATED BASS RUSH YYZ GEDDY LEE."[67]

However, being able to use their devices is not the same as being data literate. MDSs have little real-world experience and are naïve, unsophisticated, and untrained. And because they have disposable income, idle time, and groupthink, they are highly desirable targets for surveillance capitalists. As such, they are worthy of societal protection from the vast armies of data predators inhabiting the Internet.

Action: We assign MDSs #**surf** as their meme. They surf through enormous amounts of data via social media like Twitter, Facebook, MeWe, Parler, and others. MDSs rely on social structures to spread information and access. Importantly, popular Internet applications regularly evolve to stay a step ahead of authorities (e.g., parents and teachers). Limiting data access to a MDS threatens a significant source of data value to the MDS and data poachers—both of whom will complain loudly if access is cut off.

Affects: MDSs typically interact via a network of friends who share new digital content. Many considered the content to have no value; however, companies later developed ways to monetize their content. As a result, MDS created entirely new markets and created new societal fads and longer-term norms. For example, one of the earliest mobile spreader fads was the ever-popular selfie. What was once a young person's amusement has turned into new forms of business through 'sponsored' Internet influencers. Later, influencers evolved their single-frame images into more sophisticated video content, describing an impossibly diverse array of topics.

Producing: MDSs produce massive amounts of digital content such as selfies, Tweets, and videos. A MDS creates this content for their amusement and to "fit in" with other MDSs. At first glance, many considered the content to be worthless digital debris. Still, it can become pure gold to data poachers.

Using: MDSs use social media-related technologies. Improved software and tremendous computing power help MDS explore the world of big data, digital connections, and alluringly sensitive and potentially dangerous Internet content. This same technology is often turned 180º to focus on behaviors of MDSs. This turnaround is another form of poaching—observing what individuals do and getting them to change their behavior. Even more frighteningly, MDSs often escape parental control and go deeper into darker and more threatening parts of the Internet where child molesters and other criminals lurk.

To: MDSs use the Internet primarily for entertainment and social interaction. The convenience of mobile access encourages exploration. There are already some objectives, specific levels of data literacy required, as evidenced by the parental control and screen time functionality built into the iOS™ and Android™ mobile operating systems.

Data Acumen: MDSs have virtually no understanding of data and operate at the most basic data literacy levels. For MDS, technology and data are the same—that is, MDS are typically not mature enough to recognize the distinctions between and roles played by the two. As a result, they fail to connect data to online risk and real-world danger. For MDSs, privacy concepts do not exist, so they offer personal information without understanding the injury that sharing could produce. MDSs may give up personal information to gain access to enticing Internet services. Similarly, laws prevent children under 13 from participating in some Internet activities like registering and contributing to adult websites and sharing adult materials. However, MDSs routinely skirt these laws to their detriment. Their current, specific data acumen is low but needs to meet minimal protective standards to ensure their safety.

Ethical Perspective: From a moral perspective, a goal shared by both MDSs and ADSs is to avoid being fooled or manipulated. The problem is that they are unaware of the attempts to deceive and manipulate. The MDSs are, by definition, new to the process of interacting with the data world. MDSs encounter novel issues, such as privacy policies and digital shopping, almost immediately. We must teach MDSs to assume a defensive posture by default and believe that others attempt to fool and manipulate them when using data. This is because your data behavior has to be perfect, and your adversaries just have to be lucky once!

Behavioral Focus: MDSs (and ADSs) focus on themselves. Far too many MDSs learn only from their own misadventures instead of learning from others' lessons. If nothing else, this is inefficient. Absent a higher calling (professional or employer-based), MDSs and ADSs will generally choose what they perceive is best for themselves and their families regarding their online behavior. As a result, they often do not see their own role in the bigger picture of how online data is used.

Pair each MDS with a responsible ADS

Obviously, it is not within our power to mandate how 2.5 billion MDSs and their families behave online. But improving the data literacy of MDSs as a class is a goal that we must strive to achieve. One promising way to do this is by pairing every MDS with at least one Responsible ADS (R-ADS).

Ideally, every MDS has an R-ADS to engage in an ongoing dialog as they discover the Internet's data. An excellent way to begin is to initiate a regular data discussion among household members. Adults should establish a line of communication between themselves and non-adults. Sitting down as a unit to discuss data topics will help develop a common vocabulary, designate it as an essential family matter, and increase the family's collective data literacy. The need for this communication vehicle is particularly strong between MDSs and R-ADSs.

As the MDSs discover various aspects of being online, we recommend that formal discussions and learning take place weekly at first. As data literacy grows, monthly discussions are appropriate. Most importantly, these discussions eliminate the "we have never had that discussion" problem that always occurs when a need arises. Regularly exchanging family information about new sources of data inputs, access attempts, new features, and capabilities can be both informative and fun, and sharing data stories can provide a fun basis for future data storytelling skills. While beyond our control scope, this is a potential tool to help leverage societal efforts. As a starting point, we urge R-ADSs to set devices to contacts-only mode and teach their MDSs about this functionality (more about this when we cover CDKA02). Only through these discussions do we see a reasonable alternative to being dropped into the deep end of a pool to sink or swim. We have summarized useful types of conversations in Appendix A.

MDS data knowledge areas (needs & responses)

We postulate these nine specific CDKAs as prerequisites to granting access to mobile devices. We cover each for the remainder of this chapter. We can't enforce it, but we hope that society will band together to put peer pressure on parents (ADSs) who may point their future MDSs to knowledge and skills that they should master as a prerequisite to unlocking further data capabilities. We provide suggested exercises to help ADSs teach these lessons.

CDKA01: Limiting and unlocking additional capabilities

Need: Demonstrate an ability to understand the reasons for and rules around adding entries into device capabilities such as address books and the relationship to unlocking additional data capabilities in reward for demonstrated good behavior.

Response: Objectively quantify the nature and quality of the regular expansions of the contacts entries.

Like driving skills, we must establish good data habits from the start. Since we're focusing on objective behaviors, getting the MDS off on the correct foot is vital. We have emphasized the importance of regular conversations between MDSs and R-ADS. An important component of such conversations is an understanding that continued good behavior (as defined by the R-ADS) is equated with continued device use as the MDS demonstrates their increasing data literacy. It is also important to realize that the initial device is limited in capabilities—analogous to training wheels on a bicycle. There is more to be unlocked in response to a proven track record.

Part of growing up is understanding that privileges come with responsibilities: at sixteen you can drive a car, but you have the responsibility to do so safely. The same applies to data-spreading devices. We recommend that families hold weekly meetings to review connection requests, use and growth of the address book, screen time utilization, financial costs incurred every week, etc. These meetings are used as disciplinary checkpoints to educate the MDSs and ADSs of the household. The participants should use the meetings until they have reviewed all the material. When everyone is comfortable with the concepts, the participants can relax the schedule and meet monthly or quarterly. If the group adds a new family member, they can return to a more frequent program and focus on the fundamental data literacy concepts. Other topics can include digital costs and privileges and in-app purchases, keeping and earning more digital capabilities, fragility, and the criteria for keeping existing and unlocking additional digital capabilities. We also recommend that families discuss annual data costs, data plans, and data usage. Throughout this process, families should focus on the data, not the kinds of technology they use. Other examples include cutting the cable and combining home and mobile data plans to reduce expenses.

Exercise: Tangibly reward the family member with the largest annual savings in data costs.

CDKA02: Communication protocols—contacts only

Need: Demonstrate an ability to understand the reasons for and rules related to adding access to their device-for example, entries to their contacts list.

Response: Explain and implement ContactsOnlyMode—objectively review the nature and types of requests for adding entries to the Contacts.

In the old days, you answered the phone with the question "hello" because you didn't know who was calling. Today the default mode to unsolicited approaches should be suspicion. Consider how many of the scams that you have heard about citizens falling for, could have been avoided if not knowing the caller would have perhaps altered their behavior during the scam, first alerting them and then encouraging them to double-check some of the scam assertions.

Soon, we are promised secure communication ids using the stirred and shaken protocols permitting caller receivers to securely establish the identity of the called or the call will not be permitted on the device. Devices will function much more as walkie-talkies than phones with many options available.

Our devices now have options to block all communication from anyone not already in the device's address book. In theory, MDS should be equipped with devices incapable of getting inputs from unsolicited communications, connecting with only pre-approved contacts. IOS labels that setting as "Silence Unknown Callers." When enabled, all calls are blocked–the device user gets no notification–unless the calling device identification exists already in the device address book. If you want to let calls from your mother ring on your device, then you must correctly identify her in your address book. Of course, with this setting enabled, all calls from technical support, gig economy logistics coordination, etc., go straight to voice mail (if enabled). You get the picture. Yes, a MDS needs to understand these settings or have their device setting controllable (IOS Parental Control). There needs to be a clear understanding of how often check-ins/PoL need to occur and what types are required.

Device sophistication has advanced to the point that it's possible to create a fixed set of contacts. You can use the device to screen out all data input from everyone that isn't whitelisted. Only those who appear in the device user's address book can exchange data with the device. Parents can set up an MDS's device to reject all data inputs (text, email, phone call) from anyone except (for example) three individuals: mom, dad, and sibling. This security setting creates safe and useful "training wheels" for the younger citizens as they learn how to navigate their new devices.

It's also essential that R-ADSs explain this functionality to MDSs as part of their data literacy training: If the person you want to contact isn't in your address book, you can't exchange data with them. Control over adding entries to the contacts or address book is a privilege MDSs can earn. It also motivates the MDS to carefully maintain the contact data to stay in contact with their friends.

The key is that ADSs must be appropriately data literate to look for this set of capabilities and then learn to implement them. If you are data illiterate, you won't likely think to attempt to restrict your associated MDSs. The data illiterate will not know to configure their own devices against the intrusion of surveillance capitalists.

Consider how many scams people could have avoided if a system could detect a new caller and warned the other party. The system could put the receiver on notice that the caller is unknown. Also, the system could recommend that the receiver double-check some of the scam assertions. We are close to having solutions like this one. Soon people will be able to communicate using IDs that represent verified caller identities securely. If a caller doesn't have a registered ID, the system won't allow them to speak with a receiver.

Exercise: Review the full call logs with the MDSs and discuss various missed calls due to the ContactsOnly setting.

CDKA03: Securing data

Need: Demonstrate an ability to secure data using device-provided capabilities. This includes both strong password/passphrase and device encryption.

Response: Demonstrate objectively that their devices are encrypted and secured with a strong password and biometric capabilities such as fingerprint or facial recognition.

It's important to consider the device as the equivalent of the data it contains–they are one and the same. Losing the device is losing the data! Now that your device can be used as a "key" for your automobile, it's critical that the MDS understand specifically how much is at stake if care and attention are not paid to the devices' whereabouts. Losing a phone can now mean that anyone finding it has access to the car, dwelling, and the associated finances. It's necessary to introduce fundamental data security principles confidentially, integrity, and assurance (CIA) through device-centrism—that is, the device functionality. The device costs money to purchase and use. The device provides the user with access to the ability to use and make purchases. It needs to be secure, and the user needs to develop habits (that often materialize) of constant access. Securing the device's data includes (passcodes, door locks, access credentials/tickets) as well as keys to transportation and physical locations.

Best here is to leverage device manufacturers to provide rigorous guidance to learn about and encourage the use of these capabilities. The default should be opt-in to strong security practices. Careful evaluation of the general intro/on-ramping processes can determine practices around which educational materials need to be developed, vetted, and made available as widely as possible. This might leave a new Android purchaser with good information on how to secure the device but leaves for another group to develop the contextual information providing the motivation for practicing data security. All of these should be contributed and maintained across all languages so that no one ever must do these basics again! It's important to consider the device as the equivalent of the data it contains–they are one and the same.

Citizens must view the device as equivalent to the data it contains. Losing the device is losing the information. This convergence is significant because a device serves many purposes, including being a key for your car in some cases! The MDSs must understand what is at stake and always know where their devices are. Losing a phone can now mean that anyone finds it has access to the car, dwelling, and the associated finances. It's necessary to introduce fundamental data security principles confidentially, with integrity and assurance (CIA) through device-centrism—that is, the device functionality. The device costs money to purchase and use. The tool provides the user with access to the ability to use and make purchases. It needs to be secure, and the user needs to develop habits of constant access. Securing the device's data includes using passcodes, door locks, access credentials/tickets, and keys to transportation and physical locations.

Leverage the device's tools to provide rigorous guidance to learn about and encourage the use of these capabilities. The default should opt-in to healthy security practices. Careful evaluation of the general introduction processes can determine procedures around which educational materials schools should develop, vet, and make available as widely as possible. This process might leave a new Android purchaser with useful information on securing the device but leaves another group to develop contextual information that motivates practicing data security. These should be contributed and maintained across all languages so that no one ever has to do these basics again!

This CDKA encompasses understanding the strengths and weaknesses of on-device capabilities that require no additional download or maintenance. These include encryption, facial fingerprint recognition, password managers, "lockers," and more—in addition to passcodes. Begin with and encourage the use of passphrases where possible. Understand the relationship between your device and your data. Understand the risks associated with device control of household and workplace access and function. We increasingly use mobile devices to unlock homes, offices, vehicles, etc. Good data security works best when learned as habits like that of children who learn to buckle their seatbelts when traveling by car continue to buckle throughout their lives as the action becomes automatic. This has the same desired result: automated use of available security and knowledge of how "safe" it is.

But the physical device is not the only thing that needs to be secure. We must also protect the data on the device from hackers.

Exercise: Reward the best story of someone losing control over their data in the media for the past week. Follow up on previous stories—discuss what type of bad guys may have been after the data based on data sighting reports.

CDKA04: Identify trustworthy data

Need: Demonstrate an ability to take a defensive approach to trusting received data or when sending data to others. Doubt by rule; trust by exception.

Response: Develop habits for accessing trusted data via trusted methods—objectively review device connections and scan for malware.

Unfortunately, connecting to the Internet inevitably results in some degree of surveillance. EULAs are virtually useless in stopping this (primarily due to the inclusion of the word "other") and reading them does not necessarily provide useful information about what happens to the data you share. Evaluating the trade-offs between surveillance and convenience is an excellent habit to learn even early in life. Everyone must make these trade-offs; the goal is to learn to use them in a healthy manner. MDSs should learn about the following:

- Allowing access to various device capabilities (location, audio/video ports, address book, etc.)
- Locating reputable sources about the apps making the requests
- Recovering when inevitable mistakes are made.

There are a couple of different concepts here. A very important one addresses secure networks. If you are on a public system, you must behave differently than when on a private network. (For example, you take additional care when entering passwords or storing user information on public machines.) It's similar to how you behave at home versus in public (as our moms used to say). Thus, it is essential to set MDS devices to access only permissible (whitelisted) networks and convey this restriction's importance to the MDS as part of the lesson. To teach this concept, it's likely that examples of current headline threats need to be made real to the learner. It is possible to envision learning objectives around:

- Understanding browser connections
- What encryption can and can't accomplish

- Specific avoidance of being fooled.

These could be made current annually, just like the annual cyber awareness refresher.

The other big idea here is trusted *data* or information. How do you know what you see is what you think it is? How do you know what services to trust or when and where to share private information? If there is any room for doubt, then do not extend trust.

Understand that stepping into the mobile world *requires an immediate understanding of the concept of trusted data*. Begin with authorized network access and concepts such as, why is the service's data made available for free? And what else could be done with that data? We must drill these concepts into novices. Installing a defensive default approach will help young minds develop a questioning approach to data requests of all types. This discussion must include an understanding of governing laws and regulations. MDS should have a good sense of what governance structures exist beyond the family unit and what types of conceptual boundaries these can provide.

It is essential to differentiate between the concept of trusted data and a trusted place. It may become impossible to know whether what you see is what you think it is with data. Therefore, it will become critical to understand the further distinction between trusted data and trusted data sources. With malware traffic so prevalent, people should never presume that they're dealing with the person they expect.

Defensively approach each request to add/connect a new device type/instance. Regularly prune your 'known' network connections and actively scan for malware.

Response: When an MDS enters the online community, companies bombard them with different data access types requests. The MDS must develop an approach to these requests to increase their uniformity. If one responded to data requests randomly, some things would work, and others wouldn't go without apparent rhyme or reason. A general approach will help MDS rapidly recognize and evaluate data requests. Internet companies will continually present MDS with this type of request, and it's crucial to develop a specific framework for responding. A response method will allow MDS to recognize routine requests and rapidly respond, objectively reviewing the nature, types, and response to tradeoff requests. For example, we know of a current MDS who has adopted a "don't care" attitude toward sharing. Lack of interest has already proven costly for someone applying for a law-enforcement position using a shared social media password. Today the default attitude towards unsolicited data requests should be one of suspicion.

Exercise: Have a weekly conversation about newly discovered parts of the Internet with R-ADA and the appropriate initial trust to extend to it. Discuss new types of connectivity that become available. Demonstrate the results of weekly malware scans. Have a weekly conversation with an adult about what apps had requested information from the MDS this week.

CDKA05: Urgent protocols and emergency capabilities

Need: Demonstrate an ability to identify when to use emergency protocols and capabilities within the family or group unit.

Response: Demonstrate the ability to recognize and respond to emergency protocols—objectively run household-wide tests and evaluate the results.

Not fun but extremely useful. Learning to use these capabilities appropriately in various situations can be a life-saving skill. Examine these and establish and practice a family emergency contact plan periodically.

Response: Develop and practice specific protocols built into devices for urgent communications and emergencies. Many devices support an urgent call protocol. Calling twice in two minutes inactivates device do-not-disturb settings. Automated cutoff services can be useful in urgent or non-emergency situations. Data settings can be helpful in emergencies via redial, GPS, 911 protocols.

In your device settings, you can activate two types of exceptions to your Do Not Disturb. The first type is contact-based—you can select to have specific contacts calls always ring through. Automated routing is useful if you can't miss a call from a particular connection. The second type of exception is frequency-based—you can select to have repeated calls (defined as a second call from the same person within three minutes) to ring through. This exception helps you address pressing matters when people are most likely trying to reach you. Unfortunately, emergencies do occur, and the device can provide adequate support under differing conditions. It's possible to:

- Silence the device with a single switch to prevent the device from attracting attention
- Contact law enforcement by clicking predetermined sequences (such as a triple-click on a specific button)
- Send location notices
- Take and send photos
- Record and transmit and stream events.

Exercise: Think about the "fire drills" practiced in school. They become so routine that students would hopefully know exactly what to do in the case of a real emergency. Apply the same principles at home—practice data emergency drills using communication and technology.

CDKA06: Device Data Capabilities

Need: All MDS must demonstrate their mastery of device data utilities–a good example is restoring from an automated backup.

Response: Understand the use of the device (including cloud) capabilities–objectively demonstrate an ability to restore the device from backup and review device access.

Device replacement costs, data replacement costs, data storage costs–numerous different characteristics come together to constitute a device. Just knowing that your device can record hours of video with the existing storage can encourage safe behavior. The MDS should be able to:

- Describe the device's last backup
- Restore data from an existing backup
- Understand what the users request from the device (i.e., the Facebook app wants access to your microphone).

While a backup is an easily understandable example, CDKA06 extends to virus and malware protection, device search optimization, wireless sharing, and other devices and OS-specific capabilities.

Devices are capable of many data management capabilities. Storage has been optimized for the faster, flash-based memories accessible in parallel via multi-core processing. Understand and take advantage of low-level capabilities, such as data store and data retrieval. Install and explain data restriction technologies. We will go as far as saying that all MDS should be equipped (software) with a 'transponder' indicating this device belongs to an MDS and should be considered off-limits by data collectors.

This opens an entirely new class of data practices based on these transponders. Right now, we require the device to determine on a case-by-case basis whether the various connections and requests are responsible and valid. Imagine how the behavior would be altered if the collectors were fined for even making a data request of an MDS device. Consider a scenario illustrating the existence and extent of device logging capabilities. Consider the following two scenarios:

	Scenario #1/Device Log File		**Scenario #2/Device Log File**
1 -	Device lifted during an automobile ride	1 -	Siri activated/authenticated by voice command
2 -	Manual entry of passcode and phone number	2 -	Siri dials the phone number

3- Call terminated by operator
4- Automobile stops
5- Start recording video

3- Call terminated by Siri
4- Automobile stops
5- Start recording video

Suppose the police pulled over the automobile in question. In that case, the log file for scenario #2 could provide key evidence keeping the driver from facing a traffic summons or other consequences, understanding that the computer records every action that it takes but that one must generally take affirmative action to access this valuable record of contemporaneous happenings.

The MDS requires this sort of knowledge to understand that when stuff hits the Internet, it tends to stick. Being able to find stuff on everyone under a certain age fundamentally changes society. Understanding that data persists even after user deletion, will keep the Tom Brady's of the world from further embarrassment as they discover that a copy of every message, emoji, picture, audio file, or video that is shared is also copied to some cloud server and those logs will record the event.

It's fascinating how many forget that their device makes an excellent calculator with capabilities right up to the supercomputing level. Further, MDSs should consider the vast possibilities and useful tools available to them through their devices. Beyond these abilities are also wonderful apps and extensions for monitoring and tracking (citizens, metadata, advertising, convenience, geofencing, and device/system logging).

It can check to see if its software and malware virus protection is the latest version. Regular checkups by a unit can help encourage this habit. Identify the update tester who installs the update first to ensure the entire unit communications aren't shut down when all download a bad update and break their devices simultaneously.

Know of the existence of deep fakes and their purpose to fool individuals, such as a message from mom asking for her password.

Exercise: Implement full device restoration from backup.

CDKA07: The appropriateness of data requests

Need: Demonstrate a mastery of the numerous types of data requests that come with device ownership.

Response: Demonstrate an ability to respond appropriately to a range of specific requests.

One of the essential concepts in this book—that is, the best way to deal with data requests (at the MDS/ADS levels) and when dealing with data in general, is opt-in by default or opt-out by default.

Let's look at an example to see the difference between opt-in and opt-out activities. In most of the United States, voter registration is an opt-in activity: citizens must act—filling out a form—to be registered to vote. However, some states have an automatic voter registration system in which all eligible citizens are registered automatically unless they take specific action to opt-out.

The selection of opt-in and opt-out approaches represents society's most fundamental decisions and is especially important for data decisions. For example, a unit could share a whitelist permitting unrestricted data exchange among trusted individuals in addition to generally improved data control and maintenance. This is important because generally when you authorize access to some data on your device, you grant it going forward from today onward.

Bottom line: the citizen should be careful when giving access to device data. Suppose sufficient apps, websites, and organizations are granted access to device capabilities that the battery drains noticeably more rapidly. In such cases, the device is spending too many cycles satisfying data requests. As a result, tasks such as opening apps, accessing websites, playing games, etc., slows—at which point citizens play into industry's hands by purchasing and renting a machine with increased capabilities.

Even the label "data request" is incorrect. In most instances, it should be labeled: "Request to permanently and continuously receive unspecified data feeds from your mobile device on an unspecified schedule with unspecified regularity?"

A data request sounds like a one-time request. For example: "What is your passcode?" or "Show me your face, please." **Most data requests are attempts to implement a data acquisition stream for an unspecified purpose**. The difference between sharing your passcode with an authorized requestor and telling an (often unknown) entity that they have permission to use your device's battery and computing power to send them unspecified amounts of your data forever is enormous! And yet, the same request covers both extremities.

When an MDS agrees to a requested data stream, i.e., "clicks," it's often difficult to tell that your device battery is also being used to send a location ping to an unknown server perhaps multiple times per minute. It is difficult to tell that your battery no longer powers your device as long as it used to, as many data surveillance activities encumber your device with unrequested activities.

Response: We need to change how ADSs currently view various transactions and change our perception to view these as data transactions. Of course, some data transactions are necessary and beneficial. For example, it would be best to have your bank require your passcode before it relays your balance information to you. On the other hand, there is likely no reason that a single-brand, retail app on your phone needs to know your location all the time. This is an unreasonable data request. Retail apps would like to capture all data you are willing to share about your location, including anything else that you authorize the app to ingest, such as the contents of your contact book, past messages you have sent and received, your email, etc.

Data access also requires a reframing of our perspective.

Old question:	Where are you?
Reformulation:	I want to know where you go, what time you go, how fast you go, everywhere. Possible responses should minimally be ("no," "only while the app is open," or "always") whereas most options are only "yes" or "no"

Appropriateness of data requests is a further criterion that should be applied after trustworthiness has been determined and verified. When an app or an individual asks for access to data, the user must understand the nature of the request and (in the case of MDSs) ask for assistance before granting access. Everyone should be willing to at least Google the request before blindly saying yes or no. Legislation around these standards is likely upcoming.

As MDSs mature into an ADS, they must form a coherent internal approach to these risks. Granting them all will kill your device performance via multitudinous, onerous data requests. Remember: each data request and transfer is logged, thereby incurring additional overhead. We should approach most requests programmatically.

As part of their data education, MDSs must begin to understand appropriate and inappropriate data requests. These requests will be an increasing part of the MDSs' lives and will be increasingly disguised as innocuous. A regular conversation about which apps are requesting which data capabilities and why, would be an excellent means of learning more about which should be granted and denied. The goal is to draw together a relationship between your data and your safety through a series of conversations with the responsible ADS.

Data request from an app or organization

Internet actors bombard MDSs and ADSs with new messages requesting access to systems, software, and tools all the time. These requests grow, and software programs collect vast amounts of personal data. But these websites rarely return or destroy that personal information. Instead, they keep it and use it for other purposes. Many websites and software applications make their terms of use unclear to registrants. There are countless complaints about the readability of these terms. Many people believe the agreements are overly complicated and deliberately confusing. And there are examples to back up their claims. For example, software programs often ask permission to access seemingly unrelated system capabilities, such as cameras. Often there is no apparent need for the software program to access the camera. Although users do not understand the consequences of these requests, they compliantly grant access. What happens then? Different software programs operate in different ways. But when malicious software gets permission, *those systems can scan photos, travel documents, and payment information without a user ever knowing*. Also, other data, like credit card information, vouchers, and additional financial information, is vulnerable to risk.

Modern systems are only beginning to recognize this problem and take steps to prevent them from happening. For example, new systems constrain external channels and participants. Smart systems use blacklists to flag malicious websites, and they use programmatic tools to prevent software programs from accessing system services when they want. However, unethical data harvesters will always probe and push the boundaries justifying the defensive posture.

Organizations may also request confirmation of passwords or other PII. Reputable organizations have trained KWs who won't make inappropriate requests of customers. If MDSs recognize the difference between appropriate and inappropriate data requests, they will be better equipped to identify new threats to their data quickly.

Data request from an individual

The rise of social media has redefined relationships in hazardous ways. By referring to your hundreds of contacts as "friends," social media encourages more sharing. After all, you would certainly share with your real-life friends when you have a nice meal at a specific location. However, it isn't always wise to share that information with your cousin's friend that you met once at a party.

When you have lots of connections, you can influence them, and the thing you most want them to do is behavior based, that is, subscribe, like, purchase, and vote. **NOTE: all four options-subscribe, like, connect, and vote involve data requests and exchanges.** Just as there are appropriate and inappropriate data requests from devices (apps), influencers can greatly influence resulting behavior. Notice how the parent-child (formerly family-based) functions have been subsumed into this more populous group? Until influencing (the practice) can be brought under a code of conduct, it will be up to recipients to discern appropriate from inappropriate behavior that is used to influence their behavior.

Exercise: Devise data "tricks" to toughen group/unit data strength and resilience in the same manner that Netflix IT uses the chaos monkey to make its technology operations resilient. The 'monkey' literally goes around breaking stuff that doesn't usually break. This has successfully forced Netflix KWs to 'harden' their data and processes against these imminent threats.[68] Active fooling attempts among the group will increase the entire group's abilities to fend off data predators.

CDKA08: Device data capabilities

Need: Demonstrate a mastery of device data utilities, including cloud capabilities.

Response: Demonstrate ability to restore the device from backup and review device access.

Learn how to learn about your device. Understand the device's various capabilities, not so much memorizing them, but so that you can investigate further when the powers are needed and dealing programmatically with inappropriate data requests. Know your device. Understand the device's various capabilities. You don't need to memorize them; just know how to find necessary information when capabilities are needed to deal programmatically with inappropriate data requests.

Device replacement costs, data replacement costs, data storage costs. Numerous different characteristics come together to constitute a device. Just knowing that your device can record hours of video with the existing storage can encourage safe behavior. The MDS should describe the device's last backup, restore data from an existing backup, and understand what the users request from the device (e.g., the Facebook app wants access to your microphone). While backup is an easily understandable example, CDKA06 extends to virus and malware protection, device search optimization, wireless sharing, and other operating system-specific capabilities.

Response: MDSs should objectively demonstrate their ability to use these device functions. Devices are capable of many data management capabilities. Storage has been optimized for the (10X) faster, flash-based memories accessible in parallel via multi-core processing. Understand and take advantage of low-level stuff, such as data storage and data retrieval.

The MDS must also understand that the device can also check to see if its software and malware virus protection is the latest version. Obvious regular checkups by the R-ADS can help encourage this habit. R-ADS can have an excellent discussion regarding who tests the installs. Observing a family software upgrade plan can ensure that all family unit communications aren't shut down when all download a lousy update and break their devices simultaneously.

Exercise: Critically review data use rate, automation incorporation, data sharing, etc., for validity.

CDKA09: Overcoming bad internet behavior

Need: Demonstrate understanding of the range of bad behavior potentially encountered on the Internet.

Response: Objectively respond appropriately to a range of Internet behaviors.

MDSs need to understand what constitutes bad Internet behavior. (This should be linked to a broader discussion as to what constitutes "bad behavior.") Begin to educate yourself on the worst of the Internet and understand what constitutes, how to avoid, and what to do when encountering trolling, harassment, stalking, click-baiting, and cyberbullying. Introduce copyright laws. Instead of asking, "Can I?" ask yourself, "Should I?"

We do not have the space for a full discourse on social media, but we present this list of the "O'Reilly Principles" as a starting point for incorporating ideas into an unenforceable online code of conduct.

- Take responsibility—not just for your own words, but for the comments you allow.
- Label your tolerance level for abusive comments.
- Consider eliminating anonymous comments.
- Ignore the trolls.
- Take the conversation offline and talk directly—or find an intermediary who can do so.
- If you know someone who is behaving badly, tell them so.
- Don't say anything online that you wouldn't say in person.[69]

All of this may be a bit much for the MDS, so try to get them to understand that the golden rule applies online and IRL (In Real Life). It's good to introduce MSD to social media with constraints regarding the number of connections, time, and financial obligations. If people perceive a capability as not being free, immediately prioritizing activities becomes more useful. If I only have 30 minutes of screen time remaining, which of the many things I want to do, do I have time to accomplish well? We discuss specific ADS constraints expected in CDKA10: Manage Online Reputations.

Exercise: Weekly discussion participants nominate the worst Internet behavior examples they've seen and describe a better approach to the situation.

Chapter conclusions–Educating future citizens

We have described characteristics shared by 2.5 billion citizens (or future citizens). These characteristics underpin the derivation of shared data literacy needs. We have specified nine CDKAs constituting an objective level of data literacy that we believe prerequisite to being handed a supercomputer connected to the Internet at a young age:

- Securing data belonging to you and others.

- Understand there exists some data that is trustworthy and some that isn't.
- Effectively evaluate surveillance/convenience tradeoffs poised routinely to citizens.
- Understand both the rationale and incentives upon which ContactsOnly connecting is based.
- Implement emergency protocols during practice and an actual emergency.
- Successfully leverage device data capabilities.
- Appropriately evaluate specific data requests.
- Recognize and navigate bad Internet behavior.
- Successfully demonstrate your data literacy by achieving specific verifiable 'good' behaviors by unlocking additional device capabilities/services/bandwidth.

If you cannot achieve these levels of competency, quite frankly, the rest of us would just as soon that you stayed off the Internet as you will be a magnet for bad behavior, malware, and attacks. Your data illiteracy will be a threat to wherever you live.

CHAPTER 8

Adult Data Spreader (ADS)

About 1.5 billion people of adult age are using mobile devices connected to the Internet. We call these Adult Data Spreaders (ADSs) with the emphasis on the word **adult**.

Adulthood comes with a combination of civic rights, duties, and privileges. For example, in the United States, a citizen must be eighteen years old to vote in a federal election or twenty-one years old to drink alcohol. Many cultures consider these activities to be steppingstones to adulthood and taking responsibility for actions in society. Likewise, we believe adults must understand how to use the data corresponding to these and other adult-related data activities.

Consider this example. How does the law measure intoxication? The law defines intoxication as the measure of the amount of alcohol circulating in your bloodstream. The relationship between alcohol and blood is called blood alcohol content (BAC). The blood alcohol content is the amount of alcohol present in a blood volume equal to 100 milliliters (ml) or its equivalent of 1 deciliter (dL). For example:80 mg is 0.08 grams (0.08 grams of alcohol in 100 ml is 0.08%; people also express this value as 80 mg/dL or a BAC of 0.08).

In the United States, a blood-alcohol content of 0.1 (0.1% or one-tenth of 1%) means that there are 0.10 grams of alcohol for every deciliter of blood in the person's body at the time of the test. Of course, results also vary by body type, food consumption, energy levels, etc. Factoring all of these at age 18 can be difficult, even for the few capable of doing the math—and that, of course, assumes that they have the correct data! It is no wonder so many have encountered challenges around this concept. Consider the fall 2016 US elections when Donald Trump went into the final stretch with 28.6% chance of winning (according to 538.com). Most citizens do not comprehend that this is the same as playing Russian Roulette with two of the six cylinders loaded! Normally the game is played with only one cylinder loaded. Citizens generally prefer not to play against these odds. While these examples are common, other examples are not so obvious. Citizens must understand and follow digital data trails to conclude all messages have motives. Failure to understand the data basics of the election caused a national moment of surprise in the US.

ADSs can be a bit more focused than MDSs because they do not have time to be as unfocused as a youth. Maturity is often accompanied by more concrete forms of safety—a steady job, a clear sense of right and wrong, a sense of property, etc.

Not learning the necessary data security requirements, motivations, accounting, and other risks can have disastrous consequences for individuals and society. In this chapter, we establish minimum standards for data literacy among adults. We will describe an ADS and eight additional CDKAs that this group of 1.5 billion citizens will benefit from immensely. Society, in turn, will be immensely grateful. This content represents a natural maturation of the data literacy presented in the previous chapter.

As we stated in the previous chapter, MDSs (and ADSs) are the perfect targets for surveillance capitalists of all kinds. Building data literacy concepts into the educational system will make these citizens less vulnerable to data poachers. However, if MDSs and ADSs do not understand basic data concepts, these groups will be pawns for the data matrix. Changing the system and putting social reins on the data matrix is a massive legal endeavor.

Adult data spreader description

Actor: Level 2 actors are called Adult Data Spreaders (ADSs). Adults are responsible for the actions and consequences of themselves and their wards. A key difference between adult and mobile data spreaders is the amount of time the actors have. Where MDSs seemingly have limitless amounts of time, ADSs have less time due to responsibilities. Another key difference between the actors is that ADSs are full participants in society. They contribute to and consume resources. ADSs are distinguished from others because they focus on individuals and family safety. Their meme is a reminder that they **#vote** and have the power to change the rules about data. This tag can often be more powerful than money.

Action: The scope of ADSs' data actions is generally constrained to children, immediate family, and work colleagues. Social media, however, also allows ADSs to affect a wider circle. For example, ADSs can affect others outside their immediate sphere of influence when others "follow" them on social media. The rise of these unregulated influencers represents a challenge. This trend is growing and showing no sign of slowing any time soon. We can see this by the number of young citizens who aspire to become influencers as a profession.

Affects: Because ADSs play an active role in social governance, ADSs can affect broader societal rules and behaviors. ADSs exercise more general civic influence by participating in political processes. In more recent years, politicians have recognized social media's power to craft and deliver their messages to an increasingly wider audience.

Producing: an ability to create endless data consumed by the surveillance capitalist economy. For example, ADSs have larger buying power than MDSs. Social media giants monitor and exploit ADSs' shopping habits, information consumption, and medical information to deliver more targeted advertising.

Using: ADSs can use their influence to nurture and guide others. The best example is a parent raising a child. Parental influence, education, guidance, and nurturing all help to prepare children to become full-fledged members of society. As part of this, ADSs help MDSs understand and use the Internet's power and the dangers as one of many elements of a complex society.

To: One significant goal of the ADS should be to protect MDSs. Because MDSs are children and start with no real understanding of the Internet and the risks it presents, ADSs play an essential role in teaching them about the digital world. We have already described the role of the R-ADS in Chapter 7. They help MDSs understand the differences between computing platforms like cell phones, desktop computers, and other Internet-enabled devices. ADSs teach MDSs about appropriate content sharing and cyberbullying.

Data Acumen: Like MDSs, ADSs learn by doing, resulting in unnecessary bleeding from thousands of small cuts. ADSs understand data mainly through personal experiences and have not participated in formal educational or professional programs. We hope this will change in the future as data education becomes standardized.

Ethical Perspective: ADSs' ethics relative to data are self-assigned; there are a few outside forces (community, church, social groups, etc.) that set digital ethical expectations for some ADSs. When ADSs interact with MDSs, ADSs operate along with inherited ethical definitions, which they try to impart to their wards. ADSs expect other societal actors to operate along similar ethical lines. For example, when vendors make claims using data, ADSs expect those claims to be accurate and verifiable—something others can objectively measure. However, it's still wise to operate as if others attempt to fool and manipulate you regarding the data you encounter.

Behavioral Focus: ADSs mostly operate individually, devoting large amounts of time with MDSs and co-workers. ADSs often collaborate with others to seek advice and share experiences. And like MDSs, ADSs consume enormous amounts of digital content and other resources like food, clothing, and entertainment items. The hot spots from a behavioral perspective are family and immediate environment.

ADS data knowledge areas (needs & responses)

We postulate these eight additional CDKAs as prerequisites for being a contributing adult citizen today.

Online reputations	Automated data management
Consider the source	Data fiduciary relationships
Sensitive personal data protection	Influencing
Automated data restraints	Data investments

We cover each for the remainder of this chapter. Unfortunately, we can't enforce, but we hope that society will band together to put peer pressure on citizens who may benefit from additional education in these areas to raise the entire citizenry's data literacy level.

CDKA10: Managing online reputations

Need: Demonstrate an ability to review, improve and monitor their online reputations.

Response: Objectively illustrate knowledge of how to view and maintain existing online reputation scores.

It takes conscious effort to establish your online reputation and even more to repair a damaged reputation. Adults are required to spend an increasing amount of their time and effort in maintaining multiple online profiles. Matrix operators penalize those adults if they don't keep those accounts—those accounts, including LinkedIn, social media, Amazon, among many others.

As an adult, one is expected to maintain several scores, including the number of 'points' on their driving record, credit score, gig economy rating, LinkedIn profile, etc. First of all, these are all data points under the control of the individual. When a judge checks on your driving record and determines that you have accumulated safe driving points and waives a fee or penalty based on your 'good' driving record, this is an example of how a data point that you have control over (just don't drive unsafely) requires maintenance. When it comes to social media, the control loop can be shorter and more consequential. As surely as someone in an e-mail addressed to ALL will hit the REPLY-ALL button, stories abound about individuals posting to social media not realizing that "others could read it!"

A true story–someone tweets something racist (10:36 pm 25 Jul 2016). A quick google yields that individual's social media presence, an examination of which reveals their occupation in the home loan industry. This resulted in public tweets at the individual's employer (2:18 am 26 Jul 2016), resulting in a public announcement of the individual's termination, less than 18 hours after the offensive tweet (1:28 pm 26 Jul 2016). [70]

If you are an ADS, you must understand that others maintain data about you and that it is your responsibility to maintain your personal online data. Your reputational risk is a combination of the "relative proximity" of three factors:

1. Who you ARE. Your identity in the real life.
2. Who YOU SAY you are. The image you wish to display to the public.
3. Who Citizens SAY you are. The way others describe you or your business.

Understanding these is crucial to ensuring your online reputation well reflects the reality.

Response: A good online reputation proves that you, as an individual, have sufficiently matured in society's eyes, followed applicable laws, and taken responsibility for your actions. For example, it is critical to understand what happens when you sign up for a social website using your employer's email account. Be aware of applicable laws and enforcement mechanisms. Recognize what data issues can affect your employment status. Recognize what data issues jeopardize your freedom.

Exercise: Each participant is assigned a different participant to research online. What did you find out about the other person? Discuss what is real and what is incorrect.

CDKA11: Consider the source: The online reputation of others

Need: Demonstrate an ability to review and evaluate the online reputation of various sources and use this ability to enhance their ability to trust certain data sources.

Response: Objectively respond appropriately to a range of approaches demonstrating an ability to differentiate between informed and uninformed commentary.

In some ways, the need to "consider the source" has always been around. Consider those subjected to Chicken Little's communications about the end of the world. After repeated warnings with no results, the general populace learns to ignore Chicken Little's rants. In many ways, this cause leads to no effect pattern that should have translated easily into the online realm. However, the mystique associated with computing and the wonder of being able to google everything combine to lead novices (significantly) not to challenge information from the Internet. Learning to consider the source of all data is a critical skill required of all ADSs.

People have a healthy skeptical distrust of data coming from an unsolicited source. There are many ways for citizens to get confused on the Internet. A common way to become confused is to overlook the source of information.

There are, though, ways to figure out what the source is. Consider the following.

`whitehouse.com | whitehouse.org | whitehouse.gov`

Each website contains "whitehouse." But the suffix for each website is different. The suffix denotes the kind of website it purports to be. For example, ".com" means the website is a commercial entity. The ".org" suffix indicates the website belongs to a non-specific entity (generally an association), and the ".gov" suffix means the website belongs to a governmental entity. An excellent way to explain the differences between these types of websites is to explore these websites cautiously.

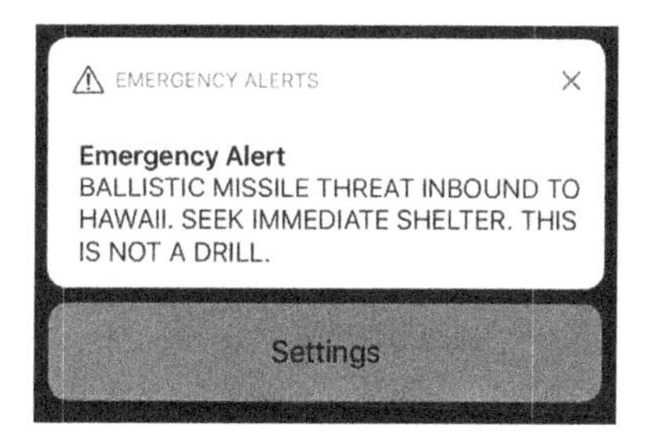

Figure 8.1— Hawaii's false alarm

Just because a communication originated from a seemingly reputable source, such as the US Emergency Alert System, that doesn't always make the data valid either! The screenshot above was widely transmitted in Hawaii on the morning of Saturday, January 13, 2018. This text advised residents to seek shelter, closing with the phrase "this isn't a drill." Happily, it was not a drill or an emergency either, but a "miscommunication" between employees.

ADSs receive a massive number of unsolicited communications. Employing common security practices provides up-to-date protection and filters out large amounts of junk communications. It should be a shared goal to understand appropriate and inappropriate data sharing as a responsible adult in an increasingly transparent society. Shunning friends who repeatedly forward unwanted materials should be standard.

An excellent digital citizen doesn't allow hackers to access their communication devices. An important reason is that hackers target the personal communication devices address book—it's instantly uploaded for future exploitation. This means that everyone in the hacked phone book begins to receive unwanted communications, and it usually isn't difficult to determine who is responsible for the breach. Repeated hacking causes sloppy data citizens to be unfriended digitally as annoying. No one stays connected with 'friends' who get repeatedly hacked.

Exercise: Pick a "celebrity influencer" and determine objective qualifications. Just what objective authority does that influencer actually have?

CDKA12: Individual policies and data practices regarding sensitive personal data

Need: Demonstrate an ability to identify and protect sensitive data (especially personal data).

Response: Demonstrate an ability to safeguard and steward your own PII as well as that of others.

Develop policies around essential data practices. Understand the role that your credit score, social media profiles, etc., play in today's world. Understand data surveillance, monitoring, tracking capabilities, and the strengths and weaknesses of the various technical systems. Understand the role of capabilities such as route optimizing and reporting to gain contextual perspective. Evolve the tradeoff between convenience and privacy at a process level instead of individually. Finally, understand the costs and benefits related to maintaining personal data.

Response: Adult thinking abstracts individual instances to classes of events to reduce stress and increase consistency. Take, for example, a request to access by an app to access part of your device's memory. Is this the first time an app has made such a request? Have you developed a policy for responding to requests of this type? Resolving to not be too liberal in "friending" to avoid spam is entirely rational behavior. Individual data requests can be approached from a policy perspective—for example, approaching data requests with a predefined set of responses might include:

1. Grant, conditionally if possible
2. Deny
3. Requires further study before responding.

When legitimate companies request data, grant them as perhaps mutually beneficial. Refusing doesn't necessarily result in the denial of services desired. Useful analogies give citizens an increasing amount of control in these situations. ADS should adopt an approach that refuses data requests from organizations with which they have no fiduciary relationship. Working like this will eliminate most data requests.

Exercise: Determine an ever-growing list of data requiring familial safeguarding.

CDKA13: Automated data restraints

Need: Demonstrate an ability to learn how to use new automated data controls to their benefit.

Response: Objectively demonstrate successful use of automated data restrictions beyond what is required by system and malware updates.

Use data to enable programmatic controls to restrict incoming data. Ranging from virus filters to whitelisting subscriptions to malware "fingerprints," today's digital citizens have a wide variety of automated, semi-automated, and validation controls to assist with the incoming data tsunami. Data controls have two primary benefits to ADSs: increasing safety and reducing distractions. Data controls can range from 'safe' browsing settings to whitelist-only website restrictions. Today's Internet devices are built for multitasking, and apps will send you as many notifications as you will let them. But ADSs should understand that multitasking is the enemy of productivity. They must learn how and when to use their devices' controls to filter out unnecessary incoming distractions.

Response: It's an ADS's decision to opt-in or opt-out of new communications, but these should be governed by and default to an opt-in process. ADSs' devices come equipped to encourage communication only between address book parties (ContactsOnly). This should not be viewed or presented as a limiting factor but instead as a beneficial feature. These technologies work under most circumstances. We have already described one class of challenges—a call back from a technical support number will go straight to voicemail when using ContactsOnly. Someone calling back within a 2-minute window gets classed as an urgent call. Evidence indicates increased productivity results from turning off individual new mail alerts and push notifications.

Exercise: As a group, incorporate into your device capabilities various levels and types of filtering such as ad-blockers, blacklists, firewall controls, VPN capabilities, etc.

CDKA14: Responsible automated data management

Need: Demonstrate an ability to use automated data management capabilities to their benefit.

Response: Demonstrate knowledgeable use of smart lists, macros, and other data time savers.

ADSs must use tools to help them manage and secure their data. Popular software like Apple's Photos, MusicBee, and others help citizens manage their photographs, music, and documents. Learning how to use these kinds of tools has gotten so commonplace that we describe that knowledge as life skills. And a lifetime of teaching convinces us that the sooner citizens started using them, the greater the lifetime benefit.

One of the most popular data management tools is the ubiquitous cloud-based backup utilities. These tools allow citizens to access their data where they are (and have a network connection) and recover lost or destroyed files. But your data is probably not safe. Tech giants troll through billions of documents looking for clues to help advertisers target customers with high precision. One way to help make sure your private information stays private is to use encryption technology and integrate it across all your work and personal habits. ADSs must understand their data is always at risk, and they are responsible for protecting it at all times.

A further example is data organization. Organization does not happen by magic; it must be planned, executed, and maintained, or data will descend into chaos.

Take, for example, the way an average user organizes their music on an application such as Music (formerly iTunes). We can surmise that this is representative of how they treat data organization. One of your co-authors has more than 10,000 songs belonging to thousands of artists' combinations. One specific playlist entitled "Wordless" contains more than 6,000 instrumental songs, totaling more than twenty days' worth of music. The purpose of this playlist is to provide ambient music that is beneficial for concentration. It wouldn't work to toss all 10,000 songs into the library and then hit "skip" each time the play encountered a piece with words. This "mega-playlist" combines all the songs on several smaller lists of instrumental music. It can only be maintained efficiently using the built-in app data management capabilities to organize smart folders.

While some users care more than others about music, those who do are generally pretty good at organizing access to their collections. After all, it wouldn't make sense to acquire music and then not access it when desired. Skills such as the ability to organize your music, photos, documents, and more, are useful throughout your lifetime. The earlier that people learn about them, the sooner people can get more value from them. We mentioned in Chapter 1 that some agencies requested the passwords to applicants' social media accounts. Perhaps it would also be beneficial to the candidates' address book or music library to get a sense of their organizational abilities!

Response: The device (in this case, the operating system) can and will give an increasingly useful means of organizing individual data collections, as we illustrated describing the music playlist management. Understand best practices around email management, use of folders, and file naming conventions—there are boundless topics to become educated. These are also great topics for family unit conversations. Explore the various capabilities, learn how to organize your photos, etc.

Exercise: Describe how you can determine the degree of trust you should have in data knowing that everything can be preserved forever. Everything can also be doctored to any degree. This relates to understanding that data access is recorded, but that access can also easily be faked. Evaluate how the ADS acts under evolving circumstances.

CDKA15: Understand data fiduciary relationships

Need: Demonstrate knowledge of data fiduciary relationships.

Response: Demonstrate the ability to treat data differently when it is governed by fiduciary obligations.

A "fiduciary obligation" is an obligation that an ADS has based on professional responsibilities. One of these obligations is to protect the data of others when it is in their possession. For example, physicians, lawyers, and bankers have access to the private information of their patients or clients and must be sure that it doesn't fall into the wrong hands. In these kinds of data-sharing relationships, the ADS must understand the following concepts:

- What terms and conditions are typically governed by the terms of a fiduciary data relationship?
- How should data sharing occur within the confines of a fiduciary relationship?
- Who can influence fiduciary data relationships?
- How does data inform fiduciary-based choices like investing or health?

Response: If we ran the world, anyone with whom you exchanged data would be governed by a fiduciary relationship. It's the responsibility of anyone entrusted with someone else's data to protect it in several different ways. (We will dive further into these in a later chapter.) In this manner, our organization's data loss would be the crime of not caring for it professionally. The future points increasingly toward this outcome.

While we believe that what we outlined above is what should be, it doesn't reflect today's reality. Understand that at least four types of fiduciary relationships are recognized by society. Individuals who are trusted with your financial, health, legal, and governmental data exchanges are governed by statutes that might include the:

- 1996 Clinger-Cohen Act
- 1996 HIPAA
- 2002 Data Quality Act
- 2002 Sarbanes-Oxley
- 2003 CA Senate Bill 1386
- 2006 Basel II Capital Accord
- 2007 USA Patriot Act
- 2018 GDPR
- 2018 Federal Rules of Civil Procedure (FRCP)
- 2018 FEPA
- 2018 CCPA.

While the industries governed by these laws have some employees qualified to exchange data under these statutes, most lack the specific training required to comply. All instances above represent examples of data exchanges taking place between parties with direct fiduciary relationships. It's essential to recognize what these are and under what circumstances they apply. As a result, ADSs should have a very low expectation of privacy in most data exchanges, even those that should be confidential.

Exercise: Role-play various fiduciary parties encountering data requests. Discuss what data to exchange, if at all.

CDKA16: Responsible influencing

Need: Demonstrate an ability to distinguish between responsible and irresponsible influencing.

Response: Demonstrate knowledge of responsible and irresponsible use of influencing data.

In June 2018, Instagram reached one billion active users. Folk heroes ranging from Betty Bowers to flash-in-the-pan celebrities all have the power to be influential. This isn't new, but the direct amplification power of social networks is the critical new ingredient. Whether you are a parent influencing your wards or have made a legitimate business providing the desired service.

Response: People who do not live in a vacuum influence each other. Some make a more conscious effort to influence others. Others discover a monetary motive to become influencers, particularly through their social media presence. Influencers typically have zero fiduciary responsibilities. Like the guidelines presented in "CDKA09: Overcoming Bad Internet Behavior," influencers must develop a similar code and provide toothy enforcement mechanisms. Governing influencers are the key to exerting any influence over this rapidly growing force in society.

Additionally, ADSs need to understand that all incoming messages from influencers are a form of marking. As such, their purpose is to change your personal choices in areas such as voting, shopping, or travel. Statements will claim to inform, but the reality is that all marketing aims to influence behavior. ADSs must be able to:

- recognize misleading marketing practices and compensate for erroneous information
- understand the motives behind the data streams aimed at you
- understand how data informs ADSs about various personal choices.

CDKA17: Data investments: features and expectations

Need: Demonstrate an ability to understand and effectively manage the component costs of their data consumption.

Response: Demonstrate knowledge of data and data processing costs with an eye towards process improvement.

Since MDSs are generally prohibited from entering into contractual relationships, ADSs are solely responsible for factoring financial costs into the data equation. Even in 2021, we still hear people and organizations say, "You can't quantify data's value." We believe they are incorrect. Just because it is a difficult challenge and not much practical experience exists, doesn't mean that we cannot achieve meaningful successes.

Quarantined at home in early 2020, entire families were suddenly forced to cooperatively manage home download data capabilities.[71] Consider two ADSs, each with a Zoom meeting and multiple MDSs attempting to "attend" school simultaneously. This clearly put a strain on existing infrastructure. That wasn't helped by the fact Zoom and other organizations set the default video streams to be 1080p instead of the much more efficient 480p. (Is it really necessary for everyone in a weekly staff meeting to be in HI-DEF?)

The ability to deliver high volumes of prepaid Internet (which they have trained us to call "free") has forced individuals and families to make immediate choices about the types, volumes, and frequencies with which a household can consume data. The existing infrastructure was not designed to support a family of four—each streaming a different video signal simultaneously! Data choice must now become a topic of discussion and individual focus.

Response: ADS should be able to:

- learn more about cutting the cord
- comprehend streaming versus downloading options
- evaluate various offered bundled data plan options
- understand the consequences of unlocking digital capabilities
- understand that "free long distance" really means "prepaid long distance"
- evaluate various bundle options against data describing current usage levels.

Exercise: In response to changes in the market, evaluate the costs/benefits of various offers and the impact of that understanding on the current suppliers.

Chapter conclusions–Codifying adult data responsibilities

We have described the characteristics shared by 1.5 billion adults. These characteristics permit the derivation of shared data literacy needs. We have specified eight additional CDKAs representing an objective level of data proficiency that we believe to be a prerequisite to meaningfully participating today as a citizen.

In addition to all the CDKAs of MDSs, an ADS must:

- actively manage online reputations
- maintain defense posture against digital inputs
- protect sensitive personal data
- implement and evolve automated data restraints
- leverage automated data management capabilities
- identify and respect fiduciary data relationships
- assist the community in establishing influencing boundaries
- make the right data investment decisions.

The more ADS that can achieve these objective data literacy measures, the better off all citizens will be.

CHAPTER 9

Knowledge Worker (KW)

Organizations can become data literate if they are willing to invest sufficient resources in a foundational curriculum. This begins with thoroughly educating Knowledge Workers (KWs) to reach the level of data acumen.

As described in Chapter 5, a Knowledge Worker is someone who "thinks for a living." We have found that many KWs are skilled in using technology but ham-fisted using data. We expect readers to be surprised at this, but we're not. Throughout our careers, we've encountered citizens who self-identify as being "data literate." However, in many cases, they didn't know how much they didn't know. To recall a concept from Chapter 1, many KWs cannot use data assets to their fullest ability.

The most objective attribute difference between KWs and ADSs is employment status. Only the subset of employed KWs can be required to sign a data conduct code governing them. KWs can voluntarily also subscribe to data conduct codes by affiliating with professional organizations and associations. Organizations will benefit by immediately adopting data literacy screening to refine similar candidates further. This screening will significantly facilitate the process of educating organizational KWs about the organization's ethics.

As Stephen Hawkins noted, "The greatest enemy of knowledge isn't ignorance; it's the illusion of knowledge." If organizations want to embrace evidence-based practices and data-driven decisions, there is only one logical starting point: understanding that instincts and intuitions may be wrong. Organizations must be humble, self-critical, and curious to accept this point. But adopting this posture will help organizations avoid being fooled by intuition even when it may feel good to corporate decision-makers.

Today's poor state of data education means that every KW in your organization learned data management individually without uniform guidance. Imagine if all your KWs were implementing their individual versions of what they believed your HR policies to be. If that approach were better, we would see a movement to "decentralize HR." That isn't happening because organizations understand that uniform HR policies are beneficial. Yet this same principle is rarely applied to data policies.

KWs are likely to become or interact with data stewards who will help systematize the organization's approach. Stewards are data governance individuals with a fiduciary responsibility to maintain a subset of organizational data.

KWs can interact with a specific data subset and often become an expert with its management.

As a bonus, KWs produce ideas faster if they can concentrate on their primary tasks by simply reducing the amount of time spent locating required data (again, see Chapter 5). There is also a reduced risk of introducing errors and acting on erroneous information at the individual, workgroup, and organizational levels. Integrating existing systems to easily search and find similar or identical tests can reduce expenses, improve the client's competitive edge and customer service, increase time savings, and improve operational capabilities.

To illustrate the importance of knowing more about an organization's data, here is a story from the early 1990s. The Pentagon wanted to know how many employees were listed within the 37 different personnel systems in use across DoD personnel operations. It seemed like a simple question. It wasn't. Instead of providing a precise answer, all 37 respondents answered: "What do you mean by "employee?'"

The Pentagon, confused by this response, quickly learned that up to 30% of service members around the world worked a second job within the Department of Defense. So, there was no standard answer to the question, "What is an employee?" After spending time trying to work through the babble, the Pentagon decided to establish a formal definition of critical business terms such as "employee." Standardizing business terms helped the organization save millions of dollars.[72]

This story reminds us of the problem we have yet to solve. We produce more data each day, making it harder to use and to integrate within systems. Because there are still problems like this, we MUST have a standard working data vocabulary (some call it a data dictionary). The penalty for not having a data dictionary is high. In this instance, data professionals did not participate in the discussion which took place among business analysts. Whether working at the Pentagon or one of its locations, all would have classified themselves as KWs.

In this chapter, we will again read the description of the actor, followed by a set of needs and responses. From here onward in our literacy journey, all control will be in the hands of organizations that will set standards (perhaps globally, perhaps by industry, perhaps by culture)—interested organizations will likely precisely determine the control specifics. We change the control label from "exercise" to "demonstrate" accordingly. These demonstrations will be indicators that organizations can use to identify whether a KW has attained the required level of data literacy.

Knowledge worker description

Actor: Level 3 actors are KWs. Recent estimates show there are more than a billion citizens worldwide working in this capacity. KWs are professionals typically working in a specific industry. They understand some technologies designed for business purposes. As fully contributing members of society, they have resources and are targets for marketers and industry, in general. Their hashtag would be #contribute, but it's unlikely that KWs will organize as a group and adopt a single data acumen standard.

Action: KWs provide organizations with more value than they cost. But instead of the production of goods, knowledge workers produce data.

Affecting: KWs differ from the general population in a few essential ways. Their superpower is that, in addition to being ADSs, they possess a greater capacity to impact society. These are generally opportunities to view processes holistically and materially influence outcomes. The opportunity to work together as an organization permits the greater application of leverage. Whether the concept is that of a "labor-saving device" or a new form of infotainment, the opportunity here is to positively impact the lives of others with goods and services.

Producing: These advances have societal upside potential due to a mature understanding of automation capabilities.

It is desired that the KW's societal impacts be positive, but very little enforces this beyond general expectations of good behavior on the part of organizations and individuals. In some instances, KWs must assess what is best for aspects of society. Proper understanding of both the systems and the impact of system designs on society are essential.

Using: KWs typically understand sophisticated technologies. For example, KWs routinely use word processing, customer resource management tools, and presentation software across hundreds of different domains: manufacturing, supply-side management, and sales, for example. To do these tasks effectively, KWs should manipulate, interpret, and draw conclusions about data.

To: KWs are adults hired to create value by thinking instead of creating value from physical labor. KWs work for both private and public sectors, and all focus on shared goals of advancing some aspect of society. This could range from selling retail items to making citizen taxation policies more effective.

Data Acumen: KWs must demonstrate a data competency that derives from professional acumen, showing their ability to understand basic data concepts and use data as an asset that adds value to their organizations. This embodies the first 3-levels, whereby outside ratings and assessments (certifications) can help individuals prove to organizations that they possess a desired data competency level. KWs pursue academic degrees in specialty fields and seek industry credentials to demonstrate mastery over different disciplines. Specific data acumen characteristics will be developed and customized by discipline. While most organizations do not consider screening applicants for data literacy to be important, we predict that, in the future, organizations will start testing prospective employees to ensure they have the requisite data competency.

Ethical Perspective: Level 3 is the first level where we believe many citizens will begin learning about data ethics. Employers must screen all KW applicants for concepts such as:

- basic ethical analysis
- accepting responsibility for the potential costs, duties, and obligations for decisions
- recognition in their accountability in implementing mechanisms
- demonstrated understanding of prevailing legal requirements and how those impact the organizational mission.

Organizations can (and increasingly will) hold KWs to strict data ethics standards. Only employees of a specific caliber of data literacy will be able to enforce organizational data conduct codes. Different ethical principles guide individual and group behaviors relative to organizational goals. In the future, we expect society to hold KWs to a strict code relative to data, primarily to manage corporate liability. An essential part of that liability will be relying on properly qualified employees who can uphold specifics mandated by data conduct codes.

From an ethical standpoint, KWs are on the data frontlines, always watching for questionable data behavior. They will be encouraged individually towards and away from certain activities and behaviors by the Code of Conduct (CoC) required by their employer and potentially by professional associations. These CoCs will likely be public and, consequently, pro-data literacy. Companies don't want the reputation of being illegitimate or having the tagline "Be evil."

This sort of organizational guidance can provide a clear context for data decision-making. A basic example already exists in many organizations—the "No Free Lunch" Rule: assume that virtually all tangible and intangible objects are owned by someone unless there is a specific declaration otherwise. This assumption immediately puts the default suspicion on the data gift giver in the same manner that the MDS should be instantly suspicious of a call originating outside of the ContactsOnly list.

Behavioral Focus: Because KWs can be held to a code of conduct, organizations can prescribe KW data behavior. KWs use data to carefully craft information for the organization's consumption as organizations use data to support their assertions and defend their gains. KWs are key to corporate initiatives. Because organizations can incur severe financial injury resulting from bad decisions, KWs work tirelessly to ensure organizations use the right data as part of their decision-making processes. (We outlined the immense cost of inefficient use of organizational KW capabilities in Chapter 5.)

Organizations must provide employees with the tools, processes, and methodologies to use data as required and meet business goals. Further, more expert users should make investments in solutions that quickly deliver data that's ready for analysis, monetization, and productization.

Close the data literacy skills gap

Just 20% of the current global workforce reports that they are confident in their data literacy skills. The two primary options for correcting this are either training the existing workforce or training replacements. Given that 37% of all employees believe that data literacy training would make them more productive and 22% think it would reduce stress, it's clear that there is an excellent appetite among employees to improve their data skillsets. This hunger for new skills presents an exciting opportunity for business leaders, given the critical role data literacy plays in future-proofing organizations in a data-saturated world.

Data literacy training can take many forms. Some companies integrate it into existing skills initiatives, provide standalone e-learning courses, or offer specialized classroom training. Free e-learning courses and resources are available from the Data Literacy Project, including an initial assessment that helps users identify current data literacy levels. Training should not focus solely on the hard, technical skills needed for data processes, but should also encompass soft skills that help citizens realize the full value of data, such as collaboration, curiosity, critical thinking, and storytelling.

Being self-sufficient to work with data isn't the same as having self-service data and analytics available. No matter how consumable the information, employees need to be curious and capable of understanding, questioning, and taking the right action based on their insights. In turn, such actions improve their experience with and confidence in using data. For example, employees who identify as data literate were at least 50% more likely than data novices to say that they feel empowered to make better decisions and trusted to make better decisions.

Data literacy training has improved employees' self-confidence to ask the right questions and assess the recommended insights. These insights have helped them better understand the trends and the rationale behind them, leading to more confident decision-making and meaningful discussions with other colleagues. – Shahid Younis, CEO of Data Whizz Academy[73]

KW data knowledge areas (needs & responses)

Five CDKAs are prerequisites for understanding how to use data as an asset.

data stewardship	demonstrating value
data currency	organizational data fiduciary responsibilities
shared fate	

We cover each prerequisite in the remainder of this chapter. Education and training can enforce these data literacy standards for existing KWs. Screening future hires for these characteristics will become mandatory. Organizations that adopt this mindset early will gain a sustained competitive advantage. If enough organizations adopt these standards, they will raise societal standards and abilities.

CDKA18: Data steward responsibilities

Need: Demonstrate an ability to be stewards of organizational data.

Response: Demonstrate knowledge of data processing and uses.

A great way to imagine the additional responsibilities that we're asking all KWs to take on is to hear them directly from a KW who fully understands the role of steward.

> *As a KW, my organization entrusted me to care for a set of specific, enumerated data items. I know the sources of my data, and I can profile its characteristics. I know the potential upstream data quality issues that are associated with this data. I can document these hidden data factories because we anticipate the data errors and regularly incorporate time and resources to correct them. I understand the downstream needs that other KWs have for the data products that I produce. I can process its frequency and volume in time to deliver value to the data's next destination. I can do this while conforming to general data standards and workplace data restrictions, including confidentiality and security. I understand why workplaces need to govern data with policy and differ greatly from personal practices.*

This statement represents a repeatable learning unit of widely applicable skills that educators could design for annual refresher data training. All KWs with data stewardship responsibilities would be required to pass a yearly knowledge exam and case study.

Response: Demonstrate how your role as a steward contributes tangibly to the organizational data value chain. Recite the various penalties (including imprisonment) that could accrue to you through mishandling or data neglect. Demonstrate your role in amplifying or coding data values. Illustrate how you enforce data standards for data in your stewardship. Demonstrate your role, recognizing data is certified as safe for organizational use. Recite your employee data responsibilities.

CDKA19: Add value

Need: Demonstrate an ability to learn how the data they steward adds value to the organization.

Response: Demonstrate the ability to improve aspects of organizational data.

KWs must understand their role in the organizational value chain. It will continue to be difficult for them to contribute holistically to organizational success if they do not. Their value will be recognized as data that can be input into some system. Understanding that value explicitly will influence and alter behavior. For example, if you reward shirt-sales-staff based on the number of shirt orders they complete, you can be certain that the average number of shirts per order will rapidly approach 1! Check the various data relationships for the expectation of a fiduciary relationship. Use data to determine if the value can be improved in a variety of ways, including:

- Identifying ways to improve data usage
- Inferring organizational behavioral focus from the data expertise of its KWs
- Increasing understanding of the importance of communication and charisma
- Understanding different data sources and how they impact a given profession
- Using data as metadata (e.g., quality, timeliness, source, etc.)
- Leveraging various combinatorial and multiplicative effects
- Understanding your role in getting value from data
- Improving feedback from data and processes to improve organizational outcomes.

Response: Be aware of the organization's behavioral focus, specifically regarding workplace data restrictions, standards, security. Demonstrate an understanding of the requirement of context for all data items. Articulate your role in the broader organizational data value chain(s). Describe specific items available via automated processes data collection to provide inputs to corporate improvement efforts. Account for the value that you give the organization. Prioritize how to create value from data.

Most organizations are unskilled at various approaches to adding value. Our guidance is to pick one and a primary and a second as a backup and practice, practice, practice getting good at that course of action. Organizations must pick one of these and get better at their citizens, processes, and technology applications. Technology should occupy only 10% of the investment. If you are spending $1M on data technology, a similarly detailed plan should exist to invest $9M in citizens and processes. Importantly, technology continues to remain the last data investments that you should consider. (Technology-first approaches have resulted in the current state.) Our focus here is on the role of KWs as enablers of both service delivery product improvement and innovation and as customer interaction points.

CDKA20: Keep current

Need: Demonstrate an ability to learn how to apply organization policies to the recency of data and supporting IT components.

Response: Demonstrate ability to quickly and efficiently validate and install software updates.

Keeping both data and supporting infrastructure current are important goals for organizations, especially in a post-GDPR[74] data handling world. Because of our increasing dependence on the built-in app and OS capabilities such as file syncing, KWs must now understand that part of their job includes ensuring that their organization's data is processed using the correct (generally, the latest) version of the data, the app, and the operating system. Knowledge of data-helpful utilities is often non-existent among KWs—sample your own organization by asking how many know of the existence of Excel macros. The organizational data machine requires that KWs understand concepts such as data trusts, branding and use of DMBOK-based practices, appropriate use of cloud-based utilities, enforcement of measurable data standards, and monitoring and tracking services.

Response: KWs must demonstrate their ability to do the following:

- Select appropriate automated support
- Construct trusted data environments, data branding, and other supplemental utilities relevant to their mission
- Leverage existing monitoring and tracking implemented by their organizations
- Illustrate how to use data and process feedback to improve organizational performance

- Use a corporate data feedback loop to improve performance
- Practice self-reinforcing data protection
- Indicate how data accounting needs contribute to the specified process
- Describe how to use technology to improve the quality and value of data asset
- Illustrate knowledge of the software upon which your data security depends.

CDKA21: Uphold organizational fiduciary responsibilities

Need: Demonstrate an ability to identify and comprehend specific roles that are governed by fiduciary responsibilities.

Response: Demonstrate knowledge of organizational data fiduciary relationships.

Organizations are continually surprised upon discovering that they receive data that originated outside or are constrained by a designated fiduciary responsibility situation. For example, a manufacturer might be surprised to learn that it does not have direct access to supplier data—relegating its ability to monitor quality to a post event audit. It is important to know how to search for the existence of such conditional data. Equally important is the proactive duty-to-report clauses calling out specific organizational responsibilities that they must take in response to getting hacked.

Response: Much like other specialized training areas, data fiduciary responsibilities will quickly become a means of better managing this type of risk. Qualified KWs may demonstrate their ability to:

- Understand the organization's stated ethical framework and expectations of data for which it has a fiduciary responsibility
- Support organizational strategy using sound data judgment and quick data decisions
- Act in a fiduciary role concerning that portion of the organizational data that has been entrusted to them
- Name, categorize, and itemize items covered by the known data fiduciary exchange partners
- Describe the organization's self-reinforcing data protection—specifically addressing repetitional risk
- Explain how fiduciary data impacts them professionally.

CDKA22: Shared fate: everyone is swimming in the same pool

Need: Demonstrate their ability to learn how their data is sourced from and is used by other parts of the organization.

Response: Demonstrate an understanding of how data is sourced and used by other parts of the organization.

All KWs must understand that, from a data perspective, an organization collectively sinks or swims! If the data isn't fit for purpose, the entire organization suffers as a result. Therefore, organizations need to create contexts that reinforce the "we're all in it together" focus that motivates its components toward the same objectives. Data stewardship responsibilities include an explicit mandate to understand the sources and uses of the data entrusted to the stewards as such environment leads directly to a series of benefits:

- Every KW using data to help the organization achieve its mission
- Self-reinforcing organizational data protection
- Intolerance of malicious behavior in the organization
- Confidence that your organization's data is properly prepared to be used safely

- Important feedback from data management processes, procedures, and measures.

Response: Improved communication and understanding resulting from a clear understanding of how technology and data analytics interact. Citizen data should be broadly perceived as a community resource. Failure of components must be understood to negatively impact the organization as well as the population. It is important to demonstrate how an individual KW would alert others to data and data standards failures not within their realm. It is equally important for KWs to demonstrate the ability to use technology to enhance efforts required by the togetherness. Our data pools can and should be considered shared resources. Failure of components can negatively impact the organization as well as the population. Illustrate how you alert others to data standards failures not in your stewardship realm. KWs must be able to:

- Understand how to use data better to help the organization achieve its mission should be taught to every KW

- Understand why organizational data protection reinforces itself

- Report malicious behavior in the organization as a data attack on one of us is an attack on the workgroup

- Prepare data to safely use according to the organization's data safety regime
- Use feedback from data management processes, procedures, and measures to improve the organizational use of data
- Understand how technology and data analytics can visually improve communication and charisma.

Chapter conclusions–Knowledge workers and data

We have described the characteristics shared by 1 billion KW/citizens. We have specified five additional CDKAs representing an objective level of data acumen that we believe to be a prerequisite when working as a KW. KWs must be able to:

- assist with formalizing the role of data in your job,
- demonstrate how data adds differing value to different processes,
- prove adherence to organizational software update policies,
- identify with whom the corporate has fiduciary data relationships, and

- provide examples of upstream and downstream data pollution.

Otherwise, it will be easy enough to replace those who cannot with someone who can.

As a result, the entire workforce will be measurably more data literate. Recall that only 1 in 3 business decision-makers fell confident that they can understand, analyze, and argue with data. Increasing this number to 2 in 3 would represent a doubling of data capabilities over today's average results.

CHAPTER 10

Data Teacher (DT)

Data Teachers (DTs) must be on the front lines of the war on data illiteracy, but as described in Chapter 4, few educators specifically focus on teaching data literacy. We need to rethink the way we produce and develop more data literate citizens. Because the demand for data literacy exceeds supply, it's necessary to invest in proven accelerating technologies, innovative course materials, and new approaches.

The approach we prescribe involves a two-way educational mission not implemented in other disciplines to our knowledge. We need to design this program so that teachers receive almost real-time feedback regarding the success of their teaching to refine their practices constantly. In other words, DTs may spend as much time improving their delivery and contributing to overall throughput as they deliver.

We will be asking data teachers to simultaneously:

- Collaborate with peers in a formal organized process that will guide a set of best data teaching practices

- Plan to constantly evolve their actual teaching topics and materials to take advantage of the knowledge coming from the practices
- Efficiently and effectively bring the participants up through Level 3.

This is a lot to ask of any professional teacher and we are talking about large numbers of citizens who will need this. Some funding will likely come directly from larger organizations that can benefit from the acceleration.

Data teacher description

Actor: Level 4 actors are called Data Teachers (DTs). Companies may hire them to educate their workers, or they may work within traditional educational institutions. Given that there are about 1 billion KWs worldwide, there are not nearly enough DTs, and not all of them are well equipped enough to teach data management efficiently and effectively. The number of data literate teachers is relatively small when compared to the global need for data education. Likewise, as the societal need for KWs increases, so too does the need for DTs. The hashtag for this level is #catchup. Their superpower is reducing the epidemic of data illiteracy.

Action: DTs are explicitly skilled at rapidly imparting data information to students. This prepares students to be productive members of society. Data teachers develop curricula and instill academic discipline in students to share technical information, life lessons, and wisdom. DTs interact with students in a structured and repeatable manner to provide information for others to access.

Produces: DTs prepare citizens to contribute to and interact with a digital society safely.

Affecting: DTs affect a wide range of populations, namely MDS, ADS, and KWs. The impact of DTs is rapidly multiplied as the analyst gap narrows and is (hopefully) eliminated.

Using: DTs have a literal pulpit from which data knowledge flows. DTs use new and old information to shape and mold future KWs. They organize that information into structured and repeatable knowledge packages for students to absorb. DTs also impart data ethics to students and help them operate within acceptable social boundaries relating to collecting and using data. For example, they explain the conditions under which it's appropriate to collect data while protecting individual privacy.

To: There are additional objective data knowledge levels required to teach efficiently and effectively. It becomes incumbent on individual DTs to ensure that their data-related education efforts do not support fooling or manipulating. These lessons will be easy to deliver if a data teacher professional organization adopts a code of conduct.

Data Acumen: DTs need varying degrees of data competency depending on the comprehension level of their students. For example, if a data teacher instructs MDSs, they need a measurably lower data competency than those teaching KWs.

Ethical Perspective: A DT's ethical goal is to help others understand data and not be fooled or manipulated by it. For example, DTs will help students put statistics into context and interpret them as significant or insignificant. They will also train KWs to behave ethically in their dealings with data in their various fields.

Behavioral Focus: DTs almost always operate as organized groups. Generally, they represent educational institutions or commercial enterprises designed to impart information to others. Common examples include elementary schools, colleges, and universities, as well as professional training companies.

DT data knowledge areas (needs & responses)

We suggest four additional CDKAs as prerequisites because they provide the basis for the monumental effort required to remove organizational and societal data debt:

great teaching	the role of certification
designed feedback	people, process, technology

We cover each for the remainder of this chapter. These data teacher-data literacy standards can be enforced and will evolve based on the feedback.

CDKA23: Teach effectively

Need: Demonstrate an ability to contribute to the elimination of the data debt.

Response: Objectively demonstrate that your great teaching will support data literacy.

Note: it is possible to interpret this CDKA narrowly. Instead, the way to consider it is to eliminate some aspect(s) of organizational data debt as the first object of focus for most organizations—as this area represents the greatest potential data leverage.

All of us remember from our time in school that teachers vary greatly in their effectiveness. Some imparted a deep knowledge of their content and made us want to continue learning about it, while others did quite the opposite. It is imperative that DTs, whether in an educational institution or otherwise, fall into the first category. DTs must effectively identify, divert, scale up, study results, and evolve in response to feedback.

Many DTs work and continue to work within businesses. Some of their students are business users who need to review relevant data and act quickly. Whether it's nurses managing hospital beds or supply chain managers identifying and addressing potential issues, taking action based on insights will improve performance while boosting organizational efficiency and productivity. Most general business users need quite simple information presented in an easily consumable way to make better decisions.

At the other end of the scale are data scientists who will deliver value by improving existing models and developing new ones—in between sit analysts who will focus on the "why" and provide deeper insights to business users. Then, discovery users will deploy advanced data skills to explore and prove the value of new use cases, ultimately working toward industrializing new ideas. Thus, each type of user has a vital role in using data to deliver their organization's goals.

Response: The DTs must demonstrate their ability to:

- Deliver specific levels of instruction efficiently and effectively. Indicate how you will demonstrate both certifications and the fiduciaries of the student and teacher relationship.
- Achieve the required data learning speed and comprehension measures.
- Comment on the utility of the applicable teaching standards for learning about data-profession specific workplace standards, including confidentiality, security, and physical restrictions.
- Describe what it means to approach data holistically and how you will help provide students with information that puts their roles into perspective.
- Illustrate how and why the functions of data persistence and data malleability are relevant to various data careers.

For example, a DT could ask students in professional or career-focused programs to consider who has the authority within their study areas and the origins of that authority. Ask students to find several scholarly sources on the same topic that take very different stands. How was it that the authors came to different conclusions? Must it do with authority? Ask students to brainstorm situations when traditional peer review might not accomplish its purpose. Of specific interest here would be work done around the subject of document literacy, defined as the knowledge and skills needed to perform document tasks (i.e., to search, comprehend, and use non-continuous texts in various formats). Examples include job applications, payroll forms, transportation schedules, maps, tables, and drug or food labels.

CDKA24: Feedback is designed into the teaching

Need: Demonstrate an ability to contribute to the improvement of the data teaching process.

Response: Objectively demonstrate knowledge of how inputs are used in a downstream evaluation.

Data, as a collective profession, is relatively immature when compared to the accounting profession. Consider two objective differences: 1) the existence of and reliance on Generally Accepted Accounting Principles[75] (aka GAAP) and 2) the tenure of financial leaders is much longer than IS/IT and data leaders. It is sufficient to state that we do not know the best way to implement educational and training programs addressing data and data literacy. The key to overall data education program effectiveness will be the requirement for data teachers to be actively involved in research designed to improve current practices! DTs must have the ability to participate vigorously in the meta-conversation required to develop an active learning environment to improve data literacy. This requires the ability to teach and simultaneously observe the effectiveness of their efforts. This can evolve into as sophisticated a system of A/B testing as the ones run by Amazon continuously.[76]

Response: The DT must be able to demonstrate the ability to do the following:

- Understand how what you do in the classroom will be used as data to feed instruction, data improvements, and the machine. Part of the DT's job is to gather information from students to funnel into a research project focused on making data teaching more effective.
- Contribute to the classroom portions and the process improvement portion of our collective mission to make the world more data literate.
- Illustrate feedback loops to guide the education process.
- Engage with educational materials to refine further, ensuring that they are appropriate and correct for the task.
- Possess the various prerequisites.

CDKA25: Do not over emphasize technology

Need: Demonstrate an ability to place appropriate amounts of attention on respective data-people, process, and technology components.

Response: Objectively demonstrate knowledge and topic coverage.

Right now, we have precious little beyond anecdotal experiences in defining the 'right' data/people-processes. For the moment, we must limit discussions on the technology aspects. DTs must teach students to avoid focusing too much on technology when solving problems or planning projects, focusing instead on gathering and interpreting the appropriate data.

Nearly all of us have heard the following statement: "Too much was spent on technology early in the project." Perhaps because it has remained so tangible, technology has been the far too pre-eminent focus of data improvement efforts.

If technology is addressed during the initial requirements phase of a project, it represents time not spent focusing on the requirements—a common pattern in far too many IS/IT disasters. Only when the requirements are largely understood is it appropriate to discuss the technology needed for implementation. Until data needs are understood, any technology discussion is both 1) premature and 2) taking oxygen from the more critical requirements discussion. Be similarly wary of the overpromise of anything hyped.

Response: In the data world, we often say that the hardest thing to do during requirements isn't designing anything. By this, we mean that it requires the skill to focus on what is important without letting your mind wander toward details irrelevant to the task at hand. Not many know that using the word "database" during the SDLC requirements phase is considered premature. At the requirements stage, we should only speak of "data stores." The selection of a specific database or even the use of a database is a design decision. It is essential to understand that any time spent discussing design issues during the requirements phase represents resources not spent on analyses. Similarly, DTs must demonstrate an understanding of under what conditions it is permissible to discuss technology solutions.

CDKA26: Ongoing educational requirements

Need: Demonstrate a commitment to achieving ongoing educational requirements.

Response: Objectively demonstrate knowledge of feedback and certification linkages.

Individuals who wish to succeed in IS/IT or management, in general, must excel at lifelong learning. Similarly, all

DTs must rapidly adapt and evolve their techniques as we learn more about what it will take to educate 2.5 billion citizens about data. Signing up as a DT carries an explicit commitment to staying current and continuing to be curious. Many current certification programs establish educational co-requisites, which the data profession also incorporates. The key is to incorporate these into the people, processes, and technology systems as it will be easier to remain self-reinforcing. Understanding that the subject materials and methods will continue to evolve in response to feedback that you and the students give is key to successfully and effectively making DT work.

Response: The feedback focus will drive ongoing educational requirements. This will lead to evolving data academic requirements. Recognize what you do not know and what you are not teaching.

DTs will need to hold relevant certifications. Doing so will require documentation of work experience, educational achievements, and endorsements.

Chapter conclusions–Why a new form of education is required

We have described the characteristics required to rapidly make up for lost time by turning as many citizens data literate as possible. This will require a vastly different process with many changes to the traditional data teaching. Four additional CDKAs can address these. Their achievement represents an objective level of data acumen DT that we believe to be a prerequisite to developing the highest quality teaching cadre possible. As a prerequisite to becoming a DT, you must be able to:

- demonstrate exceptional abilities to educate students efficiently and effectively,
- work with more built-in feedback and evolution permitting program more and faster growth and improvements than is possible outside of this integrated effort,
- adopt a systems approach emphasizing people, process, and technology (in that order of priority), and commit to ongoing educational requirements.

CHAPTER 11

Data Professional (DP)

The fifth framework level addresses the data professional. Only data professionals are qualified to perform useful basic research into causes and remediation to data challenges. They are equally responsible for improving relative societal data knowledge levels. Only when armed with data knowledge metadata can one contribute to improvements in this aspect of data management.

This group must have the most stringent data knowledge requirements, including concepts such as data responsiveness, innovation, strategy, etc. As data professionals, we all must improve our practices and collectively improve society as a direct result. Unfortunately, more data management efforts fail than succeed. When IS/IT projects fail to meet schedule deadlines, functionality imperatives, or cost requirements, data management efforts fail. This is because people treat data and IT as the same type of work. On LinkedIn, the number of data scientists keeps even with the number of data engineers indicating the market is still sorting itself out.

Data professional description

Actor: Level 5 actors are called data professionals (DPs). Likely, the data profession employs millions. DPs represent the most sophisticated and competent level in the framework. This term should be required (certification preferred) of anyone working in the data industry. It signifies an objective ability to 'self-actualize' with data and understand the individual's role in the organizational data ecosystem. This ability includes the range of specialized data skills described so far, including all prior CDKAs. Data professionals have hashtag #improve, as they should seek to improve society through both research and education. Also, data professionals have a superpower, leverage.

Action: Data professionals need to leverage their knowledge to educate the public about data. DPs have a deep and broad data understanding, supported by an excellent mix of knowledge and skills to improve the overall human experience.

Affects: When all members of society have a baseline level of data literacy, the data industry's effectiveness will increase. The scope of data professionals' actions is broad. There is potential to form a trade-wide union that could effectively block certain types of work, much as the APA has examined its role in past national actions.[77] The organization can do this work as various data groups subscribe to specific codes relevant to practice areas that establish a (hopefully simplified) ethical framework.

Producing: Data professionals manipulate data in novel ways to create new insights.

Using: Data professionals interrogate data using new techniques, strategies, and technologies.

To: Often, data professionals address some of society's most profound and most difficult questions. For example, what chemical compounds directly affect the spread of the COVID-19?

Ethical Perspective: Society holds medical professionals to the highest ethical standards because the risk of failure could have negative societal consequences. In principle, society holds data professionals to similarly high standards. For example, it is considered malpractice for research scientists to publish conclusions without sufficiently vetting process, data, and conclusions. Over time, data professionals created oversight bodies to monitor their work and ensure that their concessions meet the highest scrutiny level. Because society places its highest trust level in data professionals, they do not deviate from agreed ethical norms.

Data Acumen: Data professionals invent and discover things. They develop new methods to combine and compute data to reveal new information. For example, data professionals are experts who created data mining, artificial intelligence, and machine learning. DPs' products should be part of any KWs, ADS, and MDS curricula.

Behavior: Data professionals work differently than other actors. Individual work preferences and problem characteristics drive the organizational model a professional DP chooses.

DP data knowledge areas (needs & responses)

We believe these four final CDKAs to be prerequisites to work as a data professional in today's workplace. They create a guild of data professionals who are collectively working on behalf of citizens everywhere to contribute to a better society. These most important are:

- continuous recertification
- holders of specialized data knowledge
- data storytelling
- building data discipline knowledge.

Organizations can use these criteria to screen for or certifications and credentials. We cover each for the remainder of this chapter.

CDKA27: Certification and recertification mechanisms

Need: Demonstrate an ability to maintain current certification valued across industries.

Response: Objectively demonstrate knowledge of continuous professional certification requirements.

To become DPs, citizens will need access to proof that they can perform at each of the five levels of the data literacy scale. Certification requires continuous education to maintain currency—periodic recertification will be necessary. In addition, certifications must be specialized based on the DP's industry. This will prove the ability to comprehend and implement compliance with domain specific data policies like IDMP (pharmacology), GDPR (Europe), and CCPA.

The question of who controls data literacy certification is key. It will likely come down to a question of supply and demand. If **organizations** hold certifications, they will have the ability to increase or refine requirements that improve outcomes important to them. If the **professionals** hold the certifications, the shoe will be on the other foot. Professionals will be able to significantly alter and respond to supply and demand using data industry-wide reporting. A third possibility is that both situations will co-exist, with organizations (such as ACM, IEEE, IIBA,

DAMA) supplementing existing workplace capability coverage.

Automated certification will be required because of the volume required and the rapidly evolving curricula (a desirable feature). A respected governing body must adhere to fiduciary relationships (teacher-student/research subject) and understanding formal governance roles and laws and policies regarding data research subjects.

Response: All data professionals would need to demonstrate proven ability to achieve and maintain certification/recertification.

CDKA28: Possession of valuable knowledge

Need: Demonstrate knowledge of and ability to access data reference knowledge required by data professional specialization.

Response: Objectively demonstrate improved understanding of BoK contents.

DPs require access to a respected body of knowledge to get the industry *singing off the same sheet of music.* Various certifications exist so that this vocabulary can be formally recognized. More discussion around these topics can be found in an excellent analysis of the DMBOK and DCAM.[78]

Response: Citizens who correspond with DPs will likely not understand many data concepts—unless they have read this book—for example, data held in a fiduciary relationship. The rules, roles, requisites, and responsibilities require precise explanations and agreements. These should be codified across professions and posted to governmental websites as required standards of care.

Every DP should be willing to give back their specialized knowledge to the community. The data profession should host annual events rewarding the best use of data by citizens and many other types of events facilitating the ease with which everyone can become more data literate.

CNLN29: Data storytelling capabilities

Response: Objectively demonstrate improving data storytelling capabilities.

Need: Demonstrate an ability to communicate their various data stories successfully.

DPs need to understand that data must tell a story and take steps to ensure they tell a story that accurately represents the data. This is critical when explaining data to a nontechnical audience. One dire illustration of this necessity is via the lectures of Professor Edward Tufte. The picture below is a reproduction of the fax that engineers at

Morton Thiakol sent to NASA, attempting to communicate a hesitancy to launch the next morning. The engineers were unsuccessful at communicating their warning, and the Challenger blew apart on launch—killing the entire crew.

In his lectures at the time, Tufte later presented the data reorganized to tell a better story. In this case, the lower the temperature, the more often dangerous booster rocket structural failures occurred. When coupled with the information that the planned launch was happening at a 20 degrees temperature below the lowest launch temperature so far experienced by the program, the hesitation was easier to understand.

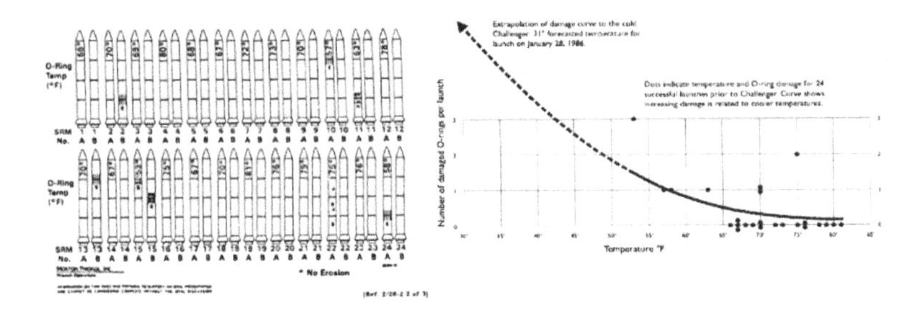

Figure 11.1—The Challenger Chartjunk Data Story[79]

Powerful stories with human repercussions are just some of the necessary data storytelling skills. We're also looking for ways to:

- improve the data experiences of non-DPs

- recognize complex data processing like finances, drug approval, and engineering research
- understand the best ways to bring about data experience improvements.

Communicating results more effectively and efficiently is of key interest, and technology's role is only now being understood.[80]

Response: All DPs must have adequate communication skills so that messages do not get mangled during delivery. One component of this is making their communications interesting enough that people will listen! Leverage technology to enhance communication efforts through backgrounds, animation, scripting, prototyping, etc.

It should never be the case that a certified DP can't express a result and concern due to inarticulateness because they were too mathematical or could only "speak" using the R programming language. The sad story of the Challenger reminded us of Claude Shannon's Information Theory based charge that the message must be received, not just transmitted.[81] All DP certifications must include a demonstration of storytelling abilities. Formal curricula should contain topics including toastmasters and Dale Carnegie, data visualization, data journalism, etc. There is especially promising work in prose literacy. Prose literacy is the knowledge and skills needed to perform prose tasks—that is, to search, comprehend, and use continuous texts. Examples include editorials, news stories, brochures, and instructional materials.

CDKA30: Building the foundation for the data discipline

Need: Demonstrate an ability to contribute to the profession and the broader citizenry by standardizing knowledge and education.

Response: Objectively demonstrate contributions to the discipline.

There is still no degree program at any university in "data management." It remains to data professionals to develop discipline-specific bodies of knowledge and codes of conduct. So, as a first step, we need to create and adopt a body of knowledge that can be considered standard for all other DPs. This effort will ensure that each subsequent generation doesn't have to relearn data by the seats of their pants. Each sub-domain or subsection of data professionals must carry on the process of building integrated bodies of knowledge to:

- recognize specialized supporting technologies
- use technology to improve the quality and value of data assets

- use technology to enhance communication and charisma efforts
- use automated data collection processes to improve organizational conditions
- understand how data persistence and data malleability are relevant.

As DPs, we have access to trusted data that is not understandable by non-DPs. We have a duty as citizens to use this knowledge to help society improve and make this knowledge more accessible. Simple stories such as garbage-in/garbage-out need to pervade IT thinking.

Response: Other ways that DPs should contribute to the profession include decreasing the data debt and increasing society's data literacy. We must continue the work required to transform an underappreciated craft into widespread practice. The profession must come together and form standard bodies of knowledge to increase data literacy. Key is to instill a mission of service to the profession to help the world get smarter about data. The following characteristics would be desirable.

- Sort of need a Peace Corps vibe about having joined the data tribe.
- Realize that if we don't attempt to make the difference, no one will

- Uses data to identify problems in environment, policies, economics, scientific, etc.
- Understand relevant data methods/tools systematically
- Assess project/process risks/costs
- Supports an environment that fosters critical use of data for learning and research.

Chapter conclusions–Starting data professionals from the same sheet of music

We have described the characteristics shared by data professionals and specified the four additional CDKAs representing an objective level of data acumen-DP that we believe prerequisite to obtaining the highest quality data professionals possible. To remain a card-carrying DP, you must:

1. continuously update your recertification requirements
2. demonstrate specialized data knowledge in service of your organization
3. produce lucid data storytelling examples to add value
4. continue to build data discipline knowledge.

PART 3

Developing Data Literate Organizations

So far we have described an approach to significantly improve citizen data literacy and reduce the percentage of PIDD population. Part 3 builds on the framework described in Part 2 to explain in more depth and specificity how organizations can increase their data literacy with a programmatic approach.

Chapter 12 describes a program for repairing neglected organizational data and addressing organizational data debt. The program involves a rather public ritual to enforce commitment and sustainment.

Chapter 13 presents an updated version of our previously published Data Doctrine. The doctrine details specific, objective criteria required to begin practicing getting good at data at the organizational level.

Chapter 14 describes the barriers to and benefits of increasing the general level of data literacy at each level of data user, from MDSs to DPs.

CHAPTER 12

A 12-step Approach to Improving Organizational Data Literacy

This chapter describes what to do from an organizational perspective. It describes the people, processes, and corporate activities that need to occur so that communities can implement a data doctrine. Recall that we have hyper-focused on the technical aspects of data. This hyper-focus has happened at the expense of improving the people and process aspects of data. It has resulted in a more massive than necessary data debt. Companies can ensure data literacy through employment agreements and codes of conduct. These two tools give organizations the necessary leverage over the people (data literate KWs) and processes (work rules).

We outline the steps required if organizations are to effect the necessary changes. These changes will ensure that their KWs and data practitioners have conditions supportive of increasing organizational data literacy. These organizational changes will necessitate patience and first focus on repairing neglected data and data infrastructure and measurably working off accumulated data debt. Putting it in project management terms, this kind of work can only work when implemented as a **program**. Once initiated, this program must continue until the organization decides it no longer needs to perform data work or when the organization ceases to exist. Likely, your organization will no longer need a data program when it no longer needs an HR program! To create a sustainable plan, organizations must understand and incorporate an increased data focus into everything they do. Organizations consistently rate these challenges as comprising 90% of issues encountered when becoming more data focused.

Twelve-step programs are ritualistic for a precise reason—to stop bad habits, you must carefully replace them with better habits. We debated internally whether this framework was appropriate for communicating our purpose. We since validated our concept with our peers to ensure that 1) our presentation conforms to twelve-step programs[82], and 2) this type of approach made sense to them. They told us that it did. Inevitably someone sitting around the table knows a least one individual who has benefitted from a 12-step program and appreciated the seriousness of the required commitment. We also need everyone involved to understand those simple techniques can't solve data literacy, especially at the organizational level, any more than society can eliminate data illiteracy by just acquiring the technology. But by committing to 12 steps upfront, we will find it easier to achieve the critical mass required. Organizations can embark on their data improvement journey with their eyes wide open.

The materials below are the HOW to do WHAT (needs to be done) and ensure that implementation will be successful. The focus is on specific objective achievements. Changing organizational behavior will result in these outcomes. Still, they can't be the focus of the change efforts as the actions are symptomatic. Changing specific behaviors will be required to support data literate KWs and DPs objectively. Each can mature to better use data in support of the strategy.

How the steps are organized

We can address the 12-steps systematically, grouping them into DCF-levels. Experienced executives will recognize the validity of these step descriptions and the correspondence to the levels. The parallel between this and Maslow's Hierarchy of Needs is intentional, mostly the necessary but insufficient prerequisite of organizations to achieve a fundamental level before attempting any next-level steps. Note: while these concepts apply to the organization and not to any specific types of individuals, they are roughly equated to the groups we have illustrated. We expand on each step below. We have also specified a group story across each level's steps and offer suggested group exercises to illustrate each step's key point.

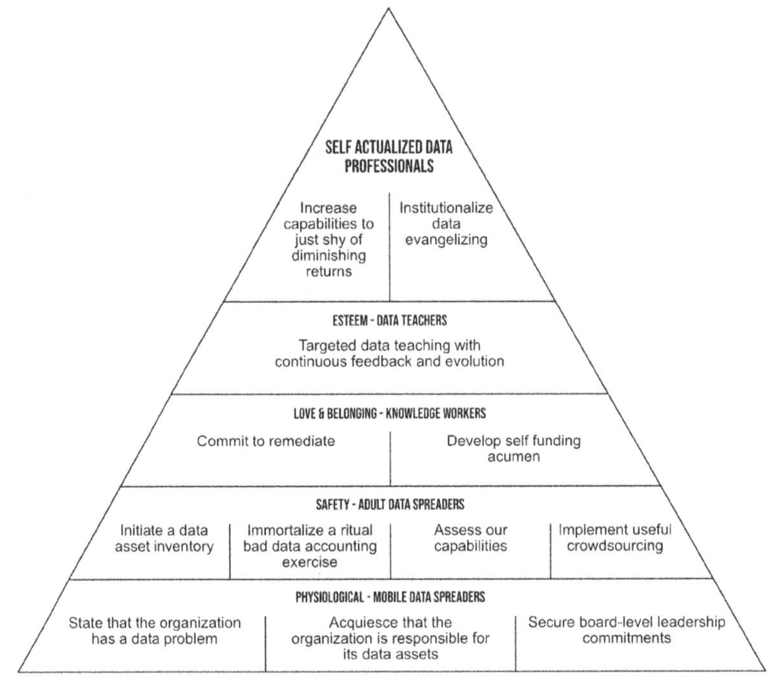

Figure 12.1— A 12-step approach to improving organizational data literacy

Three steps comprising Level 1: Physiological—mobile data spreaders

We present the first three steps as a wake-up call to citizens. The measures will raise their awareness and expectations and secure the resources to fund societal change. It's easier to keep an organization in motion than to start the organization moving in the first place. Often, some crises precipitated an increased focus on data. (If your organization isn't reacting to a challenge, you are in the minority and should consider yourself lucky!) The most challenging part of becoming better with data is just getting started.

Step 1 Admitting there is a problem

> *We admit that we are currently powerless with respect to getting better at managing our data if we continue on our present course—that our organizational lives will become less and less manageable—this is evident individually and organizationally. [Sample organizational statement]*

People often feel that admitting that there's a problem reflects poorly on them, especially in leadership positions. It might. However, true leaders can recognize a crisis and acknowledge that they contributed to the chaos and confusion. To this extend, people are not powerless. They have the strength to make changes and improve their conditions. Before systematic change occurs, however, society must address and resolve twelve steps. Each builds on and complements previous steps. These twelve steps help communities manage data literacy and forge a path towards establishing a social baseline competency and objective standards for moving forward.

The first step is to publicly acknowledge that society has a systemic data management problem that will overwhelm the bureaucracy and its administrators. If a community doesn't resolve data literacy, its citizens remain ignorant and become contributors to the data matrix.

This admission doesn't need to be a press conference or considerable fanfare. It should, however, be a topic of civic conversation, among other organizational issues. It has been interesting to learn that the 'secret sauce' is just better data programs for many communities. Of course, the Data Matrix doesn't want people to know that data illiteracy is the key to social control.

It is useful to put this assertion into some perspective. As a citizen, consider making a big announcement to friends and family that you will publish a weekly blog on a topic. There is a reason that most such efforts fizzle—it is hard work, and it is challenging to come up with content continually. One highly motivating factor is peer pressure knowing that blog failure, not publishing the newsletter for example, will result in the event being missed.

Admitting to a data problem (organizationally) permits everyone (internally) who witnesses future bad data behavior (as described by data governance) to call it out as inconsistent. If the organization doesn't proclaim that it will follow a data doctrine, it will not feel the pressure of continuity. It must be enough that a journalist will be able to ask in 3 years—whatever happened to that data stuff you all were working on?

Unfortunately, most organizations are unaware of their individual and organizational data literacy levels. Therefore, they don't know if corporate data literacy indicators are rising or falling (they are falling!). We have presented much evidence that organizations are currently unconcerned about employee data literacy. Improvement begins by drawing a line in the sand and saying publicly:

Here, we stop accumulating data debt, and citizens begin managing their data!

Of course, this can happen anywhere along your journey, so why not now? First, understand what it means to make this admission. It's one thing to make a courageous step towards a changed organizational life, especially your own. It's another thing entirely to change the behavior of an entire organization. This is a deep commitment with meaningful measures taken annually—nothing will be corrected by Friday!

The key to Step-1 success is to set realistic expectations. The organization (like individuals) will experience setbacks. Still, with everyone pulling in the same direction for a sustained period—things will get better rapidly. The goal must be to practice getting better as opposed to achieving some perfection.

Group Story: A group depends on an individual to hold their tickets for a live event. It's time to go, yet the individual can't locate their electronic tickets because all emails go to a single inbox, and access is blocked to many messages. Tension builds as the group pressures the individual to locate the e-tickets in time. (Perhaps illustrate the e-ticket sellers can also be poor data managers?)

Exercise:

- Hand a large dataset over and ask participants to locate 1 of 10 specific emails challenging to distinguish from the remainder.
- Illustrate a range of tools available and the applicability to classes of data problems to be solved.
- Measure how much time is saved, locating the messages using proper (usually just advanced) tools.

Step 2 To accept as true data's promise

We accept that data mastery and the power of data management can restore us to sane data processing and reverse our accumulated data debt.

Step two involves accepting that data mastery and the power of data management can restore us to sane data processing and reverse our accumulated data debt. In this step, people understand that the road to better data practices begins with an awareness of the challenge's nature. Realize that society must effectively manage its data with formal methods that use external authoritative references from a generally accepted body of knowledge. The organization is ready to improve suboptimal data practices by scoping and executing an iteration of the data management strategy. Since the heart of the hidden data factories causes organizations to bleed unnecessarily from thousands of small cuts, everyone must begin with the same baseline expectations. The most critical aspect is knowing what it means to start a new initiative to address the existing practices and how immediate benefits will be accruable.

Only with the promise of immediate benefit accrual and addressing the data debt with programmatic effort can the organization believe the change will be sustainable. Just knowing that there is a set of practices available to help folks get organized, finding more about upcoming is a terrific first message to the populace. Further details such as Department X will be the first to prototype this new class of solutions—will help everyone understand the low-level but persistent nature of these changes. Nothing here about what we (the organization) will do. Instead, the organization should lay out the vision for its data as inspiration.

Continuing the Group Story: A mysterious stranger overhears the consternation and offers to help—showing how to use the search capabilities to locate the missing e-tickets and permitting the group to attend. Once inside, the group notes this isn't the first time that this has happened and comes to agree that the pattern exists and is a challenge to group enjoyment.

Exercise: Change to more massive (10X) datasets and answer all ten queries from above more effectively than searching by scrolling. Illustrate the dependency upon accurate metadata.

Step 3 Commit to mastering a data doctrine

Made a decision to submit to the tenets of a data doctrine.

Step three requires leadership to commit to the tenets of a data doctrine. As part of this commitment, leadership saves resources to improve prioritized societal data deficiencies. Executives commit to enhancing their own individual data literacy and improving the organization's data management capabilities. Now we (the organization) save for the program. The critical thing here is to be clear about what society's commitment entails, including potentially:

This commitment should include reengineering the entire IT and data supply chains, reeducating key knowledge worker communities, and funding a long-term effort. Suppose civic leaders commit to a data program. In that case, this will provide the needed momentum to overcome the typical organizational inertia. Implementation is always tempered by size, subject matter, complexity, and more.

- Reengineering the entire IT/data supply chains
- Reeducation of key knowledge worker communities
- Restructuring the executive team
- Funding a long-term effort.

This act chisels these requirements in stone. For example:

- In X months, we will begin the process of searching for data leaders
- The first priority for data cleanup is the data originating from Department Y
- The CIO and the CDO will be peers.

Suppose the decision is made public to commit to a data program. Often this will provide the needed momentum to overcome the typical organizational inertia.

Continuing the Group Story: Others in the group use their newfound search capabilities to find many items that had been previously considered lost. Discounts are found for beverages, a rideshare home, and admission to a future event. Include as the last example, one that involves diminishing returns. All also realize that everything cannot be managed formally. The group confronts a fundamental question—under what conditions should data be formally organized—they decide to solve collectively, illustrating an aspect of data governance. Illustrate the costs of not applying proper data management in the context of a system development (configuration) effort—develop specific individual criteria for determining when an individual or workgroup data asset should be formally managed by understanding the 'size and shape' of problems capable of being addressed by data management techniques.

Exercise: Reuse the previous (much more extensive) email database but this time, easily export the data to at least three different environments: a) RDBMS with a drag and drop interface, b) legal transcript database, c) Outlook. Attempt to match queries with tools and reinstitute the searches.

Four steps comprising Level 2: Safety—adult data spreader

Only once the first three steps are complete must the organization focus on building foundational capabilities.

We grouped the next four steps into the Level 2 category foundation-building activities. They are:

- Initiate a **data asset inventory** (including data relevant assets such as talent, business processes, tools and technologies, and data assets) using an established model so that the organization can immediately benefit from their value.
- This creates a baseline and is immortalized as a **ritual bad data accounting exercise**. Accept the baseline assessment and prioritize remediation initiatives to first normalize and then optimize data capabilities.
- **Assess** our capabilities against objective standards and report on progress annually.
- Implement useful **crowdsourcing** of relevant data information/practices, adding to our existing inventory structure and contents—in a way that all parties can immediately use and benefit.

These four steps build teams who deeply understand the organizational data challenges, provide a capability for registering organizationally valuable data things, and initiate the annual data lessons learned event-among other accomplishments. These realizations should be in the form of prioritized initiatives and remediation steps that offer opportunities for combining and optimizing (synergy) capabilities and data.

Step 4 Inventorying data assets

Began to accumulate and understand an inventory of our data assets and to establish criteria permitting recognition of inventory-able data assets.

The organization begins inventorying its data assets and provides the capability for organizational citizens to discover them. Inventory existing data-relevant assets (e.g., talent, business processes, tools and technologies, and data assets) using an established model so that the organization can immediately benefit from their value. Establish an improvable process for maintaining access to the inventory. Note: these are two separate processes with two different goals.

While the above seem to be reasonable goals, data things are usually more complicated than they first appear. 80% of organizational data (ROT) dictates that the 'inventory' should be more culling. Data grooming changes the nature of the task from a find-everything job to an understand most everything task. Now consider the more typical conversation occurring between a new CDO and a CEO:

CEO: When will you be done inventorying our data? By Friday?
CDO: No organization has ever completed a data inventory!
CEO: Then why are we doing this??????????????????
CDO: To gain an understanding of our data assets—we can't use them if we don't know they exist!

The CEO approaches the data inventory task as a project. Unfortunately, very little about data is a project. CDO must reframe the question from "When will my inventory be complete?" to "How rapidly can we achieve the necessary capabilities to help others better use our data assets?" Organizations should immediately benefit from the wealth of preexisting classification frameworks used to jumpstart efforts. A sample data inventory might include:

1. The purpose is the goal of understanding, not definitions. Definitions are passive. Purpose statements incorporate strategic elements, the rationale, and justification based on the need for data.
2. The sharing of inventoried data assets are categorized as:
    a. Data items that are shared with external organizations
    b. Data items that are shared within the organization
    c. Data items that are not shared but are used to derive shared data items
    d. Data items not shared outside but used to support workgroup activities
3. Organizational data ROT
4. Assign each data asset inventoried, an existing subject area from which that data item best

supports the organizational mission (for example, pay is part of back-office operations)—based on (refinable) purpose statements, primary subject area allegiance is posted.

5. Identify, de-dupe, and harmonize data assets participating in synonyms and homonyms and other challenges—ensure only one item is designated as a (current) golden source.
6. Identify sensitive or personal data items and what specific controls need to be in place.
7. Document all mapping rules for data items in categories a. and b. above.

Note: this exercise can't be comprehensively performed in a single cycle, so equally as important as the exercise itself, a processing system needs to be established so that as other data items are inevitably discovered, this inventory can be easily updated.

Group Story: Describe how individuals develop systems of systems to manage their data and how some of those lessons and systems apply to the workgroup. The group seeks to learn more about exploiting existing capabilities. For example, some play in a band and want to share music playlists instead of everyone passing around a notebook of individual musical tablature sheets. Everyone thinks this is both a good idea and is also too difficult to master, given the group's advanced age (+50).

Exercise:

1. Walkthrough the process of acquiring a master list of all the songs played by the band.
2. Expand the scope to include automated updating of individual devices.
3. Solve the data inventory puzzle by creating a 'stopping rule' to determine whether to formally manage a pile of data.

Step 5 Organizationally understand the costs of bad data practices

Admitted (understanding) the individual and organizational costs of previous bad data practices.

The organization ritually presents an event where it demonstrates:

- That it's making progress against the data debt.
- That it's getting better at data improvements.
- That the cost of insufficient data for the organization continues to be reduced.

Step five aims not to achieve a final count of the total deficient data practices cost our organization. Instead, it's to get good at evaluating data's impact on the organizational mission. An excellent way to instill corporate lessons is to annually make a data confession, discuss the amount and effects of the past year's data sins, the counseled remedies, and penance. Aside from the apparent annual progress reporting, the ritual calculates the data management successes already attained with a bit of reality thrown in. While these cost estimates are not highly accurate, the goal is improvement not perfection. Over time both the effectiveness and efficiency of the measures improve. One study has repeatedly found that just measuring DQ issues actually brings about data processing performance improvements.

Continue the Group Story: The group determines that they are learning something all groups will encounter—how to best manage an evolving song list displayed on a stage iPad? Illustrate the challenges of playing the wrong song.

Exercise: Produce three examples of a positive return on investments in data management that should be directly applicable to your situation.

Step 6 Demonstrate a capacity to replace bad data practices with good ones

Are entirely ready to have good data practices replace bad practices that have led to the current data debt.

The organization presents a plan to surge and seed additional resources required to incrementally raise its data literacy by improving KW and DP literacy. Initial data improvement efforts will benefit from a careful examination. Still, almost as much good will come from the required inter-data-silo communications among team members. This is an exercise in collective, collaborative, critical design review. The worst conclusion from the study is confusion. The best—is a clear focus on obtaining organizational wisdom (a systems perspective) to improve its collective data and data practices. The goal is to plan the best use of resources, improving the organization's data assets via collaboration among the data team.

Continue the Group Story: The group runs through a practice with the new electronic set management systems. Surprised to discover the time savings going forward—increased practice results in higher performance levels and morale.

Exercise: Design solutions to the three solutions postulated in the previous step.

Step 7 Take steps to crowd source data literacy activities

Asked for and receive data management capabilities that can address our data shortcomings.

The organization actively takes steps to organize citizens to promote organizational data literacy and better data awareness. Currently, most organizations are operating in a mode that data is everyone's responsibility. The current poor results indicate potential improvement is possible. Our approach during Step 7 is to sponsor data meetups within the organization. Each rally should know of the other demonstrations and their specialties. Like IT, data is a mile wide discipline and requires team-based approaches to problem-solving. The solution is a focus on a data group supported by Wikionomics-style crowdsourcing. That is, regular data passionates participate in monthly meetups to calibrate, educate, and celebrate the past month's data happenings. The meeting participants interact with a broader circle that keeps everyone involved, focused on a common objective, and rapidly develops good ideas.[83]

Continue the Group Story: Group discovers both open-source apps and collaboration opportunities—illustrating both. Observe the meta-story as the group realizes the depth of this new rabbit hole. Vigorous discussion ensues as they know they must begin to apply ROI concepts to these investigations.

Exercise: Small example of crowdsourcing:

a. Mean commute time exercise
b. Critical design review of an individual work product from Step 6

c. Everyone exchanges papers and only improves the existing ideas.

Essential here is some strategic reverse engineering and profiling that can guide away from ROT and toward value using ROI calculations.

Two steps comprising Level 3: Love and belonging—knowledge workers

When steps 4-7 are complete, prepare a sufficient foundation to grow data literate organizational knowledge worker communities. KWs, per their Employment Agreements, are endowed with an artificial sense of belonging or at least we-are-all-in-this-together ness. The next two steps leverage this growing sense of community:

8. The organization is ready to commit to improving data practices by scoping and executing repeated data strategy iterations requiring data literate knowledge workers.
9. Request and obtain the required resources to address prioritized deficiencies to execute the strategy iterations using the enhanced organizational data management capabilities and resources. Provide resources to improve prioritized organizational weaknesses implemented in a

continuous improvement program. The organization reviews and inspects practices and assets to identify new requirements that need to be integrated with existing prioritized work.

A vital product of these steps is the detailed organizational self-knowledge surfaced from working through these organizationally impactful data challenges. This knowledge begins to harden generally after the third iteration of the data improvement cycle in each given subject area. Codified, it should be kept as part of organizational data practice assets.

Step 8 Identify candidates for data improvements

Made a list of data beneficiaries, and capably and ably offer resolutions.

The organization must organically evolve a suitable process for identifying candidate data improvement opportunities. To further cement the business case, document representative examples of the types of data-cuts the organization is experiencing. Then address these as what we call lighthouse projects. Lighthouse **projects** provide focus—occupying the intersection of three overlapping Venn diagrams comprising:

- Things that further organizational strategy
- Opportunities to practice needed data skills

- Opportunities to improve data use by the business.

And find a project at the intersection of these three foci. We describe these Lighthouse projects in more detail in Chapter 15.

Continuing the Group Story: A group of technology minded truckers band together in a conscious effort to crowdsource and learn as a group of independent operators. We come upon the group as it collectively realizes there is only so much 'mileage' past the literacy mileage savings. They immediately focus on an evaluation of the various 'next big things' in trucking analytics.

Exercise: Use diagrams from *How to Make Sense of Any Mess*[3] to map out a particular trucker data challenge from at least two differing perspectives. Indicate appropriate upstream and downstream sources and uses.

---

[3] https://www.youtube.com/watch?v=s6lXWgnTmRE and https://abbycovert.com.

Step 9 Address deficiencies with remediation

Made direct amends to such activities and organizational data beneficiaries.

The organization must get good at executing data improvements. In addition to addressing the challenges, it's also critical to say that you are sorry by tallying up various estimates of the total harm. These should be maintained on an ongoing basis so they can be updated by additional organizational learning. These realizations should be in the form of prioritized initiatives and **remediation steps** that offer opportunities for combining and optimizing (synergy) capabilities and data. This creates a baseline organizational description and is immortalized as a ritual bad data accounting exercise. Accept the baseline organizational assessment and prioritize remediation initiatives to normalize and optimize organizational capabilities and data.

Continue the Group Story: Pick just one of the requirements concepts developed in step 8 and flesh out the design aspects for just one!

Exercise: Develop integrated design specs for a second Step 8 work product. Illustrate the need to address cultural issues continuously (with props like the data convincer) to make a case for further investment in formalized data management training and education. They have initial trouble with the immediate boss, who is then converted and assists in presenting the request to the next level up.

One step comprises Level 4: Esteem~data teachers

Only after the KWs have inspirationally led the way and simultaneously surfaced indications of the data literacy levels attained by various parts of the organization can the organization legitimately design a targeted process for improving organizational literacy. Data teaching can occur within the organization or be contracted to specialized education providers. The specification below details the two-way nature of the data teacher role—whose direct responsibility is to evolve the organizational data curricula to best support the organization's strategic needs.

Organizational leadership reviews and concurs with the analysis and commits resources to improve the prioritized work so that the improvement in teaching effectiveness is measurable. It contains feedback loops. It occurs within budget cycles—limiting any scope creep.

The work product of level 4 is a data literacy improvement program capable of guiding and evolving the organization's data journey.

Step 10 Increase personal accountabilities

Continued to take personal and organizational data capabilities inventory and address evolving requirements.

Organizational leadership reviews and concurs with the analysis and commits resources to improve the prioritized work. The organization reviews and inspects practices and assets to identify new requirements to integrate with existing prioritized work. One of the primary needs for data to exist as a programmatic activity in organizations is the constantly evolving technical landscape. To appreciate the magnitude of the technology changes, consider how some of us in a lifetime have seen preferred personal music delivery evolve from:

- 78 ➔ 45 ➔ 33⅓ rpm (rotations per minute)
- Cassette tapes
- 8-track tapes
- Mp3s
- Loss-less audio
- Streaming audio.

The number of devices required to read more than ½ dozen music formats separately is prohibitively complicated and expensive. The unaccounted expense requires several KWs to learn data management skills independently and with varying degrees of success. Data management programs take a long-term view on organizational capabilities, including data exploitation. Group stories and exercises are not required outside of these SMEs.

Two steps comprising Level 5: Self actualized—data professionals

Only after achieving a proven ability to improve organizational literacy can organizations provide administrative data professionals with the necessary foundation to self-actualize. The final two steps are:

10. The organization seeks additional resources based on proven ROI to incrementally raise its data literacy by improving employees' knowledge, skills, and abilities

11. Having seen value in these efforts (the light of data), organizations institutionalize these practices by developing broad communities of interest and evangelizing the principles and practices across the organization.

Step 11 Improve organizational capabilities continuously

Sought to improve our individual and organizational data management knowledge, skills, and abilities and to articulate improving cases to secure sustainable resources.

The organization must demonstrate its commitment to maintaining high levels of individual and organizational data literacy. To be truly useful, data management must be a community-based effort involving each KW organization-wide. Regular business case reinforcement and defending will help our organization to identify and understand advanced indicators. Request and obtain the resources that address prioritized deficiencies in executing the strategy using the enhanced organizational data management capabilities and resources.

Group Story: These should now be organization-specific but illustrate the strategic cycle that the organization is attempting to improve.

Exercise: Literally take on the self-improvement process group, realizing: 1) the previous step could have been accomplished more elegantly, and 2) the process must be repeated iteratively, brainstormed, and developed hypotheses mapping data flows among shared organizational data items. Understanding the interdependencies among these permitted the development of a phased remediation strategy. Finally, develop and execute a successful communications strategy for developing a sustainable data management program, including sequencing, and segmenting big data technologies and data scientists.

Step 12 Evangelize across the organization or in other organizations

> *Having seen 'the light of data' as the result of these steps, we tried to carry this message to others and to practice these principles in all our affairs.*

There must exist now a sense of the pervasiveness of the organizational data debt. Some level of contribution to the profession—above helping the organization seems appropriate. Having seen "the light of data," organizations institutionalize principles by developing a community of interest and evangelizing the principles and practices across the organization. Have and have nots should be relatively easy to identify soon as organizations not planning will be limited to reacting instead of exploiting data opportunities. Being an evangelist can't hurt the cause of worldwide data literacy.

Continue the Group Story: Workgroup participants become evangelists within other parts of their organization.

Exercise: Validating the hypotheses created in the previous step increases the metadata's accuracy and improves understanding and subsequent data governability. Articulate the benefits accruing to your workgroup resulting from this 12-step program.

'Graduation' here doesn't mean the organization is primed for success. Instead of that, the organization has demonstrated specific knowledge and skills. The nature of the 12-step program ensures that the conditions met are necessary but insufficient to ensure success. In short, more work needs to be done! As the new habits replace the old traditions, the organization will need less and less reinforcement by the progression. New citizens joining the organization can learn new habits instead of learning the old habits and unlearn them and learn the latest practices. This is much more efficient.

The next chapter relates specific internal processes that must adhere per the data doctrine.

Chapter conclusions–Culture eats strategy

This is a major change that requires long-term organizational commitment and dedicated funding. Many more organizations have started this journey than have completed it. Serious internal discussion should precede any commitments.

CHAPTER 13

The Data Doctrine® (DDv2)

The previous chapter described the organizational steps required to address the accumulating data debt faced by society. This chapter describes what society must do from an organizational data program perspective.

"Build a data-driven enterprise, not a department" is reliable guidance provided by various advisory services. The only way to change an organization and an enterprise is to have a focused, sustained effort. The guidance to focus on data improvements enterprise-wide provides the most leverage. To effectively sustain change will require the actions of a program, not a single department.

The question still arises about what is meant by the terms data-focused, data-centric, data-driven, data-first, data-provocative, and others. How does that help organizations go about repairing neglected organizational data—eliminating the organizational data debt?

It turns out to be surprisingly challenging to get a useable answer and, as with the term 'literacy,' objectively defining data-driven (or data-focused or data-first, or data-centric or data-smart) continues to be elusive. A subject matter expert should be able to identify specific organizational behavior as definitively data-focused or not! We keep searching for substance behind the phrases and being disappointed.

A primary focus of organization-wide data management is to increase data sharing. We encoded a first version in our previous work as The Data Doctrine®. We developed it to provide clear and objective guidance for organizations and individuals who wanted to gain more value from their data. Hundreds of signatory practitioners got value from Version 1. In homage to the Agile Manifesto,[84] itself derived from the software engineering community, the doctrine we laid out consisted of four tenets:

"We are uncovering better ways of developing IT systems by doing it and helping others do it. Through this work, we have come to value:

- ***data programs*** *preceding software projects*
- ***stable data structures*** *preceding stable code*
- ***shared data*** *preceding completed software, and*
- ***reusable data*** *are preceding reusable code.*

While there is value in the items on the right, we value the things on the left more."[85]

Organizations following the data doctrine put their efforts into improving their ability to value the bolded left side of each tenant. While some organizations still maintain software development capabilities, more and more software development appear as packages and apps, offshoring, or symbiotic partnering arrangements that permit organizations to focus on core competencies. Therefore, we have updated the doctrine and added specific objective criteria to each of the tenets. The revised philosophy focuses less specifically on software development and instead on the broader category of using data practices to make IT and non-IT organization practices more effective. It now reads:

We are uncovering better ways of helping businesses use IT systems to employ data strategically by doing it and helping others do it. Through this work, we have come to value:

- ***data programs** driving IT programs*
- ***informed information investing** over technology acquisition activities*
- ***stable, shared organizational data** over IT component evolution*
- ***data reuse** over the acquisition of new data sources.*

While there is value in the items on the right, we value the things on the left more.

This valuation is demonstrated annually using objective and, if possible, industry-standard measures.

We will briefly describe each of the four data doctrine tenets as updated for the broader digital requirements. We follow this review with a description of putting the doctrine to work for organizations wishing to improve their data literacy. The chapter and book close with a bit of guidance towards creating your first Lighthouse Project! But first—a word of warning about unscrupulous consulting practices that will charge for and still not assume data risks because they know how the proverbial deck is stacked.

A warning about data consulting

We know that it seems convenient to hire a consulting firm to help sort out your data messes. But the truth is that your organization can easily accomplish a useful self-assessment. The most common finding from self-assessments is that your organization is at the beginning of its data journey, and there is no point in paying anyone to tell you what you already know! A self-assessment can also uncover useful pockets of internal data expertise and data knowledge networking to build your future data program organization and keep you from being pulled into money-sucking schemes. In full disclosure, we state this as having been on both sides of the equation—from government procurement officials to consultants and back again.

Consulting organizations bury their data consulting practices somewhere in IT projects. For example, organizations will often sell the client a software upgrade. However, they don't state that this will almost inevitably entail migrating to an Enterprise Resource Planning (ERP) system. The organization will address any data migration with a template holding spot. Partially into the conversion, the organization will discover that the source data is inadequate and that this will cost more time than initially planned to convert the insufficient data. The result is that your company pays more.

"Inadequate data" in this instance usually refers to data that is structured differently than the ERP's prescribed format. It's not necessarily bad. It just doesn't conform to the requirements. Remediation usually involves transforming the data's structure to conform to the ERP specifications. This kind of work does not regularly include data analysis. If the company does not understand the data, it will often pay for the same work at least two times, maybe more. For example, the organization may pay once to fix poorly formed or unintelligible data to ingest it into the ERP. The organization may have to pay to have someone else clean the data. Thirty percent of the customers in the ERP are over the age of 50! Another easy mistake that organizations cannot seem to avoid is installing the CRM system and then cleaning the data in the CRM system after it initially went live with unclean data.

Most business and IT professionals experience just a handful of significant system upgrades, modifications, and replacements in a career. Consultants do this all the time.

They know that the customers do not understand that the consulting organization fully expected to find that the data was "messed up." Guess who gets the work when it's "discovered" that the data conversion part will take longer? This part of the project is now pure profit as it requires more bodies than initially planned, and there are usually zero measures describing that progress should be much greater than what it actually is.

Organizations keep getting hooked by having these folks under contract, thinking it is easier not to change horses midstream. Instead, the organization should have managed the ERP installation separately. This approach to obtaining unnecessary data work is a well-known process that can be optimized by expertise.

A red flag for this type of scheme is when companies bid on data migrations for a fixed price without viewing even a sample of the real data. Speak with proposed staff about their approaches to problem-solving—data reengineering can't be approached with linear thinking. Determine a joint approach to risk management and mitigation, and on large projects, employ IV&V. Do not let your organization get sucked into a data morass.

Not all consultants are bad, but this practice is widespread in the industry and is one of the reasons that organizations spend 20-40% of their IT budgets on unnecessary data munging.

Now with that cautionary note out of the way—here is our discussion of the tenets of the data doctrine.

Data-centric Premise No. 1: Data programs driving IT programs

As discussed previously, data must be an organization-wide program, not simply a department. Because data evolves more slowly than other organization elements, building on this stability provides the organization the opportunity to "understand" itself. By understanding, we mean shared agreement (between business and IT and between IT and the connected systems) on standard terms describing the essence of various usefully shared business concept's—often persons, places, or things. Only on top of this well-understood stability should IT evaluate investments at the project level—this is a significant source business/IT misalignment.

Data programs and IT must be separated and sequenced. Only this will resolve confusion as to whose responsibility it is to manage data in the future. Traditionally data has been considered the responsibility of IT. But our studies indicate that 90% of IT organizations lack either the data leadership or organizational data literacy to manage their data competently. That required interaction between IT development and data evaluation isn't being performed effectively in most organizations.[86] Without sufficient data literacy, organizations have amassed an enormous amount of data debt.

Organizations are evolving their approach. Under DDV2, organizations create data architectures to span application system boundaries and rely upon other organizational components. Shared data is more comfortable to leverage and understand. Organizations design their data programs to derive the highest value from their data.

Organizations need to view their data program as an asset along with their data. Together these two valuable organizational assets need to be aligned—along with their other assets—to support the organization's strategic objectives. The most critical structural move for data is out of IT (unless your organization is one of the 10% who already does data well within IT). IT is complicated enough and, most importantly, has gotten us to the current, unacceptable state. The old IT standard "if they can connect, then my job is done" is insufficient to manage an organization's data assets.

As the data program increases in scope, it increases in importance to KWs. Once established, requests to the data program will grow as KWs and DPs increase their understanding of their data processing capabilities and data assets.

Improvement in data literacy can't occur without regular programs devoted to everyday specific organizational understanding and knowledge improvement efforts. Everyone must contribute to data asset enhancements. The efforts benefit from the formal accumulation of "tribal knowledge," the actual effects of compounding from application over time, and strategic first-mover advantages.

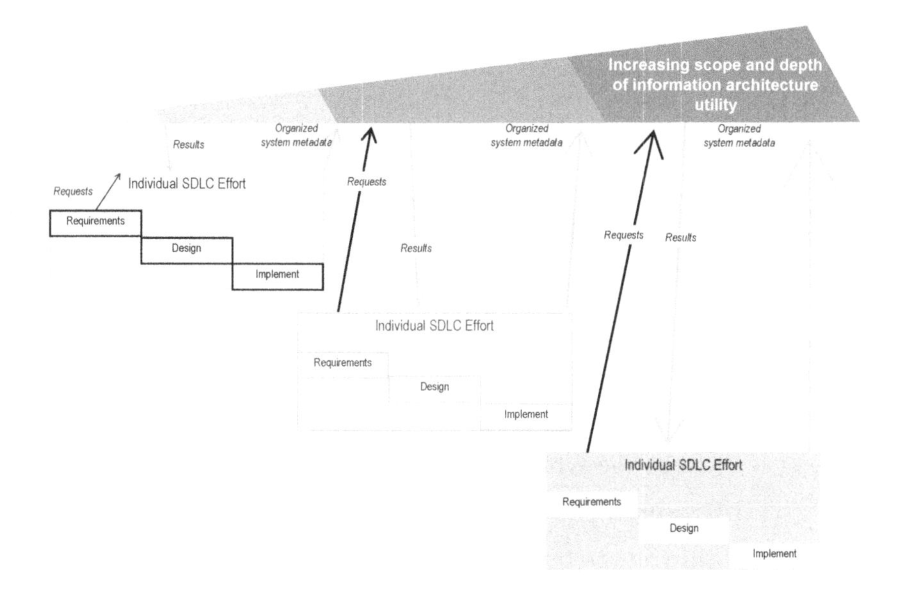

Figure 13.1—Over time, individual IT projects & business processes make increasing use of a data program

Implementation

To implement this tenant of the data doctrine, organizations must:

1. **Establish and maintain an efficient and effective data program that will continue to exist in organizational perpetuity**. Only when not worrying about imminent death can nascent data programs focus their thinking on community-oriented review.

2. **Develop a data leadership career track in your organization.** We have already made a case for stand-alone data leadership. We have also indicated the need for separate skill sets required to a) clean up the existing mess and b) manage the cleaned-up mess as we advance. Again, our guidance has been clear. First, rent a transition executive who understands data program requirements and can afford to break some eggs during the transition process setting the foundation in place. And second, identify a successor who can move the organization forward without cleaning up the mess (and apologize) simultaneously.

3. **Demonstrate positive ROI value to the organization annually.** This should be a formal expression accepted by the management of agreed upon measures. Funding comparable to HR and

other ongoing operations must be secure. Note that this doesn't eliminate the obligation on the part of the data program to illustrate the value that it adds publicly. For example, if your plan supports five FTE at 100,000/annually, then you must show 500,000 (plus overhead) in value annually! Achieving an annualized growth and controlled cost is a tall order but, indeed, keeps things focused on practical matters.

4. **Create an iterative approach.** Cyclic repetition helps organizations to understand the importance of workforce data literacy's role in organizational capability development as a goal unto itself. When organizations do this, they increase the strategic value of and the care with which they maintain their data assets and facilitate data reuse across an increasing number of systems. To achieve this, organizations must deliberately guide data reuse across various IT projects. Initially, an evolving data program results from a stepwise refinement of different IT project development cycles. Several repetitions must occur for data program activities to reach a tipping point and contribute to the organizational strategy.

5. **Document that your data strategy drives IT decisions.** First, you must get good enough at using data to better support organizational strategy

that you can document and communicate it to others. Second, you must validate that the data strategy drove IT. Data debt cannot be corrected using project thinking. Instead, it must become a data program capability.

Data-centric Premise No. 2: Informed data investing over technology acquisition activities

Data strategy must supersede IT strategy due to its much more consequential outcomes. Data practice improvement must be a fundamental component of all future IT investments! This new consideration is at the heart of the DDv2—injecting data doctrine thinking into all aspects of IT investment. There are at least two reasons why companies have failed to do this previously:

1. **Reluctance to invest long-term**. Executives tend to have financial incentives to meet short-term objectives, but data investments return value in timeframes measured in decades. We have described the wasted money surrounding ERP investments. We observe a similar pattern as organizations spend seven figures on visualization package software licenses for an entire organization and then do not achieve a positive return on the investment. Higher quality, more accessible data

makes it easier for KWs to find solutions without expensive software and with fewer individual data collections. This requires additional investments of time/resources and provides a necessary but insufficient basis for developing an organizational visualization capability.

2. **Data-less IT investment considerations**. This is an enormous area of potential savings. Organizations often purchase technology in hopes that it will solve problems. We have already presented convincing evidence that too much hope is placed on the technology alone. Too often, IT fails to consider the data implications of software development and acquisition. The organization selects the software and services that increase data debt, the number of hidden data factories, and data ROT instead of those capable of complementing the existing data assets. We agree with those who consider a best data practice to include a logical data model when evaluating any software package, application, or service. A surprisingly high percentage of organizations are happy to provide copies of the internal data models under non-disclosure agreements. Consider the value that existing shared data structures bring to the decision about which software to purchase. It becomes easy to understand which capabilities that the organization currently uses are beneficial and replicated in the new system.

> Similarly, improvements can be identified as deficiencies and tracked to new software features. This process helps determine the best data fit for the proposed data capabilities. However, core data models do not generally evolve. Whatever you start with is likely to be with you for as long as the software. All candidate packages submit these models as part of the RFP process. Some require an NDA. Those that do not submit their logical data models can't participate in the process. Objective specifications understood in light of specific options can help the organization change the granularity with which IT changes, and risks are managed. This process is typically not followed and is a primary cause of organizational data debt increase. This kind of quick analysis permits the organization to determine if the proposed solution is a good fit.

Also crucial to this process is a repeated and systematic review. Each iteration helps the team better understand the project requirements as an integrated whole. The more unified understanding that exists from simple unit functionality to overall system behavior, the more likely people will catch errors early. As noted above, if data structures change at any point during a cycle, then coding must stop until the team can address and resolve any issues related to those data structures. There are generally fewer consequences when software changes than when shared data structures change because the software is more adaptable and malleable than shared data structures. Shared data structures are foundational to every IT system, and, when they change, ripple effects can distress the entire system.

This mode of reconceptualizing IT around the support of well-documented data flows can be applied to many other current IT expenditures, from security audits to management of legal holds to maintaining customer information (the average organization maintains customer information in seventeen disparate data collections!). Once started, the amount of money saved by this approach has been staggering. Informed data investing can prevent the need for other technology acquisition activities.

Implementation

To implement this tenant of the data doctrine, organizations must:

1. **Demonstrate how making stable and shared data structures a priority has improved strategic organizational objectives**. Throughout our careers, we have seen IT systems eliminated and the associated costs reassigned more efficiently. Shifting costs is possible because data exists at a more fundamental level than IT projects, leading to more practical IT applications.

2. **Learn to quickly establish and repeatedly use an agreed-upon ROI framework to measure value.** Establishing the framework for measuring the data program value proposition and improving its utility continuity is one of the most critical measures of a well-functioning data program.

3. **Develop, adopt, or adapt a program evaluation framework.** At a minimum, require separate data processing budgets for accurate measurement. Annual assessment of the value produced by the data program will help organizations calibrate the most useful program forms. As starting points, recall from Chapter 5 how much money is wasted when KWs aren't using data to its full potential!

4. **Discourage custom, one-off, point-to-point data connections in favor of shared data sources.** Demonstrate how this will positively impact the organization's ability to achieve strategic objectives. Make it more challenging to use point-to-point connectivity than to use shared data sources. Use the resulting framework to determine a break-even rule regarding when direct data connections are cheaper than the development of data sharing facilities.

5. **Discourage the introduction of new data elements or reconfigurations.** Adding new data elements to

existing data structures is far too common a practice. Effective data governance can make it more challenging to add a new one. Accomplish this by requiring affirmative proof that the new needed data item cannot be assembled from existing data items. As above, demonstrate how this can help the organization achieve strategic objectives.

Data-centric Premise No. 3: Value stable, shared organizational data over IT component evolution

In this context, we're lumping everything that isn't data specific (such as infrastructure, security, and devices) into a category we're calling the "IT component." Changes to the IT component must be subordinated to data changes. This process applies to hardware and software upgrades, moves, and remediations. The choice of whether to buy, rent, or build organizational IT delivery capabilities is newly reliable. Far too often, the selection is made based on processing fit instead of the total cost of ownership.

The success of an IT project is often evaluated by the timely delivery of components rather than by whether it produces the correct results. Was the application made available to users at a particular time on a specific date?

Knowing this information is essential, but it can take many years to recover if a good app suffers a poor upgrade. Look no further than the 2012 fiasco that was the original Apple Maps app. It was sometimes flat-out wrong (it took one author to the middle of a cow pasture as part of a quest for a Best Buy!). Few organizations are willing to invest on the scale or for the duration during which Apple has labored intensely to recover ground by upgrading the app functionality and data quality. Consider the advantages if Apple had released an accurate app a few months later instead of a rushed product. The company would have saved itself a public embarrassment. And rather than spending resources on reactively fixing the product, they could have invested in Maps app enhancements and gained an advantage over rival Google Maps.

A similar mindset shift needs to occur regarding the challenge of IT systems delivery. The due date should be one of several success criteria. Still, users shouldn't start the application if there isn't currently, or in a specific implementation, a means of reliably delivering fit-for-purpose data to the application. Linda Bevolo of U.S. Bank contributed an excellent case study for a book on monetizing data management. In the case, she illustrates how she brought about a $50 million difference for her organization by:

- asking if the data is correct,

- valuing data more than valuing "on time and within budget"
- respecting accurate data more than proper development process, and
- auditing data rather than project documents.[87]

Promote corporate data shared among operations as a brand. Organizational data should be of higher quality, more shareable, and less in volume than other forms of data. Branding these attributes helps citizens (and KWs mainly) work more productively with data, increasing their literacy and prospects.

Consider another example. Suppose Company X invests $18 million in software, and Company X's annual return on investment is 3%. Suppose you have confidence in organizational management. In that case, you must assume that this investment will produce or help produce more than its cost in increased top-line revenue or bottom line savings within a hoped-for time. Rarely is this the case, and when we see headlines touting that Company X is investing $Y million in ERP type Z, a quick calculation of the required ROI for this investment often yields inconsistent results.

In the past, organizations often linked functionality with a specific technology. As a result, citizens became used to associating functionality with technology as well. Today's options are vast and evaluated in cycles analogous to sprints in roughly comparable timeframes, given good team experiences and (obviously) DP-level data literacy. We need to separate the data from the software application in the citizens' minds, but this can't happen unless we achieve success, separating it similarly in developers' minds.

In proactive mode, identify and eliminate point-to-point connections. Make the introduction of new data elements the exception, not the rule. Sharing data at the project level consumes more resources and impedes progress. It takes practice to obtain tremendous value from shared data. Having to wade through overly complex processes doesn't help. Only when the organization understands its data requirements can IT delivery systems optimally deliver data to KWs. To ensure organizations capture and understand those requirements, specific data program capability achievements must precede the evaluation of delivery components.

Also crucial to this process is a repeated and systematic review. Each iteration helps the team better understand the project requirements as an integrated whole. The more unified understanding that exists from simple unit functionality to overall system behavior, the more likely people will catch errors early. As noted above, if data structures change at any point during a cycle, then coding must stop until the team can address and resolve any issues related to those data structures. There are generally fewer consequences when software changes than when shared data structures change because the software is more adaptable and malleable than shared data structures. Shared data structures are foundational to every IT system, and when they change, ripple effects can distress the entire system.

Implementation

To implement this tenant of the data doctrine, organizations must:

1. **Provide evidence that they are investing appropriately in data.** It's insufficient to account for data savings properly. Once measurement systems are well functioning, the focus will turn toward process refinement. This facilitates data programs' ability to innovate.

2. **Demonstrate that using data requirements to gate development activities provides more value than implementation costs.** Data requirements are the most objective and, therefore, testable. Not finalizing data requirements means holding up other investments dependent on these requirements.

3. **Regularly illustrate how shared data structures permit significant reductions in complexity throughout the entire IT infrastructure.** Among others, our work with colleagues in IT governance shows areas ripe for simplification—reducing access time, processing requirements, and errors.[88]

Data-centric Premise No. 4: Value data reuse over new acquisition

Requiring that organizations accurately articulate resource amounts spent on new data versus on data reuse is beyond most organizations' capability to deliver. Getting good at that is the goal of this premise.

Valuing data reuse begs explicit comparison with IT investments. Given that 50% of organizational capital investments are IT-related, it's better to state unequivocally that many organizations have poorly invested in IT. A benefit of the data doctrine is that organizations can make more productive use of their IT investments. Unfortunately, data use and acquisition costs are rarely measured.

Organizations expect to reuse data, but they tend not to exercise data design principles that make it easy to do so. It is easy to see where the 80% minimal organizational data

ROT comes from as a result. Such an afterthought creates preventable problems: the practice costs more, delivers less, takes longer, and presents a more significant risk. One prominent example occurs when IT projects expect data to have been identified, specified, and documented, and it isn't! In programmatic terms, physical data structures must exist before any software project can incorporate them correctly.

Establishing the pedigree of data has been a longstanding problem. Both of us have worked for organizations where the explicit charge is to stamp out the practice of purchasing our own data—that is, data that we created originally but have now discovered that some part of the organization is purchasing from an external provider. When this sort of foundational work and documentation is produced upfront, other benefits accrue. These include better sets of project guardrails, a shared understanding of fundamental concepts, and improved resource and cost estimates.

Articulating and documenting data's origin, characteristics, and handing procedures represent data program challenges discussed previously.

Organizations need to develop processes to support the collection of data provenance as well as data requirements. If organizations were to operate in this manner, they would construct IT on shared, stable data structures, specifications, and documentation. Unfortunately, organizations are generally more comfortable with technology. They rush past the inescapable fact that individual software projects will generate project-specific data and data structures if organizations do not have stable data. When this happens, the organization positions itself to incur measurably more cost and effort when it later tries to integrate systems and share data.

Implementation

To implement this tenant of the data doctrine, organizations must:

1. **Efficiently and effectively value data.** The alternatives of data hoarding or being entirely driven by legal and risk considerations are sub-optimal. Data programs must continually improve their ability to add value to data.

2. **Determine and recognize obvious cases both for and against data reuse.** Push the task of identifying data reusability to organizational KWs incentivized to submit proposed improvements to the program.

3. **Document data and make it ready for reuse.** While these measures should improve over time, it's critical to obtain the initial (less polished) standards

to provide precise feedback to the program and orient it to productivity asap.

4. **Clearly define data guidance relative to data and its reuse.** Since the organization initially won't have experience, it must work off a stated hypothesis, collect and analyze data, and identify orienting costs from data used to data reuse.

The Data Doctrine at work as data programs support their organizations

Learning to practice the data doctrine isn't difficult. The objective criteria we have laid out permit organizations to determine what they should be doing and (equally important) what capabilities they need to develop. The question comes up more often of the form: "How does one get to Nirvana and Carnegie Hall?" The answer remains the same: practice, practice, practice. The importance of this fundamental organizational realization works hand in hand with the perceived value of the data program.

Putting together a plan needs to recognize that its first goal will be to get good at the process of exercising the cycle of continuous improvement described elsewhere. The theory of the constraints process (described in our previous work on data strategy[89]) focuses on measurable organizational things happening in response to improved data outcomes. The data program should identify DMBOK pie wedges (practice areas) that it would like to enhance its DMM score. Self-reflection and early phase problem redefinition keep the process agile, and direct interaction with sprints can be helpful in further defining challenge aspects.

When using the data doctrine in practice, the most specific goal is to focus efforts on improving the productivity of the organization's KWs. The following narrative illustrates how an organization might proceed efficiently and effectively to improve organizational KW productivity.

To start, conduct a Theory of Constraints-based analysis[90] of time spent on data-focused tasks by subject area-based groups of KWs. This can reveal a list of potentially improvable tasks and benefit quantifications. This might seem to be an academically focused research task beyond the capabilities of most organizations. Consider the same job from a different perspective: within a subject area, periodic data program participant meetings revealed the root cause of common complaints with some of the organization's data. The analysis is one of many benefits of having a more data literate organization. Focusing on ways to improve its data practices can improve organizational outcomes. The research should generally yield three candidate strategic data program initiatives designated for more substantive analysis.

The next task is to pick from among the three candidates. Devote specialized resources to evaluating how those initiatives would support business goals. Experienced data stewards vet each candidate project and other professionals who comprise the strategic data initiatives group within the data program. Evaluate these candidate projects for data-doctrine-based improvements. All analysis methods and conclusions are subject to rounds of constructive criticism and skeptical thinking. If emerging solutions meet established criteria, the group selects which initiatives to implement. This is usually through a series of cooperative projects involving a combination of process and systems reengineering techniques. Once implemented, the solutions are regularly evaluated for ongoing effectiveness, including downstream benefits.

For example, an organization could determine that many KWs spend large amounts of time requesting the subsequent analysis. These requests are printed and delivered physically. A proposal (anticipating 10% ROI) is accepted as a few significant priorities for implementation over the next two years. The group designs a series of steps to implement a new semi-automated workflow providing documented ROI above the target. The effort is publicized and registered to repeatable standards so that others can gain from the experience.

The most frequent comment we get from individual data leaders is: "I know what I am supposed to do, but I lack the resources to accomplish it."

You are likely well qualified to lead a decently functioning data program. However, it takes a different set of skills to correct data debt, implement a plan to reduce ROT, and fewer of us have had that experience. This was one reason we indicated that organizations might want to rent certain types of talent at different periods of organizational growth. Unfortunately, you may not understand, for example, how much more critical interpersonal skills are during the forming stage of your data program. Frankly, these skills are much more situation-dependent than training-based.

Creating your first lighthouse project

Recall from Chapter 12 that Lighthouse Projects provide a great overlap of these critical priorities:

- Things that need to happen to further organizational strategies
- Opportunities to improve data used by the business
- Occasions to practice required data skills.

These projects represent the type of knowledge not available to organizations currently. Let's work backward to establish what must happen for anyone to decide to start a Lighthouse Project. This will give you a picture of the activities required to operate data programs smoothly within organizations.

None of what we describe below exists in 90% of the organizations we have worked with over the past 70+ combined years. Data documentation creation, maintenance, and evolution should occupy a significant percentage of organizational data leadership time and attention.

For priority #1, identify specific occurrences/things that need to happen to achieve organizational strategic objectives. Next, indicate which data items are related to the successful accomplishment of each goal. What would make this list even more useful would be a designation along the data life cycle, indicating the business process's data items interaction. Better still, as with most things data-related, we can limit the range of values that this data interaction can take on to Create, Read, Update, and Delete. These CRUD matrices showing specific detailed interactions permit more rapid problem diagnosis and facilitate business and system reengineering efforts (see the example below).

	Process 1	Process 2	Process 3	Process 4	Process 5
Data Item A		Create	Read		Delete
Data Item B	**Read**	**Create**		**Update**	
Data Item C			Read	Update	
Data Item D	**Create**	**Update**	**Delete**	**Update**	
Data Item E		Create			

Figure 13.2— CRUD matrix shows business processes and their activity type

For priority #2, similar to the data needs identified in #1 (above), the requisite documentation won't exist initially but should describe at least the physical, as-is data model. One of the data program goals is to reduce the amount of data ROT in the organization. Reducing the data choices will make KWs more efficient (as detailed previously) as the volume of data required to perform is reduced—ultimately and ideally to one-fifth of the previous volume. The 20% remaining will be much easier to value and maintain as it evolves.

For priority #3, the organizational HR program should track the data group and all other KWs' data skills to identify the organization's most in-demand skill areas. This taxonomy and objective qualifications represent considerable attention from data leaders and, of course, information not readily available to most organizations.

The goals of an organizational data program would include each of the above data collections. Adapt systems to measure and manage—not just these, but also the management's organizational data benefits. This requires an educated KW who can suggest additional data items be handled on an organization-wide basis.

Chapter conclusions–Required objectivity

A primary reason for the success of Agile software development is a focus on its core guiding principles. Absent any specific objectives, it is difficult to see how progress can be made–much less made faster. Our goal has been to provide a specific objective starting place. As the Agile Manifesto evolved, so to shall this.

CHAPTER 14

Challenges to and Consequences of a Data Literate Citizenry

Have you ever seen the movie Idiocracy? A quick plot recap: An ordinary person wakes from a 500-year sleep and discovers the rest of the world had gotten dumber. That person is now the smartest in the world. Many people reference Mike Judge's 2006 film regularly during the pandemic. It seemed as if some understood the challenges of the pandemic, and some did not. If we were "in charge," everyone involved in data would achieve and demonstrate specific proficiency levels as a prerequisite to participation in non-PIDD aspects of society. We want to leave you with our vision of what a data literate citizenry would look like in 25 years if the proposed efforts are successful. Before describing our data literate nirvana, we will briefly discuss the barriers and challenges that citizens should overcome.

Barriers and challenges to data literacy

Barriers exist because society doesn't have control over precisely how MDSs become ADSs. We can encourage or shame, but we can't enforce data literacy Levels 1 and 2. We have encountered three attitudes in society that keep us from making progress:

1. **Looking for a quick fix.** Far too often, organizations have tried and failed at fads. People must view data literacy as a long-term program that delivers gradual improvements over time. While Lean Six-Sigma, TQM, Agile, and others have components and aspects that people should examine for potential utility. None have 'caught' on in an industry-shifting manner.
2. **Lack of perceived strategic relevance**. It is critical to present data initiatives in ways that support various societal and civic strategies. Specifics such as ensuring that voters are cognizant of factual information about candidates/issues and decision-makers are able to rely on accurate facts. This prevents data priorities from seeming to compete against other priorities.
3. **Data-induced anxiety**. Making data-driven decisions and using data insights to influence strategy is new for many non-technical employees. Introducing new tools and methods too quickly can

be overwhelming and cause significant fear and anxiety. Organizations must work hard to combat any misconceptions around what data can or can't do and build confidence in data-driven decision-making for people to engage.

4. **Not seeing the urgency**. Those not understanding pandemic math (see Chapter 2) will also not know the urgency of any of these ministrations. Getting through all this has been an ongoing challenge. As with other issues, it appears that direct personal experience facilitates comprehension.

Organizations can reduce or eliminate the impact of these barriers with careful planning. Despite the growing need to make data-driven decisions, companies trying to cultivate data literacy can encounter other challenges. We can categorize those challenges to data literacy in the following way.

Technology

Harnessing the total value of data requires infrastructure and tools that are accessible to all. Most useful would be widely available high-speed broadband connections to households. Broadband services involve correct configurations, adequate storage, organizational tools for data, access to databases, computers, and other hardware. Then once those capabilities are in place, users must have the ability to collect, store, analyze, and act on data efficiently. Cost is a factor. And many data analytics tools require specialized coding knowledge that's prohibitive to non-technical users. Additionally, organizations will have to contend with growing data compliance, and security risks and requirements cause many to keep data assets siloed or restricted entirely.

Organizational

In most companies, the language of data is spoken only by the data team, forcing them to take on the responsibility of acting as "keepers of data." Other employees become reliant on their time and ability. Exaggerated confidence can stir feelings of inadequacy and frustration that lead to a tense division culture. What's more, business teams' lines often work in silos, with no single source of data truth and no mechanisms for sharing insights or building on each other's work.

Skills and abilities

Practice, practice, practice—you can't teach the fundamental skills required—people must develop them through training, but you can teach the foundational concepts. From there, it's a matter of data practice (CMMI) maturity. Individuals must practice specifically focused data strategy cycles on concrete objectives and, in the process, exercise organizational capabilities around certain portions.

Education

We have failed to successfully modify the existing curricula to include room for course(s) on data literacy. The "new" data science curricula fail to consider context, value, and productivity concepts. Poor communication regarding student learning goals, a lack of communication about what instructors cover in courses, and what the school should develop for future studies also hamper these efforts. For example, there are several key contributors to reduced learning performance:

- differing levels of comfort and experience with technology and data
- differing levels of education (graduate vs. undergraduate), and
- age and generational differences between students.

Society needs to compensate for the lack of support and conditions for innovative learning, such as creativity and risk-taking. There are not enough skilled professors or not enough time to learn the required skills to teach a billion students effectively. All DTs require ongoing certification to maintain the critical feedback loop into our community.

Objective teaching effectiveness and efficiency standards must be required.

Visions of a data literate citizenry

Organizations expect citizens to independently seek practical knowledge and skills through alternative avenues, creating a disparity in practice and breadth of knowledge attained. We hope the vision painted below inspires everyone to overcome the barriers we have described (and others we have not anticipated). We will explain what we believe people should measure in the future!

Visions of a data literate MDS

Consider how absurd the following situation is: we give children supercomputers and connect them but don't provide them with any training. Imagine if society ensured that MDSs were data literate when they turn on the devices. What would happen? Kids would understand data and help their friends understand too. Those kids would share all kinds of tips, tricks, and workarounds as they always have. Here are a few things that would result from MDSs being data literate:

MDSs would secure their devices just as comfortably as they buckle their seatbelts. Having digital muscle memory would help MDSs protect information that' they regularly store on their mobile devices. What kind of information is at stake? How about medical information like medical conditions, recommended dietary intake, and other personal health information. Those MDSs who don't secure their mobile devices will quickly learn a valuable lesson when they fall prey to theft, intimidation. Society might exert social pressure on those who don't practice good data habits.

MDSs consider any novel communication outreach source (email, text, fax, call, etc.) as a threat by default. Personal contact lists have become essential data for MDSs. They use their contact lists to screen outsiders and serve as the first line of defense against ruthless data poachers and those that would injure unwitting MDSs.

MDSs adopt privacy expectations to the point where some trades offs are considered okay to transact for free (*determine my location when an app is in use*, for example), as long as the data is associated with random identifiers, converting the precise location where the search originated to a less-exact one after 24 hours and not retain a history of what has been searched or where a user has been. Other data tradeoffs should be made more explicit on a transaction-by-transaction basis. Ideally, social networks should give users some money for each contribution that they post.

MDSs understand the risk of communicating with people on the Internet. MDSs trust and value "ContactsOnly Connecting" and use that technique to stay safe online. Regular discussions are held within households to discuss specific additions and determine when MDSs have earned the privilege to add to their Contacts list. (Note: successful implementation means junk calls, texts, and emails are a thing of the past, and life is better—more about our vision for a data literacy citizenry in Chapter 16.) It will stay that way as the percentage of citizens adopting these practices forces bad actors to increasingly bother the data illiterate into giving up more and more of their data.

MDSs will be well-practiced using urgent call and emergency device settings capabilities to communicate with family and friends. This data exchange mode (communication) must also have a plan b as the mobile networks have been overloaded in past emergencies. Yes, items such as (non-electronic) message boards for posting pencil and paper-based data exchanges should be practiced. MDSs are exquisitely familiar with device data capabilities, such as access log files to provide verification, etc. It is now a crime to contact an MDS device for advertising or persuasion purposes. Other functions such as restoration from backup, geofencing, and malware protection are considered data skills to learn as the MDS matures.

MDSs understand the difference between appropriate and inappropriate data requests and, perhaps more importantly, where to go for assistance with novel claims. This implies a meta-level of recognition: the ability to distinguish routine data requests from a non-routine request. MDSs can identify bad Internet behavior when they see it, and they have a plan for dealing with it appropriately. Understanding the futility of arguing with unknowns on the Internet will reduce the overall intensity, just like flattening the pandemic curve.

MDSs understand the value of striving to gain increased data abilities as a reward for practicing good data behavior. They understand that good data habits are behavior patterns and that increased access comes only to demonstrated good behavior. Imagine if the MDS's toothbrush regularly reported to the responsible ADS about how long and how well each individual tooth was brushed! Today's devices give adults enormous amounts of information about how their MDSs are using them. Adults should take full advantage of that knowledge to determine the MDSs' level of maturity and responsibility.

Visions of a data literate ADS

Adults will have recognized the value of attaining a widely recognized level of data proficiency. Society recognizes data literacy is key to better understanding fiduciary relationship, finance, health, legal, and more. Friends will help data illiterate friends achieve what society now widely agrees are to keep behavioral capabilities expected of modern digital citizens. ADSs have identified and learned how to manage key reputations around the Internet. They understand that while social media and other sources of information purport to welcome user input to correct errors, the reality is that repairing a damaged reputation is difficult. All ADSs have some entry for them in a credit report or a publicly available record. It is essential to know the existence of crucial datasets such as those maintained by LinkedIn, ride-sharing apps, credit bureaus, and how they and others view you.

Additionally, ADSs understand that just googling something also requires understanding the source of that information. People know that they must question each authority of information they find on the Internet. Knowing the source of information is key to developing trust across society and what we know. One way to build trust is to build safelists for people to use collectively. ADSs can demonstrate the benefits of approaching data practices from a defensive, policy-based perspective instead of handling such requests as novel each time. Downloading a new app and hitting autocomplete may or may not be the best way to respond. ADSs require transparent sources. ASDs know how to employ best various automated software-based data restrictions. The most restrictive is a VPN-based ContactsOnly permitting no incoming signals to reach the user unless an entry exists in the Contacts List.

Integrated capabilities such as WIFI DATA ONLY will keep users from spending money on routine downloads. ASDs know how to employ best (and switch easily on and off) various automated device-based data management capabilities. For example, people use contact favorites to end distracting or repetitive tasks or prioritize incoming data requests. ASDs know of the data protection offered by fiduciary relationships. Understanding that the law governs what individuals trust with your financial, health, legal, and governmental data exchanges clarifies both parties' expectations. It also leads the ADS to ask perhaps, "Why isn't this data exchange governed fiduciarily?"

ASDs know who is and isn't governed by the specific code of data ethics on the Internet. As a result, they can recognize and report improper influencing of both ADSs and especially MDSs. Ideally, society will create an influencer code of conduct that will allow increased access to those who conform. ASDs can make meaningful, personal cost-benefit determinations concerning types of service, providers, bundling, switching costs, and more. While it would be nice to have former President Obama's vision of 25MBS to the desktop as standard, the reality is that data access costs money. ADSs should be able to make informed decisions about their cost and use.

Visions of a data literate KW

KWs understand and appreciate possessing data acumen. They know their role and the front line of defense against data malpractice and misuse. This data acumen is recognized as a useful set of skills to have in at least one family unit. KWs act as responsible data stewards. Increased capability for systems thinking will help organizations better evolve to meeting coming challenges. Key is the ability to understand the data collected by the organizational data machine used, where it comes from, and where it goes next. KW level literacy standards have become part of the resume screening process with automatic certification validation. Catchup data literacy courses help those who didn't get it the first time.

KWs can conceptualize their role as part of the organizational data machine's data value change. No longer can the KW say, "I don't understand why." Instead, each KW understands its role for data's specific ability to add value to the overall organizational output. KWs trust their automatic process updates to occur timely.

Communities can easily extend updating software processes to include various safelists and blocklists. Awareness of device configuration data and new and evolved capabilities will help speed productivity improvements as user needs are more directly addressed.

KWs are aware of various organizational fiduciary data relationships. For example, there should exist uniform standards of behavior and expectations around law enforcement of device access. Currently, not much exists for citizens beyond the unanimous decision by the US Supreme Court that law enforcement must have a warrant to access the device. Nevertheless, KWs routinely do an excellent job of maintaining and upholding corporate data fiduciary responsibilities. Society runs more smoothly as a result.

During the pandemic, most wore masks understanding that bothering to do so communicated, "I wear because I understand that we all are swimming in the same pool." However, as COVID spread among those not wearing masks, others noticed and changed their behavior. For example, a trucker might indicate that if an unsafe rig causes an accident, that might block innocents from getting to their destinations as scheduled. As a KW, it's essential to demonstrate your ability to describe this concept in terms understood by your colleagues.

Visions of a data literate DT

Citizens recognize and value Data Teachers for their substantive contributions to society for increasing the world's data IQ for more than 25 years. Success in this area means that: society appreciates Certified DTs as a revered class (complete with hazard pay). Communities overwork Teachers in the best circumstances—they all need formal appreciation. Society no longer considers data teaching a national priority because 80% of citizens are data literate and knows how to apply data concepts to different societal roles. There is still a gap between the data literate and the data illiterate. However, data illiteracy is now the exception. Data education has been incorporated into standard curricula to graduate from educational programs with the appropriate MSD, ADS, and KW data literacy levels.

DTs know the utility of the feedback-based model used to close the data literacy knowledge gap faster than any other literacy approach. As a result, the profession responds more rapidly than the traditional accreditation-bound process. Society designs feedback to be a significant part of the future educational system. Additionally, DTs insist on strict adherence to the "people-process-technology" mantra. People understand the social injury can be if the educational system exclusively focuses on technology. Communities ensure that data literacy training is part of the educational system at every level. Technology has finally become what it always was supposed to be—a commodity and a tool.

Visions of a data literate DP

The Data Profession has several unique characteristics. All will benefit from a shared holistic view of our profession. As a result:

- DPs are data literate and fluent with technology. Citizens understand that they must maintain their data credentials. The data profession created a computerized ledger system maintaining their data credentials. Listening to audio-based lessons can be tallied by the certification mechanism, as can event attendance. Most importantly, the materials for CDKAs 1-30 are standardized and are available to all practitioners.
- DPs appreciate the importance of BOKs guiding their profession. Millions of data professionals become impassioned in a massive effort to increase citizen data literacy. Industry findings and academic research refine data management processes, especially for KWs.
- DPs understand the need to increase and improve communication among data professionals and across the data world. As a result, DPs possess the

ability to tell required stories in ways that everyone understands and can use. And part of the data storytelling is accompanied by the relevant datasets.

DPs understand that some will continue to contribute to the good of all citizens. Employers build this time directly into DPs' scheduling to include one day/week for data volunteerism.

Data literacy conclusions

The existence of what we call "the Data Matrix" is the primary reason that **every** citizen should want **all** citizens to become more data literate. The data matrix is our name for all unknown, unknowable, and opaque data exchanges between organizations. Our information has historically been viewed as private and constitutionally protected. However, information leaks are becoming more common. They disproportionately impact those who have the most to lose. These same individuals are also the most unaware of the inherent danger to their freedom posed by the data matrix. Today, nothing is off-limits, and nothing stops surveillance capitalists from accessing every part of our lives. Criminals and bad actors are already using citizens' own data against them to influence their behavior unjustly.

Understanding these dangers alone might make data literate citizens pause the next time they receive a request for data. Sadly, we see little effort to make things better. Instead, we see citizens surrendering more personal data without understanding the consequences. We witness appalling data practices, a growing dependency on technology, and ruthless surveillance capitalists that track every aspect of our daily lives. Predictions were that 2020 would be remembered as the year when artificial intelligence and machine learning ran out of usable data! But we have done anything but run out of data—what's lacking is the ability to make any sort of useable meaning from most of it. The accumulated data debt wreaked havoc as algorithm after algorithm fell victim to lack of training data sets that severely limited their value! Advances are unattainable due to resource allocation imbalance. The COVID pandemic that dominated 2020 will resonate louder than the training-data shortage, but a strong case can be made that the training data shortage will have a far greater negative citizen impact!

The pandemic revealed a previously hidden societal weakness—a tangible lack of data literacy. We saw the impact of this illiteracy during the early stages of the pandemic—too many citizens could not use data to make decisions or consider various action plans suggested. Entire countries demonstrated they were incapable of distinguishing fact from fantasy, and their leaders were willing to make ultimately dangerous decisions using unreliable or insufficient data and an utter lack of consequential understanding. When leaders don't understand how data can help them understand a pandemic, society suffers, and the results are evident for all to see.

Like the pandemic, data literacy isn't constrained to any geographic area, social class, or job. It affects everyone—politicians, corporations, and the public. And their behavior shows just how widespread is the problem. There is a great danger of not preparing citizens to live in a digital society. Lowering citizen data literacy reduces risk and creates benefits for all citizens. When citizens are data literate, each one becomes part of a frontline defense for the ethical use of data. But if the citizens do not understand data and the consequences of their digital actions, the balance of societal power shifts to the data literate at the expense of everyone else.

Data nerds and others who are data literate must help the data illiterate to become data literate. We offer a framework to focus efforts, and we discuss issues related to increasing data literacy across the nation. The effort to develop and improve data literacy is no small feat by any measure and will take years to accomplish. However, we believe this effort is essential to a long-term and stable society.

APPENDICES

These appendices contain reference materials that should be more readily to citizens.

- Appendix A is a collection of data conversations useful between family unit members
- Appendix B is a succinct restatement of the data doctrine (version 2)
- Appendix C is a poor reproduction of the Open Data Institute's excellent conversation starter – their data ethics canvas and a link to the original.
- Appendix D is a consolidated list of the CDKAs
- Appendix E provides a more detailed examination of FEPA – likely the most significant new federal data law of recent time.

APPENDIX A

Suggested Conversations for Responsible ADSs (R-ADSs) to have with MDSs

Approached from a shared learning perspective, these vitally important data literacy conversations between MDSs and R-ADSs are seen as information exchanges with both parties contributing useful information. Recall that the common ethical focus of Levels 1 & 2 is to avoid being fooled manipulated.

Widely disseminated guidance should be developed to these and related topics and added to the evolving shared body of data knowledge. We recommend holding meetings every week and using these meetings as disciplinary checkpoints to educate the MDS and ADS. The participants should use the meetings until they have reviewed all the material. The most important aspect of these conversations is that they occur. When issues do arise, there is a basis for conversation, familiarity with the material, and non-confrontational discourse.

MDSs and ADSs should review the following every week any time a new MDS is added to the group:

- Connection requests
- Use and growth of address book
- Screen time utilization
- Financial data costs, data plans, and data usage costs incurred.

Over time, conversations could move to the following topics:

- Digital costs versus privileges
- In-app purchases
- Keeping and earning more digital capabilities
- Why data restrictions exist
- Downloading via Wi-Fi instead of cellular data.

When everyone is comfortable with the above concepts, the participants can relax the schedule to meet monthly or even quarterly. While basic concepts should be periodically reviewed, the group should add the following more advanced topics for discussion:

- Fragility—Often, there exists no undo capability
- Why some data privileges are withheld until the MDS matures
- Data monitoring and tracking rules for metadata, advertising, convenience, geofencing, etc.

- Examining settings to determine whether an app can download or update using the data plan or only over Wi-Fi
- Who tried to contact the MDS and why (hypothesized)?
- Cutting the cable
- Streaming versus downloading
- Service bundling
- Account monitoring
- Combining home and mobile data plans to reduce expenses
- Adding entries to the ContactsBook
- Automatically blocked contacts
- Declined contacts
- Assumption of data risk
- Instances where bad behavior online often has consequences IRL
- Objectively quantify the nature and quality of the regular expansions of the contacts entries
- Whatever topics the group finds interesting.

The Data Doctrine V2 Succinctly Stated

The Data Doctrine is a unified set of principles that states that data is the most valuable business asset in the modern business world. Therefore, organizations should deliberately manage their data assets and maximize their ability to achieve organizational goals. To follow the data doctrine, organizations must:

Value data programs over IT projects

1. Establish and maintain an efficient and effective data program that will continue to exist in organizational perpetuity.
2. Develop a data leadership career track in your organization.
3. Demonstrate positive ROI value to the organization annually.
4. Create an iterative approach.
5. Document that your data strategy drives IT decisions.

Value informed data investing over technology acquisition activities

6. Demonstrate how making stable and shared data structures a priority has improved strategic organizational objectives.
7. Learn to quickly establish and use repeatedly an agreed-upon ROI framework to measure value.
8. Develop or adapt a program evaluation framework.
9. Discourage point-to-point data connections in favor of shared data sources.
10. Discourage the introduction of new data elements or reconfigurations.

Value stable, shared organizational data over IT component evaluation

11. Provide evidence that they are investing appropriately in data.
12. Demonstrate that using data requirements to gate development activities provides more value than implementation costs.
13. Regularly illustrate how shared data structures permit significant reductions in complexity throughout the entire IT infrastructure.

Value data reuse over new acquisition

14. Efficiently and effectively value data.
15. Determine and recognize obvious cases both for and against data reuse.
16. Document data and make it ready for reuse.
17. Clearly define data guidance relative to data and its reuse.

Appendix C

Open Data Institute's Data Ethics Canvas

A great framing of data ethics considerations can be found at https://theodi.org/article/the-data-ethics-canvas-2021/. [91]

Data sources	Limitations in data sources	Sharing data with others	Ethical and legislative context	Rights around data sources
Name/describe your project's key data sources, whether you're collecting data yourself or accessing via third parties. Is any personal data involved, or data that is otherwise sensitive?	Are there limitations that could influence your project's outcomes? —bias in data collection, inclusion/exclusion, analysis, algorithms —gaps or omissions in data —provenance and data quality —other issues affecting decisions, such as team composition	Are you going to be sharing data with other organizations? If so, who? Are you planning to publish any of the data? Under what conditions?	What existing ethical codes apply to your sector or project? What legislation, policies, or other regulation shape how you use data? What requirements do they introduce? Consider: the rule of law; human rights; data protection; IP and database rights; anti- discrimination laws; and data sharing, policies, regulation and ethics codes/frameworks specific to sectors (e.g., health, employment, taxation).	Where did you get the data from? Is it produced by an organization or collected directly from individuals? Was the data collected for this project or for another purpose? Do you have permission to use this data, or another basis on which you're allowed to use it? What ongoing rights will the data source have?

Your reason for using data	Communicating your purpose	Positive effects on people	Negative effects on people	Minimizing negative impact
What is your primary purpose for collecting and using data in this project? What are your main use cases? What is your business model? Are you making things better for society? How and for whom? Are you replacing another product or service as a result of this project?	Do people understand your purpose—especially people who the data is about or who are impacted by its use? How have you been communicating your purpose? Has this communication been clear? How are you ensuring more vulnerable individuals or groups understand? How are you ensuring more vulnerable individuals or groups understand?	Which individuals, groups, demographics or organizations will be positively affected by this project? How? How are you measuring and communicating positive impact? How could you increase it?	Who could be negatively affected by this project? Could the way that data is collected, used or shared cause harm or expose individuals to risk of being re-identified? Could it be used to target, profile or prejudice people, or unfairly restrict access (e.g., exclusive arrangements)? How are limitations and risks communicated to people? Consider: people who the data is about, people impacted by its use and organizations using the data.	What steps can you take to minimize harm? How could you reduce any limitations in your data sources? How are you keeping personal and other sensitive information secure? How are you measuring, reporting and acting on potential negative impacts of your project? What benefits will these actions bring to your project?

Engaging with people	Openness and transparency	Ongoing implementation	Reviews and iterations	Your actions
How can people engage with you about the project? How can people correct information, appeal or request changes to the product/service? To what extent? Are appeal mechanisms reasonable and well understood?	How open can you be about this project? Could you publish your methodology, metadata, datasets, code or impact measurements? Can you ask peers for feedback on the project? How will you communicate it internally? Will you publish your actions and answers to this canvas openly?	Are you routinely building in thoughts, ideas and considerations of people affected in your project? How? What information or training might be needed to help people understand data issues? Are systems, processes and resources available for responding to data issues that arise in the long-term?	How will ongoing data ethics issues be measured, monitored, discussed and actioned? How often will your responses to this canvas be reviewed or updated? When?	What actions will you take before moving forward with this project? Which should take priority? Who will be responsible for these actions, and who must be involved? Will you openly publish your actions and answers to this canvas?

APPENDIX D

19 Data Lessons

Any incoming mobile call, text, shared selfie, e-mail, or other file exchange (as small as a bit) are all data requests, and your response (or lack of) will also be recorded as data as well.

Data Lesson #1

Data is more complicated than people understand. Most encounter data from one perspective and do not discover other areas. This leads to incorrect perceptions, misunderstandings, misfires and, most importantly, misallocation of resources. As our colleague, Lewis often said, "You can't productively dabble in data!"

Data Lesson #2

Data is a valuable asset! Be conscious of what you have and what you do with it.

Data Lesson #3

To be useful, the concept of data literacy must be considered a range (more literate or less literate) rather than a binary (literate or not literate).

Data Lesson #4

Citizens operating in today's world are dependent on smooth interaction with ODMs and data specifically.

Data Lesson #5

---

*Organizations are faced with both data debt and low data literacy within the workforce. There is a serious misconception that the **net generation** and **digital natives** are inherently more knowledgeable technically than past students. In reality, although younger generations may be able to "do" more with their tech, they may not be any better equipped to deal responsibly with their data.*

Data Lesson #6

Data moves between ODMs to form the data matrix–generally for the not for the good of the citizen

Data Lesson #7

Ninety percent of the US is online, increasing the importance of improving data literacy.

Data Lesson #8

Data and interactions with citizens are accelerating, posing a threat to those who are data illiterate.

Data Lesson #9

Delay in processing data impacts everyone, much as traffic affects congested commutes. We must get better at recognizing, accounting for, and addressing delays programmatically.

Data Lesson #10

This challenge can't easily be corrected, and, more importantly, the data debt will require some real effort to clean up. (Professional ministrations are required to make up for past neglect.).

Data Lesson #11

Technology can only address specific parts of the data challenges. The other 90% consists of process challenges that currently are unmet.

Data Lesson #12

Disorganized data is useless data. Organizations must standardize and organize or face hidden costs later.

Data Lesson #13

Data is increasing at an incomprehensible rate. Yet, when needed most for data literacy to be holding steady (and more importantly, not growing), it is unavailable for use by the essential citizenry, and it's just as bad or worse with organizational data literacy.

Data Lesson #14

Data education occurs via any number of means, but none deliver results efficiently or effectively, as evidenced by the unimproved longitudinal scores.

Data Lesson #15

This challenge can't easily be corrected, and, more importantly, the data debt will require some real effort to clean up. (Again, professional ministrations are required to make up for past neglect.)

Data Lesson #16

KWs can be enormously more productive when equipped with the right data knowledge and skills.

Data Lesson #17

Foundational concepts for KWs include ID tags, data protection, required fields, and maps and models.

Data Lesson #18

More technology isn't always better! Consider the long-term ROI and opportunity cost prior to adoption.

Data Lesson #19

APPENDIX E

Consolidated List of CDKAs

CDKA01: Limiting and Unlocking Additional Capabilities
Need: Demonstrate an ability to understand the reasons for and rules around adding entries into address books and the relationship to unlocking additional data capabilities in reward for demonstrated good behavior.

Remediation: Objectively quantify the nature and quality of the regular expansions of the contacts entries.

CDKA02: Communication Protocols—Contacts Only
Need: Demonstrate an ability to understand the reasons for and rules related to adding entries to their contacts list.

Response: Explain and implement ContactsOnlyMode—objectively review the nature and types of requests for adding entries to the Contacts.

CDKA03: Securing Data
Need: Demonstrate an ability to secure data using device-provided capabilities. This includes both strong password/passphrase and device encryption.

Response: Demonstrate objectively that their devices are encrypted and secured with a strong password and biometric capabilities such as fingerprint or facial recognition.

CDKA04: Identify Trustworthy Data

Need: Demonstrate an ability to take a defensive approach to trusting received data or when sending data to others. Doubt by rule; trust by exception.

Response: Develop habits for accessing trusted data via trusted methods—objectively review device connections and scan for malware.

CDKA05: Emergency protocols

Need: Demonstrate an ability to identify when to use emergency protocols and capabilities within the family or group unit.

Response: Demonstrate the ability to recognize and respond to emergency protocols—objectively run household wide test and evaluate the results.

CDKA06: Trading Convenience for Surveillance

Need: Demonstrate an ability to evaluate appropriate surveillance and convenience tradeoffs.

Response: Demonstrate an ability to rapidly respond to sharing requests in a manner that is supportive of articulate goals.

CDKA07: The Appropriateness of Data Requests

Need: Demonstrate a mastery of the numerous types of data requests that come with device ownership.

Response: Demonstrate an ability to respond appropriately to a range of specific requests.

CDKA08: Device Data Capabilities

Need: Demonstrate a mastery of device data utilities including cloud capabilities.

Response: Demonstrate ability to restore device from backup and review device access.

CDKA09: Overcoming Bad Internet Behavior

Need: Demonstrate understanding of the range of bad behavior potentially encountered on the Internet.

CDKA10: Managing Online Reputations

Need: Demonstrate an ability to review, improve and monitor their online reputations.

Response: Objectively illustrate knowledge of how to view and maintain existing online reputation scores.

CDKA11: Consider the Source: The Online Reputation of Others

Need: Demonstrate an ability to review and evaluate the online reputation of various sources and use this ability to enhance their ability to trust certain data sources.

Response: Objectively respond appropriately to a range of approaches demonstrating an ability to differentiate between informed and uninformed commentary.

CDKA12: Individual Policies and Data Practices Regarding Sensitive Personal Data

Need: Demonstrate an ability to identify and protect sensitive data (especially personal data).

Response: Demonstrate an ability to safeguard and steward your own PII as well as that of others. Automated data restraints

CDKA13: Automated Data Restraints

Need: Demonstrate an ability to learn how to use new automated data controls to their benefit.

Response: Objectively demonstrate successful use of automated data restrictions beyond what is required by system and malware updates.

CDKA14: Responsible Automated Data Management

Need: Demonstrate an ability to use automated data management capabilities to their benefit.

Response: Demonstrate knowledgeable use of smart lists, macros, and other data time savers.

CDKA15: Understand Data Fiduciary Relationships

Need: Demonstrate knowledge of data fiduciary relationships.

Response: Demonstrate the ability to treat data differently when it is governed by fiduciary obligations.

CDKA16: Responsible Influencing

Need: Demonstrate an ability to distinguish between responsible and irresponsible influencing.

Response: Demonstrate knowledge of responsible and irresponsible use of influencing data.

CDKA17: Data Investments: Features and Expectations

Need: Demonstrate an ability to understand and effectively manage the component costs of their data consumption.

Response: Demonstrate knowledge of data and data processing costs with an eye towards process improvement.

CDKA18: Data Steward Responsibilities

Need: Demonstrate an ability to be stewards of organizational data.

Response: Demonstrate knowledge of data processing and uses.

CDKA19: Add Value

Need: Demonstrate an ability to learn how the data they steward adds value to the organization.

Response: Demonstrate the ability to improve aspects of organizational data.

CDKA20: Keep Current

Need: Demonstrate an ability to learn how to apply organizations policies to the recency of data and supporting IT components.

Response: Demonstrate ability to validate and install software updates quickly and efficiently.

CDKA21: Respect Organizational Fiduciary Responsibilities

Need: Demonstrate an ability to identify and comprehend specific roles that are governed by fiduciary responsibilities.

Response: Demonstrate knowledge of organizational data fiduciary relationships.

CDKA22: Shared Fate: Everyone is Swimming in the Same Pool

Need: Demonstrate their ability to learn how their data is sourced from and is used by other parts of the organization.

Response: Demonstrate an understanding of how data is sourced and used by other parts of the organization.

CDKA23: Teach Effectively

Need: Demonstrate an ability to contribute to the elimination of the data debt.

Response: Objectively demonstrate that your great teaching will support data literacy.

CDKA24: Feedback is Designed into the Teaching

Need: Demonstrate an ability to contribute to the improvement of the data teaching process.

Response: Objectively demonstrate knowledge of how inputs are used in downstream evaluation. People, process, technology

CDKA25: Do Not Over Emphasize Technology

Need: Demonstrate an ability to place appropriate amounts of attention on respective data-people, process, and technology components.

Response: Objectively demonstrate knowledge and topic coverage.

CDKA26: Ongoing Educational Requirements

Need: Demonstrate a commitment to achieving ongoing educational requirements.

Response: Objectively demonstrate knowledge of feedback and certification linkages.

CDKA27: Certification and Recertification Mechanisms
Need: Demonstrate an ability to maintain current certification valued across industries.

Response: Objectively demonstrate knowledge of continuous professional certification requirements. Holders of specialized data knowledge

CDKA28: Possession of Valuable Knowledge
Need: Demonstrate knowledge of and ability to access data reference knowledge required by data professional specialization.

Response: Objectively demonstrate improved understanding of BoK contents.

CNLN29: Data Storytelling Capabilities
Response: Objectively demonstrate improving data storytelling capabilities.

Need: Demonstrate an ability to successfully communicate their various data stories.

CDKA30: Building the Foundation for the Data Discipline
Need: Demonstrate an ability to contribute to the profession by standardizing knowledge and education.

Response: Objectively demonstrate contributions to the discipline.

APPENDIX F

Understanding the Foundations for Evidence Based Policymaking Act (FEPA)

We originally developed this section for The International Society of Chief Data Officers.[92] Our convictions about FEPA's impact on government, the public, and society remain unchanged, and we hope you find the material reproduced here helpful.

While many Americans were shoveling their driveways and sidewalks from a series of winter storms, the federal government shut down, and the President signed the Foundations for Evidence-Based Policymaking Act of 2018 (FEPA). Much of what we know about the new law and its impact is still to be seen, but several things are readily clear. First, the Chief Data Officer (CDO) role is now incorporated into federal law and separated from the role of the Chief Information Officer (CIO). Second, government data is now open by default, and the federal government must keep its data in open standards-based formats. Third, the law requires setting up data management rigor in governmental "evidence-based decision-making." Fourth, the

Act fully recognizes the value and use of data in agency operations. Finally, the law expects that, collectively, these efforts will improve governmental decision-making and overall effectiveness.

FEPA's broad requirements present federal agencies with new opportunities and challenges. On the one hand, some enthusiastically support the arrival of CDOs and their assignment over national data. On the other hand, some are concerned that the federal government could not reasonably respond to these new expectations without new funding. There is little doubt that these changes will affect digital data across agency data systems as well as data in physical formats. Compliance with FEPA requirements could require levels of effort reaching those spent for Y2K compliance in the late nineties.

Foundations for Evidence-Based Policy Act of 2018 (FEPA)

This section is a synopsis of the new legislation, the authors' views of the new law, a preliminary assessment of the law, and its impacts on government, industry, and the public. We summarize the legislation's significant features, examine how the new law differs from earlier legislation, and review the requirement to expand the use of data across the federal landscape. Then we show outstanding questions we believe deserve further analysis and clarification.

It exclusively reflects the authors' thoughts and opinions. We received help in the form of review comments from many colleagues, and we especially thank the Bipartisan Policy Center's Dr. Nick Hart, who was one of the legislation's strongest proponents.

Let's begin with a clarifying note instigated by one of our reviewers. Natalie Evans Harris—former Senior Policy Advisor in the presidential Office of Science and Technology Policy, and now BrightHive's COO—noted that we should explicitly differentiate between open data laws and federal data laws. Open data is a subset of the suite of federal data laws. FEPA is a federal data law and is more comprehensive than open data laws. This important distinction is obscured by the new law's use of the acronym OPEN (Open, Public, Electronic, and Necessary). Evidence-based policymaking addresses processes far beyond open data; it's about data's use as a strategic asset.

There are arguably only a handful of federal data laws requiring the government to share data with its constituents. The first significant law was the Freedom of Information Act (FOIA) in 1967. FOIA requires federal agencies to show requested information to the requestor unless it falls under one of nine exemption categories (5 U.S. Code § 552). Years later, the federal government passed the Federal Funding Accountability and Transparency Act of 2006 (FFATA) to empower every American with the ability to hold the government accountable for each spending decision. This law resulted in the data sharing site, USASpending.gov, where the public can use government-provided tools to analyze more than 80% of annual government spending. The list for laws also includes GPRA (1993) and CIPSEA (2002).

A more recent data law was the Digital Accountability and Transparency Act of 2014 (The DATA Act). The DATA Act requires the federal government to transform and report its spending information into open data. The DATA Act also amended the Federal Funding Accountability and Transparency Act of 2006, addressing two fundamental issues.

- First, the Act required the Treasury Department (TRE) and the White House Office of Management and Budget (OMB) to set up government-wide data standards for reporting expenditures to TRE, OMB, and the General Services Administration (GSA). When the government collects data from the public, TRE and OMB publish that information at no cost to the public via the Internet.
- Second, the Act tried to standardize data that contractors and grantees report to the federal government. The law required OMB to determine whether data standards might relieve compliance costs for financial reporting. OMB concluded that rules were critical and would help control costs.

The DATA Act uncovered the need for standardization but did not address the lack of universal data standards. Instead, the government continued to employ *ad hoc*, agency-specific policies, procedures, and markings to safeguard, mark, and control its data, introducing a confusing bureaucratic patchwork of inconsistent markings, incongruent processes to share data, and different standards to safeguard data.

In 2018, Congress passed the FEPA to address many of the gaps left by the DATA Act. FEPA adds some new and potentially compelling elements to federal data implementation and use. FEPA follows a 2017 bipartisan commission report to Congress that advocated:

A future in which rigorous evidence is created efficiently, as a routine part of government operations, and used to construct effective public policy. Advances in technology and statistical methodology, coupled with a modern legal framework and a commitment to transparency, make it possible to do this while simultaneously providing stronger protections for the privacy and confidentiality of the citizens, businesses, and organizations from which the government collects information.

The commission focused on improving how data is used to generate evidence in support of federal policies and programs. Additional support for FEPA arrived in the 2018 President's Management Agenda, which called for developing a long-term national data strategy and the government to leverage data as a strategic asset (Hart and Shaw, 2018)[93]. Though this legislation seemed slightly "out of the blue," according to a representative from the Data Coalition (The Data Coalition, n.d.)[94], the group actually worked for more than three years with help from both political parties to help shape FEPA and position it for success in Congress. The Data Coalition is a group that advocates for the increased use of open standards by the federal government.

The following figure is reproduced with permission from the Bipartisan Policy Center and summarizes the components of the commission's recommendations as described in FEPA.

Topic	Bill Section #	CEP No.
Strengthening Privacy Protections		
Establishing an Agency Official for Data Policy	101(a) (§314)	3-3
Designation of Chief Data Officers	202(e) (§3520)	3-3
Codification of Statistical Policy Directive #1	302(a) (§3563 and §3572(b))	3-4
Conduct of Comprehensive Risk Assessment and Analysis of Data Sensitivity	303(a) (§3582)	3-1
Improving Secure Access to Data		
Establishing the Advisory Committee on Data for Evidence Building	101(a) (§315)	4-2
Creating and update Data Inventories with Metadata	202(d) (§3511)	4-5
Making Data Available for Statistical Activities	303(a) (§3581)	2-3
Developing a Single Process for Researcher Access to Data	303(a) (§3583)	2-8
Improving Transparency About Projects Using Confidential Data	303(a) (§3583(a)(6))	4-3
Enhancing Evidence-Building Capacity		
Requiring Agencies to Produce Evidence-Building Plans (learning agendas)	101(a) (§312)	5-2
Designation of Evaluation Officers and Requirements for Written Evaluation Policies	101(a) (§313)	5-1
Generation of an Inventory of Evidence-Building Units	101(c)	5-1
Establishing a Chief Data Officer Council	202(f) (§3 520A)	5-3
Improving Standard for Data Confidentiality and Disclosure Practices	302(a) (§3562)	5-3

TITLE I: Federal evidence-building activities

The federal government engages in a wide variety of activities and, where possible, tries to measure its performance in quantitative terms. For example, the US Department of Commerce (DOC) conducts the Population and Housing Census every ten years to present a count of every person living in the US. Similarly, the Bureau of Justice Statistics sends a report describing justice systems, crime, criminal offenders, and victims of crime, and the Bureau of Transportation Statistics prepares a report describing airline on-time performance, pirates at sea, transportation safety and availability, and more. These reports and many others are used to measure the health and welfare of the US and are critical inputs to legislative and executive decision-making, specifically when it comes to building federal budgets and administering services across the country.

Collectively, the analysis behind these reports is known as *evidence-building activities*. These functions include collecting, compiling, processing, analyzing, and disseminating data to create general-purpose, policy- and program-specific statistics. Evidence-building activities also include program evaluation, research, policy- and program-related analysis, performance measurement, and public health surveillance. Federal evidence building is highly decentralized, requiring each agency to carry out all the functions. While many departments and agencies have some ability to undertake at least some of this work, not every department and agency can perform them all to the consistently high, professional levels required by legislation.

Similarly, organizing principles vary by department and agency. For example, some departments have set up centralized offices to implement one or more of these functions, while others have assigned evidence-building duties across program areas. Departments conduct most statistical activities across mission areas, such as health or energy, and the statistical methods that agencies use also vary by agency and department.

Then there are federal agencies considered to be Federal Statistical Agencies (FSA) whose activities are predominantly the collection, compilation, processing, or analysis of information for statistical purposes (Confidential Information Protection and Statistical Efficiency Act of 2002 (P.L. 107-347, Section 502(8)). Within these agencies, more than 120 analytical components are likely to be changed by the new legislation. The table below shows agencies likely to have the most disruption from the FEPA.

Agency	Federal Department
Census Bureau (Census)*	Commerce
Bureau of Economic Analysis (BEA)*	Commerce
Bureau of Labor Statistics (BLS)*	Labor
Bureau of Justice Statistics (BJS)	Justice
Bureau of Transportation Statistics (BTS)	Transportation
Economic Research Service (ERS)	Agriculture
Energy Information Administration (EIA)	Energy
National Agricultural Statistics Service (NASS)	Agriculture
National Center for Education Statistics (NCES)	Education
National Center for Health Statistics (NCHS)	Health and Human Services
National Center for Science and Engineering Statistics (NCSES)	National Science Foundation
Office of Research, Evaluation, and Statistics (ORES)	Social Security Administration
Statistics of Income Division (SOI)	Treasury
Note: An * denotes Designated Statistical Agencies (DSA) from federal statistical agencies.	

Under Title I of FEPA, *all* federal agencies must manage their data using industry best practices, regularly analyze the data, and use the results to inform policymaking. These practices are intended to encourage using government data for measuring and understanding outcomes rather than merely counting outputs and activities.

Federal agencies must develop plans around statistical questions and appoint officials who represent agency equities related to analytical inquiries. Agencies must name data that they propose using to conduct qualified analyses. Researchers must also describe the methods they expect to use, legal obstacles that could impede their work, the plan they intend to follow, and any supporting information the Director of the OMB may ask.

Additionally, there is a requirement for a non-partisan chief evaluation officer who serves as a plan and implementation evaluator with proven domain ability. The selected individual is expected to correlate program evaluation activities to data production and data quality improvements over time. This positive structural enhancement is like the European Union's (EU) requirement for a neutral data quality official for all organizations.

Title I also requires OMB to establish an advisory council that reviews, analyzes, and makes recommendations for promoting the use of data for evidence-based decisions.

The group is called the Advisory Committee on Data for Evidence Building (the Committee). Membership consists of thirteen participants with at least three federal CDOs. The Committee also includes a single CIO to ensure continuity with IT.

TITLE II: Open Government Data Act

Open, Public, Electronic, and Necessary (OPEN) Government Data Act

Title II of FEPA is the OPEN Government Data Act. OPEN data is content that citizens can use without restriction. Citizens can change and share OPEN data with anyone for any purpose. The federal government collects an enormous variety of data types to deliver services to its citizens. Many argue that the government has not used its data nearly enough. With the passage of FEPA, federal data must be open and available, by default, for others to use, including other government agencies. OPEN data also includes access to analog data (i.e., not in digital form).

Where FOIA enables access to government data, by request in its original form, FEPA makes data electronically available. No specific application is needed, regardless of its original type. Instead of using exempted data categories like those found in FOIA, the federal government must now develop a release process that ensures that the government doesn't release sensitive information as part of OPEN data.

FEPA's overall legislative intent includes increased transparency, self-empowerment, new or improved products and services, potential economic innovation, and new knowledge and growth areas. The Open Government Data Act is the part of FEPA that details how OPEN data will work for federal data. For instance, Title II requires the government to supply three new foundational capabilities: 1) a government-wide data inventory, 2) a new CDO role, and 3) a data governance body that is known as the Chief Data Officer Council (CDO Council).

Data inventory and federal data catalog

All organizations keep inventory, especially for valuable assets. Organizations track information about their inventory, typically across the entire lifecycle of their processes. Inventory often includes an organization's physical assets like automobiles, buildings, and raw materials. Inventories also hold things used in daily activities, finished products, raw materials, or products for sale.

Data is now legislated to also be treated as an asset. Simply put, federal data has monetary value, and organizations must track data and its value. Data lets organizations know what they have. It also allows them to see what others need and provide it to them to save them money or potentially charge them to use it. In these cases, data can be just as valuable, sometimes more, than physical products and the processes that produce them.

To that end, the Open Government Data Act requires agencies to keep an inventory of their data assets. Agencies must inventory and give their data holdings to a centralized federal data catalog that OMB administers. From there, other federal agencies, researchers, and the public can discover data that might be valuable. In this way, federal agencies can give everyone better access to their data, including other agencies, and decrease the costs required to create the same data assets across several federal agencies.

Chief Data Officer

Data already supports strategic and operational efforts every day, from the largest and most prominent organizations, like the Department of Defense (DoD), to the most obscure, like the U.S. Board on Geographic Names (BGN). Data is also a key input for the creation and management of strategy and direction for organizations.

Effective use of data requires decision-makers have access to high-quality, fit-for-purpose data. Well-formed data can include data from other agencies with different charters, authority, and compliance requirements. The complete view of business-relevant, high-quality data needs to be accessible by the right decision-makers to determine, update, and refine data-driven policy based upon measured results under changing environmental conditions.

To that end, the new law requires every federal agency to name an individual who serves as the CDO. The CDO must:

- Set standards for data formats, negotiate terms for data sharing and develop processes for data publishing
- Coordinate with any agency officials responsible for using, protecting, disseminating, and generating data
- Review the impact of agency IT infrastructure on data accessibility and coordinate with each agency's CIO to reduce barriers that inhibit data accessibility
- Maximize the use of data in the agency to support evidence-based analysis, cybersecurity, and operational improvement

- Get and support training and certification related to confidential information protection and statistical efficiency
- Handle overall data lifecycle management.

Chief Data Officer Council

Data governance is more than clarifying who "stewards" data associated decisions; instead, data governance works to optimize the value and use of data. By itself, data is the raw ingredient for improving business performance, and the responsibility for managing those resources falls on the business side.

While more organizations talk about data governance, those same organizations recognize that governance is technically complex, organizationally challenging, and politically sensitive. Compounding matters, getting executive support for data governance is critical, and unfortunately, executives don't often realize how important this business process is. Most often, data governance lands in IT hands by default. When organizations define data as a byproduct of information technology, data typically becomes an object of computing and is treated like other IT assets.

However, FEPA separates business problems and technical problems using the Council as moderator. The Council requires that the government recognize data as the source material that enables and improves business processes, decisions, and interactions. Additionally, FEPA recognizes that data *must* remain a business asset, where business takes the decisions concerning its acquisition, use, and disposition in the pursuit of generating the highest possible return on taxpayer investments.

The Council is composed of a chair appointed by the Director OMB, CDOs from each agency, two representatives for all federal CIOs and chief evaluation officers, and the Administrator of the Office of Electronic Government (OEG). The Council meets regularly and sets policy for the following:

- Establishing government-wide best practices for the use, protection, dissemination, and generation of data
- Promoting and encouraging data sharing agreements between agencies
- Showing ways agencies can improve the production of data for analysis and policymaking
- Consulting with the public and engaging with private users of government data
- Consulting other stakeholders on how to improve access to federal data

- Finding and evaluating new technological solutions for improving the collection and use of data.

Expanding the CDO role

Within the new legislation, there is a small and seemingly insignificant reference. Most citizens might glance over the citation, but it's worth a second look. Specifically, the law says the following:

"(5) carry out the requirements of the agency under subsections (b) through (d), (f), and (i) of section 3506, section 3507, and section 3511."

These references describe the requirements for government efficiency, collection, and planning as they relate to federal data management. This means that FEPA formally requires CDOs to set the policies and procedures across the entire data lifecycle, from planning a data collection to final records disposition.

In some cases, this means CDOs take a more active and direct role. For example, CDOs must communicate regularly with the public to ensure that an agency's data collection is necessary and not overly burdensome. In cooperation with the agency Chief Financial Officer (CFO), CDOs are also required to develop "a full and accurate accounting of information technology expenditures" and goals for improving information resource management's contribution to the productivity, efficiency, and effectiveness of government operation.

TITLE III: Confidential Information Protection and the Statistical Efficiency Act of 2018

FEPA's scope is considerable and affects nearly every part of the federal government; therefore, oversight and coordination are essential to its success. OMB oversees and coordinates the development of policies to help lead these efforts. OMB expects to develop, document, and make transparent business processes for all federal agencies to ensure all agencies support the same rules and implement consistent programs. FEPA also extends the notion of a statistical agency for all agencies to centralize their data. Additionally, agency heads will supply OMB reports as needed, while designated statistical agencies (DSA) will submit annual reports to OMB, the Committee on Oversight and Government Reform of the House of Representatives, and the Committee on Homeland Security and Governmental Affairs of the Senate. Annual reports will include information on the federal government's progress relative to FEPA.

Confidential information processing protection

Perhaps the most crucial part of Title III are the requirements for protecting sensitive information. Congress found that there was no single method for collecting data, and as a result, the public's trust declined. During the Committee's investigation, the group found that different agencies used different techniques for protecting public information. Congress recognized that defending personally identifying information (PII) serves public and societal interests, and if the public distrusts the federal government with their data, the public's distrust would negatively affect the accuracy and completeness of any resulting statistical analysis.

FEPA distinguishes two types of data uses: data collected for "statistical" and "non-statistical" reasons. "Statistical use" refers to data that the federal government uses for analytical purposes as part of an analytic inquiry. Non-statistical use refers to evidence the government uses for purposes other than statistical activities and can be shared among agencies but may or may not be shareable outside the agency. Data collected for non-statistical purposes can be shared more broadly and has fewer restrictions.

Title III also restricts how the government releases another class of data, namely personally identifiable information (PII). Agencies may disclose PII only with the consent of the respondent and just for statistical purposes. The law requires agency head approval for the release, and the releasing agency is responsible for confirming there are no other restrictions to prohibit the agency from releasing the PII. For example, agencies must ensure that there are no other legal restrictions on a release, like a private contractor statutory limitation.

To help drive home the seriousness of protecting confidential data, FEPA assigns strict fines for nonconformance. Anyone who willfully discloses the data to someone who isn't entitled to receive it is guilty of a Class E felony and imprisoned for not more than five years, fined not more than $250,000, or both.

Statistical efficiency

In today's fast-paced world, business, consumers, investors, and others use data to inform their decisions. As part of their research, the Committee discovered that federal agencies met legal constraints that prevented federal agencies from sharing data and increasing the efficiency and efficacy of official statistical inquiries. At the same time, survey respondents began questioning whether the government could protect their personal information.

It became clear that the quality of research directly depended on the willingness of respondents to answer statistical surveys honestly. The Committee also recognized that lowering the reporting burdens on federal agencies would lead to more correct depictions of the economy and its health. So, for instance, if the Bureau of the Census (DOC), the Bureau of Economic Analysis, and the Bureau of Labor Statistics (DOL) share data more effectively, the federal government should have a deeper understanding of American businesses and how the landscape was changing. Also, if federal agencies used uniform data standards when categorizing industries, all agencies could drill down to identify and resolve specific industry problems related to their agencies. They could adjust for new businesses entering and exiting the national economy and to any irregularities that arise.

Furthermore, Title III expands the amount of data each agency can collect and analyze. It also extends the number of industry classifications from 135 to over 800, supplying the government more granularity when reviewing the state of the economy.

Designated statistical agencies

The title's goal is to increase the government's overall understanding of the US economy, especially in areas reflecting the nation's most important economic indicators, like income and product accounts. Accordingly, the law improves the semantic and syntactic similarity and accuracy of these agencies' federal economic statistics. Title

III explicitly authorizes the sharing of business data among the Bureau of the Census (USCB), the Bureau of Economic Analysis (BEA), and the Bureau of Labor Statistics (BLS) for statistical purposes to reduce paperwork burdens on businesses. These three are Designated Statistical Agencies (DSAs).

DSAs are doing a lot of the heavy lifting under FEPA. These agencies, or divisions of agencies, produce and disseminate relevant and timely statistical information. Title III charges these agencies with conducting credible and correct statistical inquiries and running objectively. Because FSAs hold the public's data, these agencies are the last line of defense to protect confidential information and ensure that data is used for statistical purposes only. Following OMB's guidance, each DSA will then set up policies, best practices, and other procedures to conduct their work. Each agency head will enable and support their respective organization to produce evidence for policymakers.

While DSAs are being held accountable for what you would expect—the elimination of duplicate data and improvement of data quality and cost control—they are also responsible for protecting the confidentiality of collected PII. Specifically, DSAs must ensure that leadership, staff, and agents, such as academics and contractors, are aware of the importance of keeping confidential information under tight control. In this case, awareness applies to any agencies that use confidential information. DSAs ensure organizations that are given access and use the sensitive data fully understand their legal obligation to protect PII. Protections help both document business processes as well as develop physical and electronic security for safeguarding confidential data. Security procedures also include managing an audit log of everyone who accesses sensitive data.

When DSAs share data, they must conform to new sharing requirements and written agreements reflecting binding terms. Only officers, staff, and agents who are parties to the data-sharing agreements are allowed access to the data.

Access to data for evidence

Title III presumes that DSAs local copies of data to support their analytical inquiries, while other federal agencies are compelled to make a copy of their data available upon request. The title also requires that DSAs promptly respond to data requests and provide requestors with specific statutes that prohibit a DSA from sharing their data with requestors. Title III requires agencies to set up and follow regular and transparent processes to conduct interagency data exchanges.

Expanding secure access to CIPSEA data assets

Not all federally collected data will be appropriate for public access, however. Some data has sensitive governmental information and is suitable only for interagency sharing. The Confidential Information Protection and Statistical Efficiency Act of 2002 (CIPSEA) was passed to handle these situations. This law supplies strong confidentiality protections for statistical information collecting sponsored or conducted by federal agencies.

Under FEPA, confidential information will be more specifically defined. Federal agencies need to produce a system to categorize the relative sensitivity and the corresponding level of accessibility for each data asset. The categorization system includes shared sensitivity levels, criteria for assigning sensitivity levels, rules for producing a lesser sensitive version of a data asset, and standards to improve access by redacting specific information. Title III also requires FSAs to perform a risk assessment for any data asset that the government intends to release to the public. FSAs must ensure that the evaluation is easy to understand and available on the national data catalog. Additionally, FSAs must publish their standards and procedures on the national data catalog as well.

Applying to access data assets for developing evidence

Title III also directs OMB to develop a process through which the Congressional Budget Office (CBO) as well as state, local, and tribal government researchers, or other individuals, can apply for access to data assets covered under this new law. The law explicitly requires OMB to ensure that FSAs produce *identical* processes, using a standard application form and criteria, and timeframes for turnaround, appeals, and standards. Title III also requires OMB to guide FSAs to coordinate with public and private stakeholders to develop the same processes.

Analysis

These thoughts were offered in the immediate passing of the legislation. Undoubtedly, we have missed some things, but the following represents our best guess of what FEPA means for both government and the private sector. We conclude by specifically mentioning eight areas that we feel require further analysis and welcome the ensuing discussion.

What does this mean?

Better data sharing among designated groups has various benefits, not the least of which is less spending by government agencies to produce the same data—a big win for taxpayers. The long-term impacts of this new law are difficult to measure and will be heavily dependent on the law's practical implementation. However, what is clear is that we now have a law on the books and an opportunity to track any resulting issues and measure their relative impact going forward. The effect will be that agencies must plan in writing saying which specified models will use open data to produce named outputs. The effect is to impose objective professionalism on the federal government's decision-making process and will be felt throughout the US economy. Below are some potential effects that the authors have already identified:

Overall Impact Potential. The federal government accounts for 33% of our national economy and has a considerable data asset collection. The immediate effect will be on organizations interacting with the federal government who stand to receive help from the resulting improved standardization. There will be significant impact at other levels outside government, namely on business, academia, and other organizations. What sort of consequences the new legislation creates and how those impacts affect different groups isn't readily apparent beyond a significant increase in the maturity of the involved data practices?

Greater Data Sharing Examples. The new legislation supplies specific authority to DSAs to share data, allowing those agencies to access each other's data. The government's goal is to achieve higher interoperability among the DSAs and expand the practice of using uniform confidentiality protections by respective FSAs. The federal government can create more interoperability only through detailed and carefully controlled interoperation. The success of this effort can be used as a model to apply throughout other parts of the federal government.

Knowledge Worker Value. Presently, the federal government has trouble paying market rates for data expertise. As the federal government shifts to using data for more decision-making, there are opportunities for data personnel to receive higher compensation at rates comparable to industry rates. However, with the equal increase in demand for these skills, the government may still fall yet farther behind and unable to compete for scarce resources in the market.

Data as a Gateway. To be useful across agencies, the federal government must adopt a unifying measurement framework. If the government can better manage its data, many other things become more comfortable, including decision making, process design, and standards.

According to The Center for Data Innovation, open data has enormous value for businesses, journalists, academics, civil society groups, and even other government agencies. These organizations use the vast supply of data the federal government makes freely available in open formats online to develop innovative products and services, set up critical business decisions, conduct research, and ensure accountability and oversight in government (Riley, 2019).[95]

Uniform Confidentiality Approach. When all agencies share data in the same way, individuals and organizations are more likely to trust their information is protected and more likely to share it. When this happens, this directly leads to cost reduction. Greater access to data between agencies means agencies do not need to spend money to recreate data they need or buy data from third-party sources (Bean, 2018).[96] As with unifying measurements, it's unclear whether agencies will fully adopt the same confidentiality rules or whether differing legal requirements will limit the unification of approaches.

State Government Impacts. State and local governments use federal data whenever they must through federal grants. As federal agencies change their approach to data and its usage, there is potential for state and local governments to do the same.

Remainder Impacts. Though not explicitly set up by the statute, we have seen instances with earlier federal data mandates where other "knock on" effects can occur, including:

- Continued focus in the financial and other historically numbers-driven industries
- Corresponding increases in training and other immersion opportunities for federal employees should result
- The potential for research communities to focus more on the use of data instead of just new results
- Added experiences, benchmarks, and best practices to compare against the private sector
- Governments uncover more public-private partnership opportunities
- Improved efficiencies and effectiveness afford the government greater leverage.

Potential challenges and unanswered questions

As data advocates, we believe more power over data is better. The fact that FEPA was passed so quickly compared to other federal data statutes is exciting. However, it's important to understand and track the impacts so that the government can make timely measured adjustments, and the federal government can continue to lead the way for state and local governments to drive more data usage in their constituencies.

Greater data availability helps all citizens and American businesses, but it's not without consequences. Responsible rollout and management are critical at this exciting juncture. While the statutory changes show promise in many areas, our team still sees concern and open questions in some key areas:

- For the first time, the legislation shows a clear separation of duties between the CDO and CIO. No longer is data a byproduct of technology and the responsibility of the CIO. Instead, data is the business, and how organizations use and share data are decisions that the business owns. More work needs to be done to ensure that technology doesn't eclipse these ideals.
- Information is power, or, to put it more finely, disproportionate access to information is power. While the new law gives the public greater access to massive amounts of government data, the ability to process and make sense of all that data will most likely not be equally available to all citizens.
- Based on some initial research, large companies, academia, and watchdog organizations are the most likely beneficiaries of FEPA. These

organizations stand for a tiny part of the wider public. On the other hand, companies like Experian, Equifax, Transunion, Facebook, and a host of other large companies have strong abilities to process and monetize government data to their advantage. Right now, they already collect a massive amount of data from citizens—where data is the product they sell to other companies. With the passage of FEPA, all companies will also have access to government data, which may either enrich the company "products" currently available with taxpayer data or make these products less valuable since the government will make the data available for free.

- Foreign corporations would also have access to data available under FEPA. That may allow them the opportunity to take advantage of data describing American citizens and disadvantage US companies on the world stage. Few countries have open data programs that are as sweeping as the United States'. It's not clear whether the added data availability created by FEPA will inspire other countries to do the same.
- FEPA requires OMB to set up rules about the marking and handling of federal data. President Obama signed Executive Order 13556 in 2010 that requires federal agencies to mark data using

standardized marks and tags to distinguish data that the federal government deems sensitive and worthy of control. There is a significant cost associated with complying with any standard. It's still unclear how these standards interact with one another and under what conditions.

- Industry consumes federal data and incorporates that data into products and services. As demand for industry services continues to grow, industry is appealing to customers with various claims—performance, quality, relevance, etc. Because the federal government is the originator of that industry data, the government inherits costs associated with improved data timeliness without its knowledge or consent. So, while the law has not funded this effort, industry's needs may influence the government's hand in the future.
- Businesses sell data for a profit. Governments charge taxes and tariffs on products and services, which are then used for national purposes. If data has value, why can the government not glean more revenue from it? By freely releasing other data under FEPA, the government may be devaluing it to the detriment of the American taxpayer.

What constitutes a qualified CDO is ambiguous. Depending on the bent of any agency, CDOs could come in all shapes and forms. The legislation specifies:

"(b) QUALIFICATIONS.—The Chief Data Officer of an agency shall be designated on the basis of demonstrated training and experience in data management, governance (including creation, application, and maintenance of data standards), collection, analysis, protection, use, and dissemination, including with respect to any statistical and related techniques to protect and de-identify confidential data."

How these issues translate into a formalized credentialing system is still to be seen. Were we discussing a traditional and formalized profession like dentistry, we would have shared expectations. However, because CDOs are new and academia has not designed an underlying educational curriculum, those shared expectations do not exist.

Index

References

---

[1] Wylie, Christopher **Mindf*ck Cambridge Analytica and the Plot to Break America** Profile Books (2019) ISBN-10: 1788164997.

[2] Shoshana Zuboff, "Big Other: Surveillance Capitalism and the Prospects of an Information Civilization," *Journal of Information Technology* 30, no. 1 (April 4, 2015): pp. 75-89, https://doi.org/10.1057/jit.2015.5.

[3] G. E. P. Box, "Science and statistics," *Journal of the American Statistical Association*, 71 (356): 791—799, 1971 doi:10.1080/01621459.1976.10480949.

[4] *"Editorial – We need to become channels of peace."* Daily Mirror – Sri Lanka Latest Breaking News and Headlines. (2013, March 24). http://www.dailymirror.lk/print/opinion/editorial-we-need-to-become-channels-of-peace/172-27164.

[5] Builds on Laney, D. B. (2018). *Infonomics: how to monetize, manage, and measure information as an asset for competitive advantage*. Routledge.

[6] Barlow, J. P. (2000). *Cybernomics: Toward a Theory of Information Economy*. Retrieved from http://www.ml.com/woml/forum.

[7] Adapted from McFadden, C. (2020, July 2). *A chronological history of social media*. Interesting Engineering. https://interestingengineering.com/a-chronological-history-of-social-media and https://historycooperative.org/the-history-of-social-media/.

[8] Zuboff, S. (2015). Big other: Surveillance capitalism and the prospects of an information civilization. *Journal of Information Technology, 30*(1), 75–89. https://doi.org/10.1057/jit.2015.5.

[9] Kepes, B. (2013, December 6). *Google users – you're the product, not the customer*. Forbes. https://www.forbes.com/sites/benkepes/2013/12/04/google-users-youre-the-product-not-the-customer/?sh=1235ca8a76d6.

[10] Ibid.

[11] **Nicholas Carlson** "Well, These New Zuckerberg IMs Won't Help Facebook's Privacy Problems" **Business Insider** May 13, 2010, https://www.businessinsider.com/well-these-new-zuckerberg-ims-wont-help-facebooks-privacy-problems-2010-5?IR=T.

[12] **Desjardins**, Jeff **Visual Capitalist/TECHNOLOGY The Top 20 Tech Companies by Revenue Per Employee,** August 23, 2017 https://www.visualcapitalist.com/top-20-tech-companies-revenue-per-employee/.

[13] Jonathan Haidt from: https://www.happinesshypothesis.com/index.html.

[14] Raj Vardhman **Under the Influence— 80+ Influencer Marketing Statistics (Infographic)** February 8, 2021 https://www.smallbizgenius.net/by-the-numbers/influencer-marketing-statistics/#gref.

[15] https://en.wikipedia.org/wiki/Google_Analytics.

[16] Lists from Thomas, M. *24 top Internet of things examples you should know*. Built In. https://builtin.com/Internet-things/iot-examples and

Sumathy, B. (2019). Sewage Monitoring using IoT. *International Journal of Recent Technology and Engineering*, *8*(4), 8268–8270. https://doi.org/10.35940/ijrte.d8939.118419 .

[17] Baker, P., & Haberman, M. (2020, March 31). *Behind Trump's Reversal on Reopening the Country: 2 Sets of Numbers*. The New York Times. https://www.nytimes.com/2020/03/30/us/politics/trump-coronavirus.html.

[18] Madrigal A. (2020, May 14). *How Virginia Juked Its COVID-19 Statistics*. The Atlantic. https://www.theatlantic.com/health/archive/2020/05/covid-19-tests-combine-virginia/611620.

[19] A set of mathematical instructions or rules that, especially if given to a computer, will help to calculate an answer to a problem. AI benefits from the ability to "learn" certain concepts by "studying" existing occurrences in data.

[20] Brian Christian has made an excellent case in his important work *The Alignment Problem: Machine Learning and Human Values* from W. W. Norton & Company; 1st edition (October 6, 2020).

[21] Webb, A. (2020). *The Big Nine: how the tech titans and their thinking machines could warp humanity*. PublicAffairs.

[22] Dyer, Owen "Covid-19: Study claims real global deaths are twice official figures" **thebmj** https://www.bmj.com/content/373/bmj.n1188.

[23] *The Data literacy project – building a data-literate culture for all.* The Data Literacy Project. http://thedataliteracyproject.org/.

[24] Roser, M., & Ortiz-Ospina, E. (2016, August 13). *Literacy*. Our World in Data. https://ourworldindata.org/literacy.

[25] Axelrod, T. (2021, April 14). *FBI launches operation to remove malware from computers in US*. The Hill. https://thehill.com/policy/cybersecurity/548082-doj-authorizes-fbi-to-remove-malware-on-computers.

[26] Whitmer, B. (2015). *Satan Is Real the Ballad of the Louvin Brothers*. Igniter. (audio book).

[27] Rollings, A. Duncan, A., and Logan, V. (22 May 2019). *10 ways CDOs can succeed in forging a data-driven organization*. Gartner. https://www.gartner.com/en/documents/3920325/10-ways-cdos-can-succeed-in-forging-a-data-driven-organi.

[28] Baykoucheva, Svetla (2015). *Managing Scientific Information and Research Data*. Waltham, MA: Chandos Publishing. p. 80. ISBN 9780081001950.

[29] Aiken, P. (1996). *Data reverse engineering: slaying the legacy dragon*. McGraw-Hill.

[30] Opsahl, K. (2013, June 13). *Why Metadata Matters*. Electronic Frontier Foundation. https://www.eff.org/deeplinks/2013/06/why-metadata-matters.

[31] Aiken, P. (2016). EXPERIENCE: Succeeding at Data Management. *Journal of Data and Information Quality*, *7*(1-2), 1—35. https://doi.org/10.1145/2893482

[32] Defined as "Deliberately misleading information announced publicly or leaked by a government or especially by an intelligence agency to influence public opinion or the government in another nation and untrue or incorrect information" from Stengel, R. (2020). *Information wars: how we lost the global battle against disinformation and what we can do about it*. Grove Press UK.

---

[33] Stengel, R. (2019). *Information Wars.* Atlantic Monthly Press.

[34] Statistics from http://www.domo.com/learn/infographic/data-never-sleeps-8.

[35] Marr, B. (September 5, 2019). *How much data do we create every day? The mind-blowing stats everyone should read.* Forbes. https://www.forbes.com/sites/bernardmarr/2018/05/21/how-much-data-do-we-create-every-day-the-mind-blowing-stats-everyone-should-read/?sh=d01524a60ba9.

[36] Nagle, T., & Pope, A. (May 25, 2000). It's not just the pandemic curve – squash the infodemic curve too. The Irish Times. https://www.irishtimes.com/opinion/it-s-not-just-the-pandemic-curve-squash-the-infodemic-curve-too-1.4261233.

[37] In truth, the only objective measure of your organizational legacy is the size of your current production environment, hence one of our favorite sayings: "If it's in production, then it is legacy!"

[38] Programmatically as opposed to on a project-by-project basis.

[39] Aiken, P., & Billings, J. (2013). *Monetizing data management: finding the value in your organization's most important asset.* Technics Publications, LLC.

[40] *Adapting cybersecurity for the new normal.* NetWitness.com. (2021, May 5). https://www.rsa.com/en-us/offers/adapting-cybersecurity-for-the-new-normal.

[41] *The new decision-makers: equipping frontline workers for success.* Harvard Business Review Analytic Services. https://www.scribd.com/document/469176591/HBR-ThoughtSpot-The-New-Decision-Makers-pdf.

[42] *Social-Impact Efforts That Create Real Value*. Harvard Business Review. (2020, November 5). https://hbr.org/2020/09/social-impact-efforts-that-create-real-value.

[43] The Quant Crunch: How the demand for data science skills is disrupting the job market available online at: https://www.ibm.com/downloads/cas/3RL3VXGA.

[44]. *National Assessment of Adult Literacy (NAAL)*. National Center for Education Statistics. https://nces.ed.gov/naal/.

[45] Sources: 2021 Big Data & AI Executive Survey (NewVantage Partners) https://www.newvantage.com/thoughtleadership.

[46] Siegel, E. (2016). *Predictive Analytics*. Wiley.

[47] Dresner Advisory Services **Wisdom of Crowds Business Intelligence Market Study** 3 Jun 2021— available for download at: https://dresneradvisory.com.

[48] *The new decision-makers: equipping frontline workers for success*. Harvard Business Review Analytic Services. https://www.scribd.com/document/469176591/HBR-ThoughtSpot-The-New-Decision-Makers-pdf.

[49]*The Data Literacy Project – building a data-literate culture for all. Data Literacy Project*. http://thedataliteracyproject.org/.

[50]*EDM Resources*. DataWise, Inc. (n.d.). https://datawise-inc.com/edm-resources/.

[51]*DMBoK – Data Management Body of Knowledge*. DAMA. (2020, October 20). https://www.dama.org/cpages/body-of-knowledge.

[52] *The Data literacy project – building a data-literate culture for all.* The Data Literacy Project. http://thedataliteracyproject.org/.

[53] Drucker, P. (1963).Managing for results: Economic tasks and risk-taking decisions. New York: Harper and Row.

[54] Thomas, M. A., Cipolla, J., Lambert, B., & Carter, L. (2019). *Data management maturity assessment of public sector agencies.* Government Information Quarterly, *36*(4), 101401. https://doi.org/10.1016/j.giq.2019.101401.

[55] All statistics from *The Data Literacy Project – building a data-literate culture for all. Data Literacy Project.* http://thedataliteracyproject.org/.

[56] James Manyika, Michael Chui, Brad Brown, Jacques Bughin, Richard Dobbs, Charles Roxburgh, and Angela Hung Byers "Big Data: The next frontier for innovation, competition, and productivity" 1 May 2011 McKinsey Global Institute https://www.mckinsey.com/business-functions/mckinsey-digital/our-insights/big-data-the-next-frontier-for-innovation.

[57] Olivia Rockeman and Reade Pickert Bloomberg Businessweek 23 March 2021 "**The U.S. Unemployment System Is Plagued by $63 Billion in Fraud and Dysfunction** https://www.bloomberg.com/news/articles/2021-03-23/u-s-unemployment-system-plagued-by-massive-fraud-and-dysfunction.

[58] Example from: *The Data Literacy Project – building a data-literate culture for all. Data Literacy Project.* https://thedataliteracyproject.org/posts/do-you-speak-data-retailers-and-the-data-literacy-opportunity.

[59]" *Bad Data Costs the U.S. $3 Trillion Per Year.* Harvard Business Review. (2017, October 4). https://hbr.org/2016/09/bad-data-costs-the-u-s-3-trillion-per-year.

---

[60] Roth, 2019 https://blogs.gartner.com/craig-roth/2019/12/11/2019-exceeded-1-billion-knowledge-workers/.

[61] Our thinking on this matter has been refined by the work of Daniel Kahneman and Amos Tversky. This quote from Tversky has been particularly useful for us: "When presented with new information I do not think to myself, is it true, but instead I ask myself, under what conditions can this be true?" See Lewis, M. *The undoing project.* [The Undoing Project: A Friendship That Changed Our Minds by Michael Lewis W. W. Norton & Company 2016].

[62] Merriam-Webster. *Civics*. https://www.merriam-webster.com/dictionary/civics.

[63] Google's AI Principles are posted at https://ai.google/principles/.

[64] *Privacy*. Apple. https://www.apple.com/privacy/.

[65] James Manyika, Michael Chui, Brad Brown, Jacques Bughin, Richard Dobbs, Charles Roxburgh, and Angela Hung Byers "Big Data: The next frontier for innovation, competition, and productivity" 1 May 2011 McKinsey Global Institute https://www.mckinsey.com/business-functions/mckinsey-digital/our-insights/big-data-the-next-frontier-for-innovation.

[66] Of course, there is the occasional prodigy who graduates from an Ivy League university at age 13 and becomes a KW or DP by the age of 15. However, this merely amplifies our point: the sooner these individuals are exposed to data literacy concepts, the better for us all!

[67] BaixoNatural. (November 1, 2020). *ISOLATED BASS RUSH YYZ GEDDY LEE*. YouTube. https://www.youtube.com/watch?v=tJnULQznZzI.

[68] https://en.wikipedia.org/wiki/Chaos_engineering#Chaos_Monkey.

[69] https://en.wikipedia.org/wiki/Blogger%27s_Code_of_Conduct.

[70] As reported https://thegrio.com/2016/07/27/loan-officer-gets-fired-for-racist-tweet-about-michelle-obama/.

[71] Fun fact—one of your authors has operated for decades from the end of a 2mb down .3mb upload DSL connection.

[72] Aiken, P.H., Yoon, Y., and Leong-Hong, B., *Requirements Driven Data Engineering*. Information & Management February 1999 **35**(3):155-168.

[73] *The new decision-makers: equipping frontline workers for success*. Harvard Business Review Analytic Services. https://www.scribd.com/document/469176591/HBR-ThoughtSpot-The-New-Decision-Makers-pdf.

[74] https://en.wikipedia.org/wiki/General_Data_Protection_Regulation.

[75] https://en.wikipedia.org/wiki/Generally_Accepted_Accounting_Principles_(United_States).

[76] Brillmark "What is A/B Testing?" available at https://www.brillmark.com/ab-testing/.

[77] Risen, J. (2015, April 30). *American Psychological Association Bolstered C.I.A. Torture Program, Report Says*. The New York Times. https://www.nytimes.com/2015/05/01/us/report-says-american-psychological-association-collaborated-on-torture-justification.html.

[78] Steenbeek, I. (2021, April 5). *Data Management & Data Governance 102: DAMA-DMBOK and DCAM discrepancies*. Data Crossroads. https://datacrossroads.nl/2019/10/06/dama-dmbok-vs-dcam.

---

[79] Edward Tufte, *Visual Explanations*, pp. 26-53 © Edward Rolf Tufte, *Visual Explanations*, 1997. All rights reserved— reproduced with permission.

[80] Foley, J. (2021, February 10). *12 deepfake examples that terrified and amused the Internet*. Creative Bloq. https://www.creativebloq.com/features/deepfake-examples.

[81] https://en.wikipedia.org/wiki/Claude_Shannon

[82] https://en.wikipedia.org/wiki/List_of_twelve-step_groups.

[83] Tabscott, D. & Williams, A. (2019). *Wikinomics*. Portfolio Hardcover.

[84] https://agilemanifesto.org.

[85] See Aiken & Harbour *Data Strategy and the Enterprise Data Executive: Ensuring that business and IT are in Synch in the Post-Big Data Era* Technics Publications, LLC 2016— 240 pages (ISBN: 9781634622172).

[86]See Aiken, P., Gillenson, M., Zhang, X., & Rafner, D. (2011). Data Management and Data Administration. *Journal of Database Management, 22*(3), 24—45. https://doi.org/10.4018/jdm.2011070102 and Thomas, M. A., Cipolla, J., Lambert, B., & Carter, L. (2019). Data management maturity assessment of public sector agencies. *Government Information Quarterly, 36*(4), 101401. https://doi.org/10.1016/j.giq.2019.101401.

[87] Aiken, P. H., Billings, J., *Monetizing Data Management: Finding the Value in your Organization's Most Important Asset,* New Jersey: Technics Publications, LLC 2013— 93 pages (ISBN: 978-1-935504-66-5).

[88] Aiken, P., & Joseph, L. (2015). Risky Data = Risky Business. In *Data Governance Financial Services Conference*. Jersey City, NJ.

---

[89] See Aiken & Harbour *Data Strategy and the Enterprise Data Executive: Ensuring that business and IT are in Synch in the Post-Big Data Era* Technics Publications, LLC 2016— 240 pages (ISBN: 9781634622172).

[90] Goldrat, E. **The Goal: A Process of Ongoing Improvement** (ISBN 9780884271956) 362 pages 1972 North River Press

[91] Adapted from https://theodi.org/article/data-ethics-canvas/.

[92] This material has been repurposed from a (2019) white paper prepared for the international society of Chief Data Officers (isCDO.org). We have included it to provide an overview of the new law and to highlight best practices that are now applicable to one third of the economy.

[93] Hart, N., & Shaw, T. (2018, December 22). Congress Provides New Foundation for Evidence- Based Policymaking. Retrieved February 21, 2019, from https://bipartisanpolicy.org/blog/ congress-provides-new-foundation-for-evidence-based-policymaking/.

[94] The Data Coalition. (n.d.). The Data Coalition. Retrieved February 21, 2019, from https://www.datacoalition.org/.

[95] Riley, D. (2019, January 17). Trump signs law to open government documents to public scrutiny. Retrieved February 21, 2019, from https://siliconangle.com/2019/01/16/president-trump-signs- new-law-opens-government-documents-public-scrutiny/.

[96] Bean, R. (2018, January 30). The Chief Data Officer Dilemma. Retrieved February 21, 2019, from https://www.forbes.com/sites/ciocentral/2018/01/29/the-chief-data-officer-dilemma/ #49344f53896a.

Made in United States
North Haven, CT
23 March 2022